EDWARD BLAKE

LEADER AND EXILE

Other Books by Joseph Schull

Edward Blake: The Man of the Other Way
The Legend of Ghost Lagoon
I, Jones, Soldier
The Far Distant Ships
The Salt-Water Men
Battle For The Rock
Ships of the Great Days
Laurier
The Nation Makers
The Jinker
The Century of the Sun
Rebellion

EDWARD BLAKE

LEADER AND EXILE

(1881-1912)

Joseph Schull

Macmillan of Canada
TORONTO

ISBN 0-7705-1325-5

Printed in Canada for
The Macmillan Company of Canada Limited
70 Bond Street, Toronto M5B 1X3

CONTENTS

LIST OF ILLUSTRATIONS

(following page 114)

"Dignified Attitude of the Liberals"
(*Public Archives of Canada*)
Samuel Hume Blake
(*Public Archives of Ontario*)
Margaret Cronyn Blake and Edward Blake
The member for South Longford, *Vanity Fair*, 1894
(*Public Archives of Ontario*)
Aboard the S.S. *Parisian*, 1900
(*Public Archives of Canada*)
Edward Blake, 1906

The material for the J. W. Bengough cartoons listed below was supplied by the Public Archives of Ontario.

PREFACE

In this second and concluding volume I have only to repeat the acknowledgments made in the preface to the first.

This attempt to produce a study of Blake's life has been supported by a member of the Blake family, by Blake, Cassels & Graydon, the law firm he founded, and by Canada Permanent Trust Company, now merged with Toronto General Trusts Corporation, of which Blake was president for fourteen years. My thanks are due to the University of Toronto for its administrative role in the project and to the Canada Council which provided funds for the research.

As the original inspirer of the work, as the superintendent of all arrangements, and as the man who persuaded several distinguished scholars to take an interest in its production, I have to thank my friend W. R. Wright, a great-grandson of Edward Blake.

Advising the writer was a consultative body consisting of Professors J. M. S. Careless and Robert Craig Brown of the History Department of the University of Toronto; Professor Peter B. Waite of the History Department of Dalhousie University; and Professor Margaret A. Banks, Law Librarian of the University of Western Ontario and author of the book *Edward Blake, Irish Nationalist*, which deals with Blake's work in the British parliament on behalf of Home Rule for Ireland. With Professor Frank H. Underhill, who had also agreed to be consulted, there was time only for an occasional conversation before his death. Through the kindness of Mrs. Underhill a large body of her husband's papers on Blake, accumulated over many years, was made available to the writer.

In the note on sources I have acknowledged the invaluable help of archival experts and of others who assisted in the work of research. I should like to restate my particular gratitude to Mr. Peter Yurkiw of the Dominion Archives and to Mrs. Marion Beyea of the Public Archives of Ontario, whose interest was unflagging and whose judgment and expertise were indispensable. While in no way making them responsible for anything said in the book, I should also like to acknowledge the kindness of Senator H. Carl Goldenberg and Senator Paul Martin, who were generous with their time and advice on certain questions.

To the historians of the consulting board I am indebted for advice, for guidance, for some of their own notes, for the indication of sources, for the correction of many errors, and for continual kindly encouragement. They offered their knowledge and judgment, while specifically refraining from any attempt to shape or direct the work. For the manuscript in its final form they are in no way responsible. The disclaimer, however, while made in justice to a group of distinguished historians, in no way lessens my gratitude for the help given.

As to the work itself, it is an attempt to produce a portrait of a vastly complex and many-sided man who was and still is a force in the development of the nation. In the almost twenty-four years, between July 1, 1867 and June 6, 1891, there were two Canadian Prime Ministers: John A. Macdonald and Alexander Mackenzie. Blake could have been Prime Minister in place of Mackenzie. As the leader of the Liberal party in two general elections, he was the alternative force to Macdonald and might have supplanted Macdonald. He made Laurier as a politician and a leader. Without a knowledge of Blake, it seems to me, there is a whole segment, and a very important segment, missing from the picture of the first quarter-century of the

Dominion of Canada. If this book can supply some aspects of that knowledge for the layman, it may be of use and interest.

I have to thank my sister Helen for much work in the typing of notes and manuscripts, and my wife Hélène and the children for enduring a man who, for three years, was "busy with him up there".

JOSEPH SCHULL

EDWARD BLAKE

LEADER AND EXILE

CHAPTER ONE

"IT IS ONLY BY CHANGES OF OPINION"

IN 1881, as Blake looked forward to the end of the winter session, he was Liberal leader in a parliament that had brought him massive defeat. The CPR was a project established and under way. Parliament had approved the Act for the incorporation of the syndicate and approved the terms of the contract. With the first thaws of spring actual building would commence and the Conservative Government of John A. Macdonald would be hurrying the steel on. It would be strengthening the frame of ever-climbing tariffs that embodied the National Policy. All this had to be accepted, at least for the time being; it had been decreed by this parliament. Yet it could be changed by another parliament under the hand of another leader, and perhaps changed in time. In that thought there were grounds for watchful patience and stimulus even in defeat.

The railway battle was lost, the National Policy established, and nothing could redeem or alter them while Macdonald remained in office. They were linked and vital factors in that walling-away of the Americans, the basis of his whole conception. Wrong as it was in Blake's eyes, it stood imposed on the country, distorting the lines of growth, diminishing future prospects and creating unending strain. Harm had been done already and more would be done each day, yet there could be much saved and recovered if Macdonald were ousted in time.

A new government, dealing with railway builders, might renegotiate contracts and revise and reduce plans. It might convince even industrialists of protection's dangerous excesses. What was required was public opinion, aroused, alert and informed, mustering across the country. What was needed now was another man in a hurry, determined on gaining power.

There was little to be done to that end through the tired remainder of the session, and whatever there was Macdonald himself provided. On March 18, three days before prorogation, he moved confidently and ingeniously to revive his battle with Mowat on the question of the Ontario boundary. In his previous wrestlings, though he had considered them wrestlings with Blake as much as Mowat, he had pitted the federal government against Ontario. He had established a commission that answered Mackenzie's commission by throwing out its award. Now, by "An Act to provide for the extension of the boundaries of Manitoba",[1] he involved that province in the quarrel and involved it on his side. Manitoba, the Act declared, pending a formal legal decision on its actual boundary, should be extended eastward to the westward limits of Ontario. What Manitoba gained, or how much it wanted the gain, no man presently knew. Eventually, Macdonald was sure, the matter would go for decision to the Privy Council, where he had good hopes for his case. In the meantime, for his manoeuvrings against Mowat, he had recruited in name, at least, a western ally.

Blake moved instantly to identify the real foe. By this act Manitoba was to be extended eastward into territory she had never claimed; Macdonald had claimed it for her in the earlier phases of the dispute. He was insistent on his old purpose, and it was always to reduce Ontario. He was adding "confusion to the confusion that now exists, additional uncertainty and additional elements of conflict . . . wantonly, needlessly and without any good and essential purpose." Why had the bill come forward in the last days of the session? It was to prevent adequate discussion and forestall reasonable adjustment; Macdonald had drawn his own line and intended to force it through. Ontario voters should know, said the leader of the Liberal party, that they were being deprived by the head of a Conservative government of 154,000 square miles of their territory "including all the territory down to and inclusive of Prince Arthur's Landing on Lake Superior".[2]

With that word for Ontario, it was time to think of Quebec. One shuddered a little at the prospect. "The party is completely disorganized,"[3] was Laurier's perennial complaint, and it was perennially less than the truth. Both parties were disorganized to the extent of becoming unrecognizable as anything but groups of factions. The *rouges* and *bleus* of an older day had been difficult enough in their relationships with either of the federal parties. There had always been French "nationalism", that word that meant the reverse of what it seemed, at least to the English ear. It was not the great Dominion, it was the French province and people that concerned the nationalist of Quebec. All French were nationalists in greater or less degree, and most French were Catholic — there had always been that to live with. But more and worse had come with the quarrel over Riel dividing the French from the English and redividing the parties. There had been the rise of ultramontanism as another disruptive force. The question of the New Brunswick schools, with its implied threat to the Catholic schools of Quebec, was always a lurking, underlying danger. And over these was the daily grime of politics, the pull of federal ambitions, the money of railway contracts, and the schemes of restless men. There were the ambitions, money, and commercial power of the English minority in Quebec, owning so much, controlling so much, pulling so many strings. One could hardly attempt to measure it all, still less to cope with it, from the remote fastness of Toronto.

The leader of the provincial Liberal party was Joly de Lôtbinière, an upright, cultured gentleman and a man out of his depth. Holton was dead, Dorion retired to the bench, and Huntington, as always, clever and ineffective. If there was a federal leader in Quebec Laurier was certainly the man, yet he threaded his way among rivals on treacherous and shifting ground. Joseph-Adolphe Chapleau, young, spectacular, and brilliant, was the Conservative premier of the province, unhappy with his own friends. Detested by ultramontanes, the core of his *bleu* support, he was besmirched with railway corruption, anxious for federal prominence, and not averse to establishing a *rouge* alliance. He would have liked to be allied with Laurier, or at least to swallow Laurier. The same alternatives were attractive enough to a rapidly emerging *rouge* who was quite as brilliant as Chapleau. Honoré Mercier, lawyer, journalist, and ruthless politician, was prepared for any alliance that might assist in his own rising. The official friend of Laurier, he might well destroy Chapleau. He might equally well join him, and there were already hints and manoeuvres in the direction of a coalition. It could be nothing at best but a grimy marriage of expediency, repellent to ultramontanes and blackening the name of *rouge*. It was a ruinous threat to Laurier and he was engaged in fending it off, with the taming and keeping of Mercier at the heart of an obscure struggle. It seemed the worse from Toronto since the manoeuvrings were always French, sealed in a murk of Gallicism and remote from national issues. For the English national leader there was only the one course; explain himself and his Liberalism and trust in his chosen man.

Within eight days of the close of the federal parliament, Blake was in Montreal and he came carefully prepared. He could claim certain advantages. If he was still dogged by Riel it was only as a remote shadow; he had done what he could to allay the old resentments. In the federal House he had spoken as a passionless lawyer, discreet to the point of casuistry. For whatever he had said in Ontario he had been forgiven in Quebec, which understood politics too. He was also free, as Mackenzie had never been, of western Ontario grittishness and the link with George Brown. In his casual relations, moreover, it seemed that he liked the French, made more allowance for the peccadilloes of the French, and was even easier in their company than he was with some of the English. His mother had taught him French, after the schools of Dublin and Toronto, but she had not taught him much. He had the small tags, the phrases of formal greeting and then usually withdrew to reserved silence. Yet the remoteness seemed quite natural, the chill a matter of politeness. He conformed to the French ideal of the English statesman, cold to the touch but true. Above all for the best of the French, who were at home in either speech and enriched by both cultures, there was the quality of the mind and purpose. Whatever they thought or would come to think of Blake as a politician, they trusted the essential man.

Policy was another matter. There had already been ample warning of the mood of the confused province. It was cool to the Pacific Railway but it was not bitterly opposed; it was not awake to the effects of that monstrous contract. Worse still, and particularly in Montreal, there was strong support for the tariffs of the National Policy. Free trade, as Mackenzie and Cartwright preached it and Blake had seemed to preach it, was dangerous doctrine here. The times were too good, as they also were in Ontario. There were too many thriving industries and prosperous manufacturers and too many workmen going to new-made jobs. Facts were outweighing theory and producing another fact; the party would have to adjust itself if it were to stay alive at all.

Huntington, vague and clever as usual, was all for a new departure. If free trade were to be espoused it should be presented as something else, perhaps as part of a larger national freedom. There was the question of commercial treaties with other countries, which were still made for the Dominion through imperial negotiation. Blake had pressed since the days of the Washington Treaty for the right of Canada to make her own arrangements, and it had been a popular move in Quebec. Huntington suggested more of the same now. "The treaty-making power, free trade with the States, or Independence —

are they not all the same thing? The one might perhaps be a harbour of refuge en route to the other. Young French Lower Canada is ready for any or all."[4]

If it was it did not receive them when Blake reached Montreal. He arrived on March 29 for a crowded day of conferences at the Windsor Hotel. The Young Men's Reform Club, with the assistance of wiser elders, had arranged an evening banquet "in every respect all that the most critical could have anticipated."[5] What Blake offered from his lectern at the glittering head table was the best course he could see at the present moment for a country that had been committed to wrong directions. The decision on the Pacific Railway was "a great public misfortune. . . . I may go further and say that a great public crime has been committed." The government had clung to its contract and rejected the better offer, but there was still a remedy to be applied at the next election. "I ask you when you render that verdict to punish, if you think well, those unjust stewards who have taken the onerous bargain and left the good one."[6]

So much for that. He approached the subject of the National Policy and could observe a stiffening in the faces looking up at him. Liberal faces — so many of them Liberal English. Of the twenty-one names of organizers listed on the program before him, only one was French. The others were the chosen few, the stubbornly dominant few. He was speaking here as he would be speaking in urban Ontario, to industrialists and manufacturers who were becoming powerful and rich, able to sway elections. And in addition to his own pronouncements on the subject of free trade he carried Mackenzie and Cartwright as old men of the sea.

To an extent he shouldered the burden. He was in favour of free trade — trade with all the world — that he would not deny. Yet he had never said that Canada was prepared to adopt it. "In Canada revenue must continue to be raised from indirect taxation upon a large number of articles"; customs duties were a fact of national life. They were a legitimate fact and pro-

OUR NATIVE MANUFACTURER; OR, BLAKE'S INCIDENTAL MIXTURE.

vided legitimate protection for the healthy growth of a competitive native industry. The National Policy, however, went far beyond that. It was wrong in purpose and wrong in application. For two years now tariffs had been designed in many cases for the sole purpose of protection, for the establishment of "hot-house" industry that could not exist without it. Instead of healthy growth there was a closing of natural markets, an added and unjust tax on the Canadian consumer. He did not say that all protection was wrong. He did not see that the country could quite turn back. What it could do was adjust. It should key tariffs again to the actual needs of revenue, and trade would do the rest. The legitimate manufacturer would still compete with the foreigner on at least an equal footing. John Brown of Bowmanville, buying where he could buy cheapest, would very often be induced to buy in Canada. "There is no doubt whatever that this will continue until there is some new scheme of raising the revenue propounded, and that there will be a very considerable amount of incidental protection."[7]

Incidental Protection — he had accepted a phrase that Macdonald had made his own, and the fact would be well noted. There was no helping it; if he met Macdonald there on that middle ground it was his own ground as well. He had merely a crumb for Huntington and young French Lower Canada, and it was made with a nod to the other man who was still to be tamed and held. He agreed, he said, with a suggestion made by his friend Mr. Mercier "that we ought to have a voice in the making of the commercial treaties." He had pointed out long ago that on this matter the country was drifting dangerously and should consider immediate action. "You know, with reference to our foreign policy, with reference to our commercial treaties, and with reference to all those things which are called matters of imperial concern . . . it is not all the subjects of the empire who have to pass upon the matter . . . it is the Ministers of England and the representatives of the English constituencies . . . we are, in this particular respect in a subordinate and dependent position; we are not merely subjects of the Queen, but the subjects of the Queen's subjects."[8]

For that phrase at least, whatever it was intended to mean, there was much applause with a lively Gallic tinge. He sat down to prolonged cheers. Laurier saluted the occasion as the dawn of a new era, and when Blake left for Toronto it seemed that it might have come. Only in the mail that followed him was there a slightly sour note. John Maclaren, chief organizer of the banquet, had a few remarks that diminished congratulations. "Some of our friends (chiefly French-speaking) I have heard say that they thought it a mistake that you should dwell upon even theoretical free trade."[9]

Ahead was another address in Quebec City, to be followed by a tour of the three maritime provinces. Meanwhile Toronto pressed. He made his speech there, carefully shading the emphasis he had provided in Montreal, and snatched a moment to attend to his own affairs. He was about to lose a partner and regain a brother. There was a Chancellor required for Ontario and it was not to be Samuel Blake, presently the Vice-Chancellor. John Alexander Boyd, long a member of "Blake's", was the man appointed by Macdonald. It was a deprivation of the firm and a snub to the Vice-Chancellor, acknowledged by the younger brother in the usual Blake way. "We were not much astonished," Mackenzie wrote from the sulky shades of obscurity, "at Blake's resigning in a fit."[10] The balm came with the gall, however, in Sam's return to the practice, sore, indignant, irascible, and more than ever needed.

In June came a disastrous fire in Quebec City, preventing a visit there. Politically, at least in Laurier's eyes, it might have been half a blessing. Whatever was said, he had cautioned Blake tactfully, "should be devoted chiefly to the commercial element of the city."[11] Protection was a dangerous subject, to be handled deftly if at all. Nor was there much hope that the visit would promote unity. The various factions of the party, on the verge of a provincial election, were in one of their fiercer quarrels. They would not join even in an invitation to the national leader. Blake's welcome, if it had come, would have come from an amorphous nebula to be known as "The Citizens of Quebec".[12]

Even Laurier himself, distracted by the quarrels and still manoeuvring with Mercier, seemed glad to escape his province. On July 12, when Blake arrived at Pictou to commence his maritime tour, Laurier was there to join him. It had been planned as a partial holiday, and in that was moderately successful. In each of the three provinces, with the formal meetings disposed of, there were leisurely stays with Liberals and long discussions of the faith. They were the best parts of the journey and probably the most effective, for in spite of attentive audiences the political air was cool. Nova Scotia and New Brunswick were Tupper and Tilley country, and had endorsed the government impressively at some recent by-elections. "If people prefer darkness to light," Blake wrote consolingly to one of the Liberal losers, "after all it is their fault."[13] It was undeniable philosophy and all too characteristic, but it was not a recipe for votes.

By mid-September the leader was back in Toronto, and Laurier embroiled in the Quebec provincial elections. Prospects, already bad, were becoming worse. Chapleau, sick of his own party and tied to his railway barons, was still angling for Mercier. Mercier, always for himself, was steering his zig-zag course, neither quite *rouge* nor *bleu*. There was a kaleidoscope of coalitions, a continual fog of corruption, and no hope whatever of a united Liberal front. Laurier, supporting the provincial party as a dutiful federal leader, seemed steadily losing ground.

There was other slippage in Ontario as the Quebec campaign went on. Liberalism subsided dourly on November 23, as Conservatives gathered in Toronto for a great provincial convention. The heart and soul of everything was a buoyant, confident Macdonald, immersed in great affairs, contemptuous of petty fears. "The great need of Canada, in regard to business affairs, is a permanent fiscal policy. To make capital timid and enterprise uncertain is the business of the opposition. To make the National Policy permanent is the business of the government."[14] The railway marched on, at a mile and a half a day. There was to be a great southward displacement along the whole of the prairie section, with Calgary replacing Edmonton as the western terminus. An easier route had been discovered to the north of Lake Superior, and the line there would be moved nearer to the shore. The Yellowhead Pass in the Rockies would now be too far north, and another way through the mountains still remained to be found. Yet over that, silencing all forebodings, was the one tremendous fact. The railway now, at the pace the syndicate was moving, "is likely to be built in five years instead of ten."[15]

In December, preceded by this news, Blake returned to the maritimes for a few days. He spoke long in Halifax and a little longer in Saint John, but Tupper was there to match him speech for speech. Under that thunderous verbosity the props of logic melted, and Blake returned home to think of Quebec.

With a Canadian general election less than two years off, the provincial Liberals were shattered. Chapleau was again in power and Mercier completely adrift, still a rival and still a threat to Laurier. Nor could Laurier offer much but rueful loyalty. It hardly mattered where he stood on major issues. In Quebec there were no issues. "The greatest obstacle we have to fight is the absence of honor, the lack of honesty in every class of the population, especially the educated classes. I have but faint hopes for this federal election, and the very best we can do is to carry twenty seats."[16]

It was from Mercier rather than Laurier that the definite prescriptions came. He wrote as a free agent, neither much inhibited by loyalty nor overburdened with respect, but he cut through to the bone. It was useless to fight protection, which was favoured even by a majority of Quebec Liberals. It was equally useless to fight the railway syndicate. On both these issues, "our policy, being negative, is not a program worthy of an important party."[17]

Disorganization was total and would remain so in Quebec until there was a leader, a policy, and a press. Mercier dismissed Joly as amiable but ineffective and Laurier as too poor. He suffered himself from the same affliction as Laurier, "but if I saw you raise a flag *worthy of yourself and worthy of my party*, I should perhaps decide to make additional sacrifices."

What was the worthy flag? "Our friends ask for the enunciation of a great national idea capable of arousing the people." Mercier approved mildly of the stand taken by Blake on commercial treaties, but "the young, among whom I have the presumption to count myself, and a good many who are older, are in favour of political independence and no longer see a reason for maintaining the colonial tie."

Mercier, the journalist considering further sacrifices, was in favour of the establishment of a newspaper "directed with prudence by a man of talent whose name would appeal to our people and who would be assisted by several industrious and educated writers." Finally, "as a last suggestion I would say come and pass a few days incognito in Montreal *if you have decided to play practical politics* and launch some new idea . . . you have great national prestige, but you must have a definite national program. The narrow questions of ordinary administration and the blind opposition to accomplished facts will kill your talent. Make your flight but make it boldly into the higher spheres of politics . . .

"In re-reading I see that I have written enough to be hanged. Hang me, then, but save the party and the country."[18]

So much, in the chilly days of January 1882, from the provincial maverick to the national leader of Liberals. So much for the past year's work, at least in Quebec.

"Canada has been favored with a year of great prosperity . . . her farmers have enjoyed a plentiful harvest and remunerative prices . . . her manufacturing and other industries have been and continue to be developed under favorable auspices . . . the immigrants have not confined themselves to Manitoba or the vicinity, but are scattered over the country westward to the Rocky Mountains, and from the international boundary to the banks of the North Saskatchewan."[19]

The Speech from the Throne rolled on at the opening of the fourth session of the fourth parliament on February 9, 1882.

The stilted periods were an election manifesto; there would be no waiting for a decision until 1883. Everyone was sure by now that this would be the last session. Macdonald was going to the country a year earlier than expected, and certainly in the mood of the country he was choosing his time well.

Blake listened with half an ear, his mind in Toronto. Anne Margaret was dying there, his favourite sister and the wife of James Kerr, and she would be dead by early March. When he rose in reply to the speech there was dutifully scornful dissection of almost every point, but it came with little fire. There was no great new idea. Macdonald thanked him sardonically for his "kindly and pleasant tone" and noted their respective positions on either side of the aisle. Probably they would long remain so, but "we will look at each other as pleasantly as we can."[20]

If it was a hope, it was soon abandoned. There were to be no amenities as the parties approached the brink. For Blake, faced with an election, facing that confident leader, the agonizing problem was time. Time would dispel this golden fog of prosperity, time would reveal the errors and the wrong directions, yet it was already late for change. With every day that passed, every factory that was built, protection was knit more firmly into the business fabric of the country. It was not reducing imports nor increasing external trade; the net effect was a general tax on consumption. Yet the prosperous paid their taxes and still had a little left; one could only preach the threat of a rainy day. And when the day came, what then? One could not turn back the clock.

He was in the same position on the other of the great issues. The very ease and speed with which the railway seemed to be building was proof of a bad bargain; the syndicate had been overpaid. He could see now, in this boasted immigration that was spreading through the North-West, the hard hand of the landlord taking hold. Manitoba was already complaining that she could not build local railways because of that Clause 15. There was land locked up by speculators, and there were

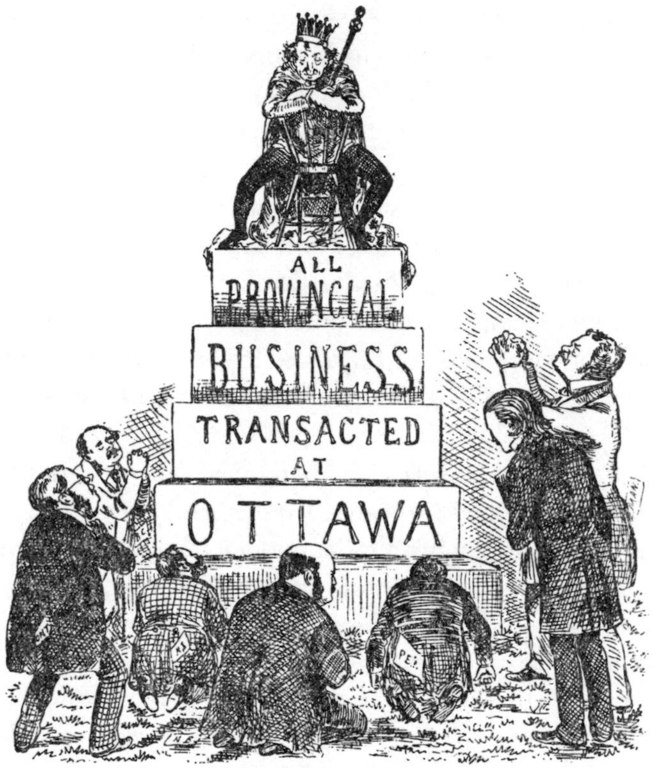

"CENTRALIZATION:"
OR, "PROVINCIAL AUTONOMY ABOLISHED."
IS THIS WHAT SIR JOHN IS AIMING AT?

settlers held to ransom. There was no farm or townsite that was not dependent on the railway and wholly in the railway's grip. Freights were already rising on completed sections of the line, and there were no means to control them. More and more, with the unfolding pattern of continental traffic, Blake saw his argument justified for the short route south of the Lakes. Yet with every mile of line and with every day that passed argument became irrelevant in the face of the accomplished fact. The country would have to live with the National Policy, and it would have to live with the Canadian Pacific Railway.

He approached the session enclosed in that rasping framework, and with little help from the collective mind of the party. Prudence seemed to be the watchword. Where there were no issues in Quebec there were too many in Ontario, yet all were tinged with localism or a pre-election caution. The truculent Mills had suddenly become wary, both of frontal assaults on the syndicate and on the broader question of the tariff. Attacks, if made, should be confined to specific items; he complained of the cost of quinine. There would be trouble soon in the west over the disposal of Indian lands, but it could hardly come in time to affect the election. He was for "a decided stand" on the matter of provincial rights, particularly the Ontario boundary. Mowat, he thought, should invade the disputed region and establish his claim by force. He was firm and wordy as always on the matter of Senate reform, but if he had been inspired to that by Blake he was now wearying Blake; it was hardly an election issue.[21]

Nor was Cartwright much more helpful. "As to the tariff, I fear that a very large number of influential men on both sides think exactly as we do . . . but are determined to make money on it." He had scatterings of potential abuse for various policies of the syndicate and the actions of various ministers. There was some hope of a cause, he thought, in "the case of the poor little factory children". Yet he was studiously vague on the one specific issue that was likely to appeal to Quebec. "There is, to be sure, the great question of independence which is always more or less under discussion, but I doubt if it is ripe for our handling. Personally, as you know, I would prefer a sort of English federation including England and the United States," but it was equally true in this case that the time was not yet ripe.[22] Time, it seemed to Ontario's leading Liberals, was only ripe for the business of re-election.

It neither promised nor produced an impressive program. Election planning was everything, Ontario was the crucial ground, and provincial issues overshadowed the session. The budget and its tariffs went through with hardly a word from Blake. When debate on the North-West came he was diverted from the problems of settlement to the effects of the mass migration. It was depleting Ontario farms. By April 14, on Ontario ground again, he was fighting another of Oliver Mowat's battles. The "Rivers and Streams Bill" was the solemn subject of debate, dignifying a quarrel of lumbermen who had high political friends. Peter McLaren of Perth, a sound Conservative, had improved a section of river line to allow passage for his logs. He had refused passage to a Liberal by the name of Caldwell, and the case had gone to law. As it ascended through numerous courts it had caught the attention of Mowat, who had passed a bill in the legislature asserting Ontario's control of provincial waters. Disallowed by Macdonald on the ground of private rights, it had been re-introduced by Mowat on the ground of provincial rights. Again in the federal House, amid clouds of acrid legalism, it was reduced to its bald essentials at the close of a long debate.

"Is it," asked Blake, grey with a night's stubble and hoarse from a two-hour speech, "because the private right of an individual is the right of a man called Peter McLaren, who is a supporter of the honorable gentleman opposite? . . . Is that a reason why an insult and a slight should be offered to an independent local legislature and a local government?"[23]

"At half-past three in the morning," rejoined a dour Macdonald, "I do not intend to occupy the House for the same length of time as the honorable gentleman who has just spoken." Yet he had time for cogent words. The bill passed by Mowat was "a wretched, flimsy and transparent device; it deceived nobody . . . it was a bill to take from Mr. McLaren his property and hand it over to Mr. Caldwell." Nor was Macdonald prepared to forget the boundary quarrel, where Mowat was inclined to follow Mills' suggestion. "Why, the belligerent premier of Ontario has threatened to march with his armies into the North-West . . . I was afraid that he might come down here like another Oliver and order our Sergeant-at-Arms to 'take away that bauble' and break us up."[24]

By six o'clock, as the bill was disallowed, McLaren's river was safe for the time being. But there had been a few votes gained for Liberals in the cause of provincial rights, and there was another cause in the making. Four days later Blake was on his feet again.

Home Rule for Ireland, that never-ending dilemma, was occupying Gladstone in England while the Irish in Canada watched. Most were Catholic, many lived in Ontario, and all were angry and vocal. By the time his speech was finished Blake had adjured Gladstone, excoriated the British government, asserted the rights of Canada and garnered the Irish vote.

What was it, he asked, that had produced "the chronically wretched state of Ireland"? It was that phalanx of landlords dominating the British parliament, absentee landlords. It was a "feeling of interfering with the sacred rights of property in land — which looked a little too much towards a denial of the divine right of landlordism, which looked a little too much like a practical recognition of the motto that property had its duties as well as its rights." What had been the course for centuries and was still the course today? "While remedies were refused, force was at the same time constantly applied." Why now, and by what right, was he speaking of Ireland in the Canadian House of Commons? "We have a right respectfully to approach our sovereign . . . we have a right to give the influence of four million of British subjects to the redress of grievances too long maintained."[25]

Whatever the political motives, he was a wrathful son of Galway speaking from a full heart. Perhaps from a guilty heart; he came of those landlords too. It seemed doubtful, however, that he had advanced the cause outside the bounds of his electorate. Macdonald, spurred by his own Irish Conservatives, permitted the passage of a diluted resolution, with a sour glance at the effect. "This Home Rule," he said acidly, "if granted at all must be granted by a parliament of landlords . . .

yet we tell the landlords that we are doing it for the purpose of removing them, for the purpose of letting Ireland be governed by Irish ideas; that a process should be adopted by which landlords would be exterminated."[26] The Colonial Secretary in London, when he received the report of the debate and the resulting resolution, had a single flat comment. "We shall do our best," he informed the Governor General, "to coldly enter into what the French call a 'fin de non reçevoir'."[27]

Blake was not yet finished. Though he had dismissed Mercier's injunctions and his hopes for independence, he maintained his own convictions on the subject of commercial treaties. They ran with Quebec's views, they were shared by Grit Ontario and even by enough Conservatives to be disconcerting to Macdonald. The day after Ireland left the order paper Blake brought up the new issue. "At home and abroad, and particularly with regard to the relations of the Empire to the colonies, while there is no system, while our whole arrangements are full of anomalies, while you cannot discover any particular plan . . . you perceive a principle of growth, of vitality, of development and of progress." That progress should be maintained; Canada, in her commerce with other nations, should negotiate her own treaties. "It is said that we cannot have the benefit of the diplomatic service of England. Much good has it done us, Mr. Speaker. The history of the diplomatic service of England, so far as Canada is concerned, has been a history of error, blunder, wrong and concession." Why not Canadian diplomats or at least negotiators, chosen in the name of the Queen? Why should they be less respected, less effective? "The Queen is Queen of Canada as well as England."[28]

Once more, speaking on this theme, he had gone beyond the drab necessities of the election. It seemed to bring its reward. He had found a lively issue and there was a surprisingly good press. But still Ontario nagged at him for more on its own concerns. To the ever-bustling Edgar there were still issues to be raised; Blake should be heard on them. He snapped back angrily. Did Edgar expect him to speak on every question?

"I will not do so. I must be allowed to judge in some degree for myself."[29]

He was irritable with good reason, for the last fight was ahead. The ground gained in Ontario was to be cut from under his feet. On April 28 Macdonald rose in the House with galley sheets in his hand, wet from the printer. They were Bill Number 153, to adjust seats in the Commons in accordance with last year's census and to revise political constituencies. The bill,

"WE'VE HIVED THE GRITS."

said Macdonald solemnly, with his tongue firmly in his cheek, would "equalize the population"[30] in many Ontario ridings. What it was actually doing, said Blake, had been better described in other words of the Prime Minister himself. It was "hiving the grits" and "it will not be our fault if the full iniquities of this measure be not exposed."[31]

The carving-up of the constituencies had been a work of many months, and it was not yet quite complete. Macdonald read from his galleys, forewarning Liberals of their counties sheared away, their strongholds clumped together, their majorities become minorities, and pocketed the bill and left. When he returned on May 6 for the business of second reading much more work had been done. There had been large and lurid revision and the bill was worse than before. It was not, said Blake, the same bill at all; it could not be accepted by the House. There was a spat of debate, prophetic of much ahead, and the Speaker ruled that the point had been well taken. The bill that was proposed for second reading had never received a first. It must receive that now, as Bill Number 158.

Under any guise, for Liberals, it was a map of chaos and disaster. Through first reading and second reading and the eighteen hours that followed they roared at their jubilant enemies, with Ontario slipping away. Blake dissected the province to expose the extent of the crime. Mills unveiled Macdonald as another Richard III, wily, treacherous, and vengeful. "We have not the axe of the executioner, but the honorable gentleman undertakes to execute us by the votes of his followers."[32]

It was not as bad as it seemed, in actual fact; there would be few constituencies lost by the gerrymander. But the statesmen shorn of their votes could not yet know it; there was only the present threat. There were only those grinning miscreants smug across the aisle, fat with their new pluralities, trading abuse for abuse. As invective begot invective and the hustings invaded parliament, twenty years of elections were fought over again with not a drop of their venom lost to time. The small hours waned, the personalities waxed, and nostalgia lost its faintest touch of sweetness . . . "the honorable gentleman was never able satisfactorily to account for $1,700. found in the manger of a stable . . . I have known that gentleman for forty years; I knew him at school and he was disliked and despised then . . . the boys were always glad to lock up their lunches when he was about."[33]

The debate was nearing its climax with no doubt of the result when Joe Rymal of Wentworth County, crowned wit of the Liberals, gathered his last resources. He was losing his seat, he knew, but there remained his reputation for the murderous shaft of humour and he had his private target. John Rykert, Conservative member for Lincoln, had favoured him with a few remarks. "He stands," said Rymal, glaring across the aisle with his finger trained on Rykert, "somewhere between a fifth and fifteenth rate lawyer . . . he is a briefless barrister practicing in police and division courts . . . ten thousand souls like that which actuates the honorable gentleman opposite could lodge in a flea's skull and then have as much room to play in as two frogs could have on the broad bosom of Lake Ontario."[34]

Mills rose, clearing his throat slightly. "As it is now two o'clock in the morning, I beg to move the adjournment of the debate."[35]

Macdonald denied the motion. There was to be neither recess nor reprieve. Once more toward six o'clock, the hour of executions, the axe of division fell.

On May 17, 1882, still more or less in the mood set by the debate, the fourth session prorogued. A day later the fourth parliament was dissolved. There were a month and three days to prepare for the general election, and Blake used them to the full. Quebec must be left to Laurier and there would be no help from Mercier; the maverick was still astray. The extent of Blake's help was to scratch up a little money for the few hopeful constituencies; there was nothing more he could do.

Ontario was the key province and the leader's place was there. In demand everywhere, he went everywhere, hammering home his program to the limits of his voice and strength. He would repair, cleanse, and reform, he would reduce tariffs where possible, he would change what could be changed. Yet he could frame no promise in any of it of a major redirection. What he offered the country essentially was himself as guiding hand.

He came home to Toronto from Goderich on the evening of June 19, hoarse, gaunt, and sensing the taste of victory, with twenty-five meetings behind him and the cheers of thousands of Liberals still ringing in his ears. Every meeting he attended had seemed to be "the best yet". The "monster gatherings", the "enthusiastic demonstrations", and the "confident, masterly speeches" had all been applauded in the *Globe*. They had been magnified and misinterpreted after the manner of Gordon Brown, while some of Brown's hirelings had achieved peaks of the inane. At one of Blake's assemblies, in the phrase of a *Globe* reporter, "his address had lasted two and three-quarter hours, yet not a man had left the hall."[36] Yet whatever the work of the *Globe* and whatever the work of the leader, nothing had been enough. On the evening of June 20 Blake turned to assess defeat.

It was not total, yet it came to a total rebuff. He had gained nine seats in Ontario, two in Manitoba and one in Prince Edward Island. He had lost five in New Brunswick and one in Nova Scotia. There had been seventeen seats in Quebec against the twenty Laurier had hoped for; it was a net loss of three. With all gains and losses the Liberal party in parliament would be in a minority of sixty-seven; Blake had improved the position by exactly one vote. He had lost Cartwright and he had lost Mills, though Laurier was safe. He was safely elected himself, and as powerless as he had been before.

"I have determined to work all the harder and spare no pains till after the next general election."[37] It was his mood in late June, and it continued throughout July. "Laying aside Quebec," he wrote to a despondent Laurier, "I see no reason to

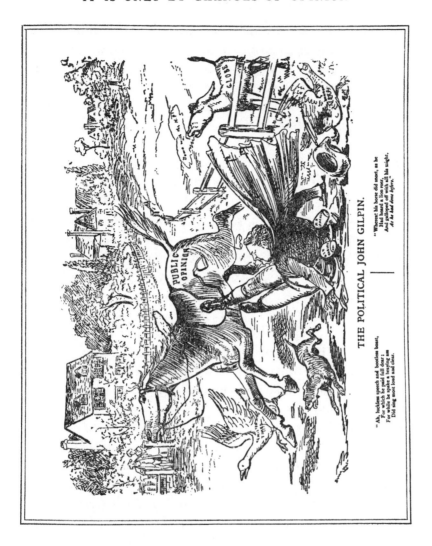

THE POLITICAL JOHN GILPIN.

"Ah, luckless speech and bootless boast,
For which he paid full dear;
For while he spake a braying ass
Did sing most loud and clear.

"Whereat his horse did snort, as he
Had heard a lion roar,
And galloped off with all his might,
As he had done before."

doubt that we have a fair prospect of carrying the elections next time." Yet it was not possible to lay aside Quebec; somehow its votes and leaders had to be won. He pleaded with Laurier in a kind of desperation. "In so large a body are there none who would be willing to combine with you to put an end to the reign of the plunderers and the jobbers? . . . I ask myself and I ask you, are *we* or *they* wholly blind? . . . God knows I don't want office or power, and I would not stoop to unworthy means to gain them. But it is only by changes of opinion that majorities become minorities and vice versa; and with you that change may begin at the top instead of the bottom. Think of these things and let me hear from you."[38]

He thought of them much himself through the late summer and autumn. He circularized party leaders in all the provinces and the answers came drifting back, answering nothing. There was little encouragement from Laurier or sign of change in Quebec, and in Ontario there was the drab business of rebuilding a wrecked party. There was the worse business of the *Globe*, which was becoming a liability. Under Gordon Brown it was raising the ghost of George, always to the belittlement of Blake. It was even turning on Quebec again in the old, disastrous way. It saw the Ontario boundary as being decided in Macdonald's cabinet, under the dominance of French Canadians. The *bleu* foot was again on the neck of Ontario. "Shall Ontario," it had asked on the very eve of the election, "at the dictation of a handful of French *bleus* be degraded to the position of a fifth-rate province?"[39]

From this the leaders in Ontario were now determined to escape. By mid-November they had persuaded Anne Brown, the widow of George and the *Globe*'s controlling shareholder. The tone of the paper must change, and it would not change while Gordon Brown remained as Managing Director. By December Gordon was out and the board of directors reorganized under the presidency of Robert Jaffray, a wealthy Toronto Liberal and an old friend of Mackenzie. He was also a friend of Blake and there were other friends on the board, with Edgar prominent among them. Gordon Brown, a friend reported to Macdonald, "spoke with much indignation of being turned out . . . and said he would start another paper."[40]

He never would, and the *Globe* without him would become an asset again. But the change had been a ruthless business, a crude example of the underside of politics, and it was only one of many. There would be more and always more, and already there had been enough. He had decided, Blake wrote to Laurier in mid-December, that it would be better for him to go. It seemed tentative and it was only half-believed; in his friend's reply there was sympathy but no release. "You may resign officially and be officially replaced," wrote Laurier, "but even then you must lead . . . you cannot resign any more than Gladstone can resign; events will bring you back."[41]

CHAPTER TWO

"I HAVE ALWAYS DETESTED MY POSITION"

LAURIER'S REASSURANCES appeared to have no effect. Toward the end of the month Blake turned to his older friend, the successful provincial premier. His gloom seemed to have deepened and his resolution stiffened with the passing of another Christmas. Advice he did not want; he was making a direct proposal. If Mowat would agree to assume the federal leadership, Blake would step out at once.

He left Mowat a distressed man in a quandary who was more than likely to refuse. Nevertheless, on January 2, 1883, Blake sat down to prepare the draft of a circular. It was to the principal men of the party; it told them what he had done, and it asked their help in support of his own approach. Since time pressed and it was impossible to call a caucus, he urged them to wire Mowat and suggest immediate acceptance. Of the reasons for his own departure "I need not say much", but on the qualifications of the other man he was emphatically and bleakly clear. Mowat's gift for leadership had been established by severe tests, and he had been as skillful with federal issues as he had been in provincial affairs. He had shown that as a politician he was at least the equal of Macdonald, and he would be the man to turn the scales at the next election. "In this view nothing succeeds like success, as nothing fails like failure."[1]

The draft with its scratched-out changes went to his files; the circular was never sent. His conversations were dropped with the relieved Mowat and party leaders were spared a new upheaval. Yet only for the time being; the essence of his mood remained. What had once been doubts had hardened to grey convictions. He lacked the ability to lead, to arouse and direct men, and without that in politics his other talents were wasted. He felt himself right in his principles and could see no way to change them, but there was neither power nor progress to show as the result of his work. He did not think that there would be while he remained leader of the party. He was the wrong man in the place.

He had been defeated on two great issues that would set the direction of the country for years to come. They would set the tone of the country's political life. He saw that and dreaded the task of facing it. On what intelligible grounds could he oppose the philosophy of protection while still upholding an essential frame of tariffs? How could he deal with this railway that had become a national goal? It rushed on, building its great hopes, showering largesse everywhere, surmounting enormous obstacles with the strength of a natural force. The man at odds with the railway seemed a man opposed to the country, and to much of the climate round him Blake was indeed opposed.

The more he studied the railway plan the more its fallacies glared at him, and the working-out was confirming the worst of his fears. With haste, with extravagant building, and with the acquiring of branches and subsidiaries came an era of political corruption that dwarfed anything in the past. He was watching its beginning now, and he knew it could only grow. As the CPR moved ever closer to government, its lobbyists swarmed in Ottawa, its jobs and retainers showered on useful members, and its contracts fattened hundreds of political friends. There were the gifts of paid-up stock, the special terms on lands, the inside information that created the private fortunes. It was the same with the colonization companies in administering their private grants. There were mineral rights and timber lands for the available and influential, and even cabinet ministers were suspected of acquiring holdings. It hardly mattered that few of the charges were proved, or that many of the charges were false; the opportunities were there. They were a part of the general atmosphere of a decade of rush and grab; the thought of them poisoned parliament and tainted every election. Politics was into the railway and the railway was into politics, disbursing legitimate millions through the hands of fallible men. There could never be any question that much would stick to the hands, and much be asked in return. "They were a hungry lot in Ottawa then," wrote W. T. R. Preston, the principal Liberal organizer, who knew whereof he spoke. He was to recall years later the deals that fed the hungers, the lobbyings in the House of Commons and the bloated Tory enemies "baldly twitting their opponents for not being in the swim."[2] A seasoned party hack, not too much to be relied on, he nevertheless conveyed the sense of the times.

To that Blake returned with the opening of the fifth parliament. He remained leader and he was leader through his own act; he had deliberately displaced Mackenzie. He was still charged by friends of the grey old man with conducting a political intrigue. The thought haunted and oppressed him, contributed to new constraint, and added to the chill surrounding the public image. If he had ever conducted an intrigue, wrote one commentator, it must have been different from that of other men. "We can imagine this singularly icy statesman treading the long, winding staircase of a solitary tower and, having reached the top which looks out into the starlit night, carrying on an intrigue with his own half-mystical ambition. Never can our imagination picture him courting his colleagues, still less courting the people for their preferences."[3]

The session of 1883 opened in February and closed in late May, with little change in the parties' respective positions.

Fresh from a prosperous election Macdonald was riding the crests. For the reluctant captain of Liberals there remained only the troughs, and he ploughed through them tiredly, doing the best he could. The progress of the railway dominated the federal scene, and it was outrunning all predictions. As the new line crossed the prairies at break-neck speed, the acquisition of older lines was creating an eastern network. On sections of completed line traffic was beginning to build and freights were better than expected. Construction costs were actually under the estimates and the railway lands were selling at handsome prices. The story unfolding so far seemed one of glowing success.

Blake could only agree, with some acid reservations. He was suspicious of much of the financing and of some of the methods of acquiring eastern railways. The story was young yet, and the prairie line was the easiest part of the building. The mountain sections and the section round Lake Superior might drastically change the picture. In any case, at the moment, it confirmed much that he had said. According to present projections the CPR would emerge not only with the railway paid for but with an additional profit of something like $37 million. Was this not proof that it had been grossly overpaid? Was this an acceptable bargain for the Canadian public? It appeared, on the whole, that it was. The public was getting its railway and seemed to be content with that.

If there was any progress for Liberals it was in the field of provincial affairs. In Ontario, in the February provincial election, Mowat came out with a reduced but safe majority. He was prepared to renew his standing battle with Macdonald, and Macdonald was prepared to accept it. The Ontario boundary question and the federal disallowance of the provincial Rivers and Streams Bill were still hanging in suspense, destined for the Judicial Committee of the Privy Council. Other potential quarrels had emerged as parliament convened. In the Throne Speech Macdonald had revived an old and cherished project, which was to amend the franchise governing

Dominion elections. Under present laws there were in effect seven franchises, each different from the other, since the provinces compiled the voters' lists and established qualifications. Always objectionable to Macdonald, it was becoming unendurable, particularly in the face of an ever-fractious Ontario. The remedy lay, to his mind, in an imposed central control. There were to be uniform qualifications for the voters in every province, and the electoral lists would be compiled by federal officers.

The bill was shelved for the session after due warning from Blake. He had opposed the measure when Macdonald first introduced it, twelve years before. He would certainly oppose it again, and for the same reasons. It would be another step toward the enlargement of the federal government and the reduction of provincial status. There were certainly diversities in the franchise but there were diversities in every province and differences had to be accepted. The alternative was "a voters' list prepared by officials to be appointed by the Administration here — a revision of that list by officials to be appointed from here — centralization, patronage and the control by the Government of the day over the whole system upon which our elections depend."[4]

Before these rumblings Macdonald had retreated for the moment, but only to return to the charge from a new direction. On March 16 he had moved for the establishment of a special committee of the House which would devise legislation by the federal parliament "to prevent the unrestrained sale of intoxicating liquors, and for that purpose to regulate the granting of shop, saloon and tavern licenses."[5] The laudable aim involved some complex problems, since there would be transfers and changes in both provincial and municipal jurisdictions. The legislation when passed, however, would have one important effect. It would remove the control of licensing and the patronage that went with it from the Ontario government and the hands of Oliver Mowat.

Among the members of his special committee Macdonald

had included Blake along with five other Liberals. They had flatly refused to serve, taking their cue from their leader. Blake himself, in his longest speech of the session, made some of his reasons clear. The government was resorting to a committee because it did not know how to proceed; it was not sure of its law. It was hoping to involve Liberals in the reduction of provincial powers, in another of Macdonald's feuds. Macdonald had said from the stumps in the last election that he was determined to reduce Mowat, "that little tyrant who had attempted to control public opinion by taking hold of every little office from that of a Division Court bailiff to a tavern keeper."[6] If he thought he could do it now, if he intended himself to control the tavern keepers, let him pass his own bill.

That Macdonald had done, but it was another bill that was bound for the Privy Council. The little feuds as they grew were shaping a general issue, and in this steadily evolving struggle to maintain the powers of the provinces, the Law Lords were becoming the referees. It was a hopeful development for Blake; at least one thing gained.

There was a gain in discontent, friend of the opposition, that was becoming loudly vocal in Manitoba. Here, particularly in Winnipeg, there were the first signs of the petering-out of the boom. Over the whole province the homestead entries that had reached 7,500 in 1882 fell to half of that in 1883. The flow of immigrants was declining, colonization companies were going bankrupt, and the CPR's policies were enraging the men on the land. The protective duties of the National Policy protected no one here. Wherever the farmer turned the hand of monopoly gripped him or the tariffs took their toll. It was eastern interests that set the price of his implements, and it was the CPR's freight rates that cut the return on his grain. He hauled to the elevator established by an eastern monopoly in a townsite chosen by the railway for its own profit and convenience. He could control nothing and change nothing, nor could his provincial government help him. John Norquay, the premier, good Conservative though he was, had failed in every attempt. Time after time, with the demand for local railways rising about him, he had issued charters for branches that were federally disallowed. Clause 15 in the contract given the syndicate was steadily invoked by the railway and steadily enforced by Macdonald. If he had not quite lost the province he was certainly on the verge of losing it; there was powder here that one bad crop would ignite.

Quebec was its usual mélange of competing chieftains, each uneasy under any federal banner. Yet even here there had been vaguely promising changes. Chapleau was gone for the moment, at least from the local scene. He had given up on provincial affairs and entered the federal cabinet, where he faced a weighty rival. Sir Hector Langevin was Macdonald's pillar in Quebec, and no friend of Chapleau. There might be prospects of useful dissension there. Provincially there was new dissension, though Conservatives were still in power. More than ever a group of embittered factions, they were steadily breaking up. Mercier was gaining on Chapleau's weak successor and attracting some of his *bleus*, reviving the talk of another coalition. If it came it would make him premier, absorb his formidable energies and unite provincial Liberals in support of the federal party. Laurier, in place of a dangerous potential rival, would have a strongly established ally.

There was a Liberal government already in Nova Scotia, and a strong man rising there. W. S. Fielding, who was to be premier within a year, had a journalist's flair for detecting political issues and they were not difficult to find. Neither the coal nor the iron industries were yet satisfied with the tariffs of the National Policy, and protection was disrupting other trade with the Americans. The great days of the sailing fleets were giving way to steamers. The province was in decline and it blamed Confederation and it blamed Macdonald. Much might be made of that, and Fielding would make the most of it.

They were all hopes and they were all distant, spread out through dreary vistas of endless political war. Autumn came on and there was frost in Manitoba, killing much of the crop.

READ LIKE A BOOK!

The land boom had collapsed, the settlers were up in arms and were even warning immigrants away from the country. The tariffs of the National Policy, that bore so hard on the Westerners seemed to have lost their magic elsewhere. Little by little the failures began in the east, and by December there were closing factories and men idle in the cities. Sir Charles Tupper, who had gone to England in March as High Commissioner, was abruptly back in Ottawa. He had been recalled by

Macdonald, it was said, because the CPR was in trouble. Somehow, for some reason, prosperity had slipped away; Blake was another Cassandra whose words were being fulfilled.

He was not surprised, nor was there anything to lift him up in the clouding-over. There was weather ahead which neither party could change, and for politicians the usual round went on. They must prepare early for the business of the next session, he wrote Laurier, "so as to begin the work of hammer, hammer."[7]

The first blows fell in January of 1884 with his reply to the Speech from the Throne. The real work, however, began on February 5. Parliament had assembled two weeks earlier than usual, and the CPR was the reason. In the mountains, on the prairies, and in the bush and muskeg fringing the Great Lakes construction was rushing on, but in the eastern offices and financial centres there was the threat of imminent collapse.

What had happened? How had those glowing prospects changed so quickly? Where had the mistakes been made? Actually, within the project's framework, there had been no mistakes at all. The railway was crossing the continent and bridging the empty west, forging the link with the Pacific. It was keeping the Americans out. It was firing the imagination of the whole country, creating an enduring legend, with the speed and skill of its building and its relentless determination. Yet it was also and simultaneously, through the force of its own imperatives, being driven beyond its means. Haste was the essence of the contract and haste meant added expense, hugely added expense. It meant far more than that. The railway now to be completed by 1885 would run for years to come through regions of scattered settlement or of no settlement at all. For years to come it would require eastern traffic to support those profitless miles of western passage. It was spending millions in Ontario and more millions in Quebec, not on new construction but to acquire existing railways, completing the eastern network that would feed from Montreal. It was making a deadly enemy of the Grand Trunk, so long entrenched in the east. It was exhausting its cash resources and being compelled to seek for more, through stock sales and land sales at a time of collapsing booms and plunging markets.

Of its authorized capital stock of $100 million about half had now been sold, all of it at a large discount and much to members of the syndicate. They could buy no more and they could not find other buyers; the price was dropping steadily on the world markets. In the late Autumn, at Stephen's desperate urging, Macdonald had agreed to attempt support of the sale. To move the shares and assure an advance in price the Dominion would guarantee payment of 3 per cent of the regular 5 per cent dividend for a period of ten years. The guarantee had been given and almost nothing had come of it; the stock continued to fall. By December, with the railway's cash exhausted, the government itself had had to plead with the banks to obtain a dribble of funds. By February 1, 1884, when Tupper rose in the House to present the first series of resolutions for the relief of the CPR, the crisis was revealed in full. There was almost nothing to be hoped for from sales of the company's stock, even supported by the government guarantee. The Canadian Pacific, in return for a mortgage covering the entire railway, would require from the Government of Canada an outright loan of $22.5 million.

It would be $30 million, said Blake. The guarantee of the dividend would pledge the credit of Canada for an additional $7.5 million. Nor had he any doubt that the CPR would get it. The country was now in the grip of its own bargain; it was the totally involved partner, and the junior partner at that.

It was equally in the grip of the National Policy, the other wing of its program. Fiscal policy must be permanent; Macdonald had said that and Blake could only agree. Protective tariffs had created a pattern of industry and induced large investment; they could not be abandoned wholesale. Nor could there be any reduction of tariffs while the railway ate up revenues, and building could not stop. Once begun, as Blake had said from the outset, it must be driven on to the end. What he saw now was the linked consequences reinforcing each other and creating a general drift. A country over-extended and artificially stimulated was inevitably beginning to react; prosperity was disappearing.

Worse than that, the strains induced by the fallacies were beginning to take their toll. What had the railway, built to Macdonald's conception, done for the North-West? In the collapsing land boom, in the deflation of "the great balloon which the Honourable Gentleman has set floating",[8] thousands were losing their money and being forced to leave their homes. The unrest in Manitoba was becoming a national issue. Settlement, instead of a compact movement, advancing region by region, was a scattering of farms and homesteads without connection or support. Nor was the railway working to support them. It was driving west for the Pacific and east round Lake Superior when it should have been building branches in Manitoba. It was using its detested monopoly to prevent the building of branches, and a province deprived of adequate southern outlets was demanding one to the north. The talk now was of a railway to Hudson's Bay, which would involve additional millions.

Yet where were the millions to come from? There had been a bad harvest, the times were turning down, the government was pressed for money. Why? Because of the partial failure of one year's crop? — it was the merest fraction of the cause. Government had created a false boom in commerce, like its false boom in land. It had taxed the people with tariffs to stimulate its pet industries, and the industries were withering away for lack of roots. "What has happened to the National Policy? Is it asleep? Has it gone upon a journey?"[9] The new industries now were the industries of the old days, those reappearing soup kitchens that had been so long blamed on Liberals.

The country had been misled, Blake told the country sombrely, but it had followed its chosen leader. He spoke on Feb-

ANOTHER CASE OF "OPEN YOUR MOUTH AND SHUT YOUR EYES."

ruary 5 as the rejected man, powerless to effect much change. His only hope was to expose and mitigate evils, for the prevention of more later. He attacked the railway's monopoly, its extravagant spending in the east, its policy of open war with the Grand Trunk. The details of the company's financing, always mysterious and fascinating, engrossed him for a long time. It appeared now that the company was building the railway while the government of Canada paid for it. Yet the company would remain the owner. It appeared that the directors of the syndicate, the holders of millions of its stock, would be assured through the guaranteed dividend of a sound return on their money. It would be rather more than sound — something like 11 per cent — on stock that had been acquired at less than half of par.

The government mortgage on the railway was formidable-looking security but Blake had doubts that the terms would ever be enforced; all experience was against it. The opposite was more likely. "I say that you may and probably will find the Company knocking at your doors again for further aid."[10] He was as convinced as ever of the wrongness of the whole policy, and convinced that it would still prevail. He began early in the evening and finished at long past midnight, but the sum of his effort came to the one conclusion. He put it in the company's mouth, and it was confirmed later by the vote. "We have a big job and we will put it through. We have the government at our back, and between the government and ourselves we shall put it through."[11]

Laurier was his desk-mate now, and would be for the rest of his days in parliament. John W. Dafoe, then an eighteen-year-old reporter for the Montreal *Star*, watched the two from the press gallery, tremendously impressed by Blake. "Laurier's political activities," so far as Dafoe observed, "consisted chiefly of being an acting secretary of sorts to the Liberal leader. He kept his references in order, handed him Hansards and blue books in turn, summoned the pages to clear away the impedimenta and to keep the glass of water replenished — little services which it was clear he was glad to do for one who engaged his ardent affection and admiration."[12]

Blake responded with growing respect and warmth. He knew more than Dafoe of Laurier's political activities, and his trust and confidence in the man were a source of strength. There were even hopes for a Quebec which had produced a man like

Laurier, and set him at Blake's side. Yet Blake's appraisal of himself remained unchanged. It had only been confirmed for him in Ottawa "since I came here and observed once again how things are going."[13] New constituencies had been found for Mills and Cartwright, and they were again back in the House. Around the leader there were the signs of a reviving party, but it was on the strength of negative hopes, on the bad times and the blunderings that would bring Conservatives down. Liberals wanted to get in — they wanted to get in with Blake — but he could neither share the hope nor endure the prospect. He saw everywhere about him a fog of blatant corruption and a maze of misdirections he had not been able to change. Either he had failed the country or the country had failed him. In either case it was better to get out now.

In late February, after defeat on the CPR, there was revived talk in the newspapers of his intrigues to supplant Mackenzie. There were new charges that he was intriguing with Quebec *bleus*, who were still bargaining with Liberals in the hope of a new alliance. He had seen no principles in the bargaining and had expressly refused to encourage it, but the pinpricks still went on. They were almost welcome now, the barbs precipitated decision, and he announced with abrupt secrecy that he had had enough of his place.

The dismay of the men he talked to came back in a wave of pleadings. Suddenly in Liberal newspapers there were fierce denials of all the charges against him, and renewed and glowing eulogies. The private letters poured in. "You are run down," Edgar wrote from Toronto. "I do not believe that at any time you realize the great and unique position which you occupy in Canada. I know that when you are depressed by ill health you seem to be utterly blind to it." In four pages of carefully plain talk, drafted and copied over, he summed up the common plea. "Do not leave us . . . do not in a time of ill health take a rash step to cut yourself off from giving the ripe fruit of your life's work to Canada."[14]

Blake, unmoved by the eloquence, had enough of his own

in reply. "I think I may fairly take my discharge and leave to others the party management which I hate and for which I am wholly unfit . . . I have always detested my position; every day I more detest it . . . Instead of wishing it I *dread* success . . . four years and a general election are enough . . . I can't pull at the galley oars any longer."[15] Yet in spite of himself the oars remained in his hands. The session was not yet over. One could not have a leaderless party. There was no one to replace Blake.

The price of retaining him, however, would be higher from now on. He made that clear on St. Patrick's day, the 17th of March. A year before, a bill had been introduced in the House to incorporate the Loyal Orange Order as a Dominion entity. It would have enabled the Order, for one thing, to establish itself in Quebec, where its presence was now forbidden. To the relief of both parties, dreading the certainty of Catholic and Protestant division, it had been given the six months' hoist. Blake had said nothing and allowed it to disappear. This time, however, as the bill came back supported by new pressure, there was to be no strategic silence.

He was not speaking at all, said the leader of the Liberal party, "in the capacity which I for the time being hold." He was speaking as a member of parliament, the governing body of the Dominion. The bill would advance bigotry, muddy the waters of politics, and promote religious strife. The Orangemen were a secret society, and "I am opposed to State recognition of secret societies." All Orangemen were Protestant, most Orangemen were Conservative, and Blake had had some experience of their electioneering methods. One fought shadows and whisperings and the *odium theologicum*; there could never be a dealing with issues as free and tolerant men. It was the story of Orangeism in Ontario and there had been a similar story in Quebec, where Liberals had fought with Catholic ultramontanes. On the one hand the Order, and on the other priests of the Church, had tainted politics with prejudice and defiled religion for votes. It was a record shameful to both parties, and for himself he consigned it to the past.

The battle with ultramontanism was beginning to be won in Quebec. He had been impressed by the change in the political attitude of the Church, and by Laurier's work in changing it. Blake would have nothing to do now with a cause inimical to that Church and almost equally inimical to the French Canadian of Quebec. "The more you set up, as a combination, a great Protestant society, which is also a great political association, the more you make coincident, or strive to make coincident, the lines of division for the religious and the political opinions of the people, and act directly in the teeth of what I believe to be for the benefit of the State." He would not do it; he was unalterably opposed to the bill. "Perhaps I am wrong; I dare say that I shall be more bitterly misrepresented than ever before . . . but I have told plainly the truth as I believe it."[16]

He had also completely alienated the Orange vote of Ontario, about twenty per cent of the total. To Orangemen of his own party it was a throwing down of the gauntlet. To all Ontario Liberals who depended on Orange support, it was an act of political madness. It appalled Cartwright, already uneasy enough with "Master Blake". He was weary of resignations, distressed by Blake's ambivalence on the question of free trade, and the differences of character went even deeper still. To Cartwright, though he was contemptuous enough of Orangemen, they were a potential pool of votes. It was worth considering, he had thought, "whether a few of our supporters having proclivities that way could not be encouraged to take an active share in the proceedings of the Order. So far we have let the whole thing go by default."[17]

Of that plan, in Cartwright's view, Blake's speech was a disastrous rejection. Almost thirty years later, brooding in his old age, he could still see nothing in the gesture but a bid for Catholic support. That it certainly got. It was a breath of new life for the tolerant Mowat in Ontario, who was slowly diluting virulence on the question of separate schools. It helped Laurier and it helped Mercier on the other ground where virulence remained to be diluted. From one old *bleu* who was now inclining toward Blake came word that his pronouncement on "la question orangiste . . . vous met à la tête du parti conservateur de Québec."[18] Yet whatever the political effects, they had now become incidental in the mind of the leader. If the fruit of his life's work was still to be given Canada it would be given in his own way. "The party management which I hate"[19] — the vote-getting — the skirting of dangerous issues – would have to be done by others for it would not be done by Blake.

The session closed in April and he was still of the same mind. Edgar was still pleading. That friend, that faithful work-horse and child of Canada First, was hardly a great man. But he represented the best of Liberal Ontario and rather more than that. He spoke French, he was a good friend of many of the Quebec leaders, and he sensed the value of their growing trust in Blake. In four previous attempts Edgar had failed to secure a seat in parliament, but he expected to succeed on the fifth. There was the hope of an acclamation, of a place at Blake's side, and it reinforced his urgency. "You cannot possibly ignore," he wrote, oblivious of some exceptions, "the fact that everybody but yourself feels your position to be one of brilliant success."[20] The position must be retained; there could be no change in the leadership. Could there not instead be a sharing of responsibilities, a relief from the distasteful work, with Mills, Cartwright, and others assuming part of the load? There could not, Blake replied. He brushed away the suggestion as more distasteful than the work. He would not stand as a figurehead and he would not lead through a committee. He remained in the detested place.

It was public property by May that he intended to retire from politics. He seemed half-heartedly to be groping about for a successor. Mowat was not to be had, and Mills could hardly be considered. Old friend though he was, and able man though he was, he had the hectoring ways of a schoolmaster and a persistent, narrow dogmatism that repelled too many people. Cartwright, for all his brilliance, could not command a following, and his relations with Blake were approaching active dislike. The thought of a leader from Quebec, unthinkable to most of the party, might have to be entertained. If it was, however, it was vague, and discouraged in its first beginnings. "Our friends in West Durham have planned a picnic on June 17," Blake wrote to Laurier on the 24th of May, "and they would much like to hear you . . . it occurred to me that perhaps you and Madam Laurier might manage to give us a week or ten days visit . . . thus we might combine pleasure with business and have you at our meeting. What do you say?"[21] What Laurier had to say, for once, was quite in the vein of Blake. He was a worried barrister faced with a neglected practice; he had too much work at home.

The picnic planned by the friends of West Durham was naturally to be held at Bowmanville. It would have meant for Laurier a shared appearance with Blake in the strong fortress of the faithful, the heart and centre of the leader's own constituency. The man at Blake's side, making the impression that he hoped Laurier would make, might well appear at least as a potential successor. It was not to be, or at least not yet to be. On the fine mid-June day Blake appeared alone, flanked as usual by a crowd of lesser luminaries.

"An immense number of people met him at the railway station," carolled the loyal Bowmanville *Statesman,* "and accompanied him to the place of meeting. A splendid body of young men and lads numbering a hundred and fifty, and mounted on the finest horses in the county served as his escort . . . Bowmanville was gay with a profusion of colours and loud cheers and the waving of handkerchiefs . . . many hundreds in wagons followed his carriage . . . along the road banners innumerable floated, triumphal arches were erected, and appropriate mottoes greeted the people's choice."[22] There was a different view, however, or a different political perspective, for a Tory writing to Macdonald. "He tried to act the gentleman and look jolly and smiling, and even lifted his hat as he passed from the railway station to the ground[23] . . . He never got one cheer from any quarter. I understand he did not like it after humiliating himself to take off his hat."[24]

Whatever the truth of Bowmanville, it left Blake unchanged. He liked nothing and could escape nothing; politics hemmed him in. Wherever he turned there was the net of the party's problems and the throb of the party's hopes. There was the baleful fascination of the continually shifting scene. Laurier's work in Quebec was bearing fruit. In July the constituency of Megantic, an old Conservative stronghold, fell to Liberals in a bitter by-election. It drew Blake to Quebec for a triumphal banquet, and even more significantly it drew Mowat too. The growing strength in the provinces was being knitted together federally, and it was knitting around Blake. It was another strand of the webwork, binding him into his place.

On the great issues he seemed to be more alone than ever before. The Treaty of Washington, governing the fisheries arrangements, was soon due to lapse. There was the need of a new agreement to be hammered out with the Americans, and it was reviving some old ideas. It was leading to talk of trade treaties and rearrangements of the tariffs, or even the abandonment of tariffs in favour of reciprocity. It was actually leading Cartwright in the direction of a commercial union, and Blake could not follow him there. He could not follow Mackenzie in the old man's new enthusiasm for the building of the CPR. Mackenzie had gone to the west on the invitation of Stephen, and had been swept away by the country and the magnificence of the great work. Blake had been invited to go and had declined the invitation. In Stephen's eyes his "blind malignity"[25] remained. In his own eyes the indisputable achievement was not the relevant point. This work that would shape the nation had been built on a defective base.

There was no doubt in his mind now that the railway would

be completed. But there would be no boom after that, and there was no promise of a boom. The hard times of the summer grew a little harder by autumn and Liberal prospects rose with that distress. By December, with the stock of the Canadian Pacific still falling on the markets, there was a warning of new trouble. Workmen struck at Port Arthur because of a delayed pay car; money was short again. Macdonald was at war with Norquay, the Premier of Manitoba, the very fact that the provincial government was Conservative was dragging Norquay down. There was hope for Liberals there, building on bad times too.

The case of the Ontario boundary, carried to the Privy Council, had been pleaded by Oliver Mowat and decided in favour of Ontario. Macdonald had lost there. He had lost on the Rivers and Streams Bill and on his Liquor Licensing Act, with the bases for both destroyed by judgments of the Lords. He was being defeated on many fronts in the face of provincial claims; it appeared at least that federalism was shaping in Blake's way.

The Liberal revival in Quebec seemed matched by Conservative disruption, federally as well as provincially. Macdonald was old, Tilley was sick; even Tupper was worn. Chapleau and Langevin in the Cabinet, almost openly at war, conducted much of their battle in the home province. At a by-election in Beauce, long impregnably Conservative, Langevin's support of a candidate had resulted in near-disaster. It had been caused, the report came, by a sudden infusion of money in support of the opposing *rouge*, and the money had come from Chapleau. "It is really amazing," Blake wrote to Laurier, commenting on that report. "Things go well for us while this disintegration proceeds . . . it may be a very important factor in the operations of the next session."[26]

The next session. He was already accepting the prospect. There had been all the familiar pressures and he could think of another now. He was required for a new reason. "I fear the recklessness of Macdonald, which now that he is near the end of his career has become more marked than ever. I think he acts on the principle, 'after me the deluge' — and the deluge is now coming."[27]

He spoke more truth than he knew. The troubles of the Red River had moved along to the Saskatchewan and the storm was gathering in the clouds. Louis Riel was back.

CHAPTER THREE

RIEL

THE THIRD SESSION of the fifth parliament was convened on January 29, 1885. The Marquess of Lansdowne, who had succeeded as Governor General two years earlier, read the Speech from the Throne. It was almost wholly innocuous, with only the return of the Franchise Bill promising a political fight. Of the real issues approaching, and the size and imminence of the dangers, nothing at all was said.

George Stephen was haunting Ottawa again, in desperate need of help for the CPR. Macdonald could see no chance of meeting his needs, and was faced with a bankrupt railway. Worse still, stretched as he was on this familiar rack, he had neglected an older problem.

With the Métis along the Saskatchewan, who had drifted west from the settlements of the Red River, all the mistakes of government had been repeated. There had been no provision for the effects of the railway's coming, nor for other and deeper change. The nomad hunters no longer followed the buffalo, for the buffalo had disappeared. The Indians said the earth had swallowed them up. Yet the half-breed squatter, forced to become a farmer, had no security for his land; civilization and the survey chain were steadily closing in. His narrow strips of river frontage were being carved into square blocks; he no longer owned what he thought he owned and there were strange men in his fields. They were denying him the use of other lands that had long been held in common, and they were appropriating some of the best. He could not understand the process, had no means of preventing it, and for years his complaints and petitions had been almost totally ignored. He lived, a French Indian in the view of a remote government, an obstacle in the course of settlement to be absorbed or brushed aside.

Since the summer of 1884 Riel had been established at Batoche, the Métis capital on the banks of the South Saskatchewan. He had come back, after restless years in exile, summoned by a deputation of Métis leaders. He had been in colleges, seminaries, and mental homes, and had at last settled in Montana. There, when the horsemen found him after their long ride from the north, he was quietly teaching school. Yet the call had come to one who was half-expecting it. It had taken little to waken the sense of destiny and stir the deep-banked fires; he dreamed of a new Church, dreamed of supplanting the Pope, he was the creator of Manitoba, and he remained his people's prophet. When he returned late in July Macdonald ought to have been warned. He was indeed warned, by many westerners and friends, but nothing had served to rouse him. He had too much work in the east, too many worries with the railway, to be troubled by the half-breed demagogue who had once accepted his bribe.

Word had come to Ottawa of stirrings in the Métis settlements. There had been still more ominous rumours from among the tribes on the reservations. Yet it was January 28, the eve of parliament's opening, before any action was taken. On that day the cabinet moved to establish a commission of inquiry, and it moved too late for Riel. He was now ahead of the Métis leaders who had summoned him and beyond the control of priests; he was priest and leader himself. With the ponderous processes of government hardly even begun, he had mobilized the bands of one-time buffalo hunters and was fomenting Indian war.

Meanwhile parliament went on. The clouds Blake saw were the old clouds, and there was little but tired irony in his reply to the Speech from the Throne. Where were the prosperous times? There had been no mention in the Speech of the affairs of the CPR; he concluded from that with heavy and sardonic emphasis that there would be no more calls for aid. He was as aware as any man of Stephen's presence in Ottawa and of the frantic necessities behind it. Yet it was only on the revived Franchise Bill that he offered the threat of battle.

The measure came to the House on March 19, once more brought down by Macdonald. It had its old virtues and its old faults. It would make the national franchise uniform, and it would centralize control. It offered some women the vote, but only unmarried women of independent property, and even that half-concession was certain to offend Quebec. Any enfranchisement of women, Laurier had reported to Blake, "will be looked at as revolutionary, and is sure to be so called from many a pulpit."[1] Some Indians were also to be given the franchise, but the bill was so loosely drawn that it was difficult to determine which. In the main it seemed to be the classes that would be susceptible to party management and usable by politicians. The bill would reduce the provinces, exalt the federal government, and the party in power would appoint the electoral officers. In all of it the one certainty was a renewal of monstrous quarrels but Macdonald, haunted by greater worries, had steeled himself to face them. They would be at least relief and distraction from the thought of that dying railway and those telegrams from the west.

Yet he could no longer control events as he controlled parliament. On the 27th of March, with Liberals girding to attack the Franchise Bill, the House adjourned for Easter. On the same day another telegram came. It was from Colonel Irvine at Prince Albert, commanding the Mounted Police. His men had been attacked by the Métis at Duck Lake, and he had twelve killed and eleven wounded to report. Madman, prophet or demagogue, Riel could not be ignored. His second rising had become actual rebellion.

By March 31 parliament was in session again, and volunteers and militia were already on their way west. Margaret Blake, driving out with Edgar to the encampment at Carleton Place, presented a flag to one of the departing units. The panache of war surrounded the many goings, and suddenly within the country there was a new sensation of power. It came from the railway, almost nearing completion, and from the brusque and ruthless magic that was characteristic of Van Horne.

On stretches of the line that rounded the Great Lakes there were still gaps in the steel, where muskeg, bush, and rock had delayed the builders. In a matter of days Van Horne bridged them all. He ran troops to the railheads, off-loaded them onto sleighs, and fought them on in the teeth of wild spring blizzards to where the steel began again. Sometimes he laid new steel, simply clamped to the ground, and drove his trains over it. His commissaries functioned smoothly, there was rough-and-ready efficiency at each of the transfer points, and he brought the contingents to Winnipeg within six days of their departure. It was a marvellous feat of logistics and its value would not be lost; Macdonald, Van Horne, and Stephen were fully aware of that. The east and the west had been joined, months had been cut to days, and it stood before the country as the work of this troubled railway.

In the House, while the telegrams came and the troops deployed in their columns on the bush and prairie, there was only the acrid fretting of helpless men. There was word of Frog Lake and of the six who had died there, this time killed by Indians. If the war was widening only soldiers could deal with it; politics could do nothing now. Yet politics still went on, for the country had to be governed. It had been ill-governed in respect to the North-West, and beyond the fears and the murk there was that issue shaping. None of the parties or leaders, neither Blake, Mackenzie, nor Macdonald, could claim to have been a friend of the native peoples. Mackenzie had barely seen the problems rising. To Blake the tribes shut in on the reservations had been children of another world, not to be fed or educated beyond their station in life. He had complained of the cost of their keep, and of "gingerbread and ribbons and some hundredweights of wax candles going to

Indians".[2] He had been at best coldly legal in his attitude to Métis claims. Yet he was not accountable for neglect, and he had at least been urgent for justice. Macdonald was the man in power, and justice had not been done.

By April 16, with this thought overhanging him and with banks refusing loans to the CPR, Macdonald had chosen the order of his coming battles. He moved on that day the second reading of the Franchise Bill, and a savage debate began. It was to be the longest the House had known, the bitterest, and the most exhausting, and the result was to be a mangled remnant of Macdonald's first proposals. Time after time, through day-long, night-long sessions, there were breaks only for food or from compelled respect for the Sabbath. "We wound up a 57-hour session exactly at twelve last night," Edgar reported to his wife on Sunday, May 3rd. "We did not let the government pass one line of the bill in that time and we could have kept it up 24 hours longer if necessary."[3]

The truculence was shared by Cartwright, who was the heart and soul of strategy. Every trick of parliament and every art of obstruction came somehow into play. As Cartwright saw the debate, twenty-seven years later, it was a heroic fight by Liberals for their very political lives. Theoretically, he conceded, there was something to be said for the bill. Practically, however, "it proposed to place the formation of the voters' lists in each riding under the control of a paid partisan of the government who would have been selected, as we well knew, for the express purpose of stuffing these lists against us . . . Had the bill passed in that shape I doubt if we could have saved twenty seats out of ninety-two in Ontario."[4]

Blake was in agreement with Cartwright but he did not share his zest. For almost two months, having said what he had to say, he left the fight to his eager politicians. He was against the bill in principle as a threat to distort federalism. He was as fearful as Mr. Gladstone, and quoted copiously from Gladstone, on the subject of votes for women. It was an enormous subject, not to be meddled with here, and not in this gimcrack way, distinguishing the married women from her still unwedded sister. On this point, with Victorian sanctity and solemnity, he was of the same mind as Quebec. Women should be sheltered from politics until a better and wiser day. Some Indians were to be enfranchised and some Indians were not; the government itself had not made clear distinctions. What it was looking for here was votes, ignorant, manageable votes, and it had neglected a first priority. Let it change its laws to declare the Indian a person, let it train and teach him for a place in modern life. The vote designed to be used in herded ignorance, would be more a curse than a blessing.

Blake would be accused, said Blake, of being against women and against Indians; he was quite indifferent to the actual course of the debate, and more to politics itself. On one occasion, during the last ten minutes of the pre-Sabbath session about which Edgar had written his wife, he had suddenly leaped to his feet without notes or warning. Obviously not prepared, and curtailed by the approach of midnight since he would not speak on a Sunday, he had had enough of foot-dragging on either side of the aisle. He had flayed the government in a "brilliant rocket of a speech",[5] cramming volumes into paragraphs and ending on the stroke of twelve. He had electrified all who heard him with the passionate flare of power, yet the passion was against delay, manoeuvring, and evasion, the very procedures and tools of party leaders. It was essentially against his place, the trap in which he was held.

Yet he was still there as the blistering session continued into its fourth and fifth month. The fight was lost on the Franchise Bill, but it would sputter on till July. In mid-May came word of the capture of Batoche, then that Riel was taken. The aftermath of rebellion would now have to be dealt with. And even before that there was the older angrier question: the justification of the railway and the needs of the CPR.

It was June 16 when John Henry Pope, Minister of Railways, introduced the resolutions respecting aid. Replacing Tupper, who had returned to England as High Commissioner, he was a rough-cut politician who knew what he was about. The CPR was desperately short of cash and it could not sell its stock. Everything it owned was mortgaged to the Dominion of Canada. In the money markets of the world it was already a dead horse, yet out beyond the foothills and among the high peaks of the Rockies it was a fiercely living thing. The steel that had spanned the prairies and put an end to rebellion was climbing into the mountains. The mountain section was driving east to meet it and the link would certainly come. Only a needless bankruptcy threatened the great achievement, and it was an obstacle to be brushed aside. Whatever the faults of conception, and whatever the railway's cost, the country wanted it finished.

"The only thing the company are going to ask from this House in the shape of money," said Pope, "is that they may be assisted temporarily to the extent of $5,000,000., and to be allowed to cancel stock of $35,000,000. and issue bonds."[6] The bonds, however, which would replace the unsaleable stock, were to be guaranteed by the government. What the Dominion would be assuming in fact was an additional burden of $40,000,000.

Pope was truculently confident that the obligation would be accepted. He believed, he said, that he spoke to a willing House. He waxed eloquent, with reason, on the work he had seen in the west and on the devoted efforts of the builders who had risked all they had. He did not mention that they would now be assured of their dividends and eventually of huge profits, nor that the actual risk was being assumed by the country. Blake would enlarge on those points as he had so often before, and he would change nothing. Pope looked across at the leader of the opposition and taunted him with the old phrase. The "sea of mountains" had been invaded and overcome; what had he to say to that?

The same day and the next Blake gave his answer. He had been seven weeks in preparing it and was seven hours in delivering it, without hope of any effect. There was all that Pope might have expected, and much that was too well-remembered, but it was paraded now in a new and final light. Through page after page of notes, quotation by endless quotation, bewildering the House with balance sheets that no man could digest, he retraced the story of the railway. He denied nothing to the magnificence of the work itself, the fault was the basic plan. He denied nothing to the builders but the title of public benefactors. Already assured of dividends of something like 12 per cent, they were to be the owners of a noble property for which the country had largely paid.

Policy had been wrong, plans had been wrong, and the fallacies stood revealed. What had been the effects of the routing, of the choice of private builders, of the haste to bridge the prairies and reach the Pacific? They were apparent now in the text of these resolutions and they were spread wide on the face of the country itself. He traced them step by step, through the deflated treasury, the collapsed booms, the discouraged immigrants leaving Manitoba and the seething west beyond. "The vast promises of material gains and immediate gains which honourable gentlemen have made have resulted in scattered settlements, in enormous expenditures, in great engagements, in widespread dissatisfaction . . . in the embarrassment of the railway company, in the distress of Canada at large and in the ruin of a great many of her citizens."[7]

He was not prepared, he concluded, encroaching on his eighth hour, to approve these resolutions to protect the directors of the syndicate. He opposed them, he protested against them, and he knew they would pass the House.

By July 6 he was on his feet again, and for another seven hours. On the desk under his hand and overflowing to Laurier's desk beside him were the records of the North-West, the long, relentless story of neglect, evasion, and delay. He had gathered the petitions of the half-breeds and the stiff replies of bureaucrats, and he read them all to the House. He was bitter on the long silences when there had been no replies at all, when the settlements seethed in ignorance and men fearful for their land had been left to live with fear. They had been left to live without help or understanding, while the great grievances and the little grievances accumulated to a monstrous wrong. "Why the record is one long cry for redress."[8] He was moved by the huge recital as he had not been moved before, for this time he had lived with it in his own study. It seemed at times he had lived with the very people. "The autumn has passed and winter is coming. What has become of the promises?"[9] He quoted from one of their cries and gave his answer. The promises had not been kept, the Métis had not known justice, the Indians had not been cared for.

Out of that had risen Riel, but he would not yet speak of Riel. There would be another day for the prisoner in Regina jail. He was speaking now of mis-government and the wreckage brought in its wake. "In older and sterner times," he concluded grimly, "men would have been impeached for conducting in this way the public affairs of the country. In these milder days we have substituted votes of censure."[10]

It was a lost vote in spite of him, and in spite of the efforts of Laurier. The French Canadian followed Blake, and there was a new power in the man. Vibrating through his words, moreover, was the throb of a new fear. The troubles of the North-West were not to be confined to the Saskatchewan nor to the second rebellion alone. The Red River was remembered and so was Thomas Scott, the Orangeman done to death by Riel's Métis court. The Métis were half-French, Riel was half-French, and the old and angry Englishness was once more rising against them. "I think the feeling permeates the very atmosphere, not only of this House but of the whole of this country . . . that if these men have rebelled it is because they are to a certain extent of French origin."[11]

The leader listened to his deskmate and recognized the sombre truth. But nothing could be done now; it would be work for next year. It would be work for another man; perhaps Laurier. On July 16, in a stinking, sweltering House that had been sitting for six months, there was a final, graceless quarrel of exhausted men. Macdonald proposed an increase in the members' indemnity; Blake fought it and lost. He was not present on the 20th when the session came to an end. He had gone home sick and seething with this last, petty defeat, magnified to a sense of failure and of total alienation. He was divorced once more from his working politicians, who felt they had earned the money and needed it more than he. He had no sense of support, of unity on the greater issues, of any general sharing of his own convictions. The days and nights of study, the endless hours of speech-making had come to their usual end. Nothing was changed, power was as distant as ever, and the thought of attaining power was the worst thought of all.

From her home with the Cronyn family his mother was writing him as usual, urging him to seek divine help and to chew his food well. The script was as fine and gentlewoman-like as ever but she was all too obviously failing; he must go to London to see her. He must go to London, England; there were briefs piled on his desk for hearings by the Privy Council. He must have time in Murray Bay, the unfailing haven of rest, and, above all and finally, he must be free of the greatest burden. In the course of the next few months, he wrote Edgar, he would inform his friends that they must choose another leader.

He was in London, Ontario, with his mother when Edgar's reply came. There was the usual dismay and the usual fears for the party, but there was no longer any surprise. There was even partial acceptance. "Perhaps," Edgar wrote, "the responsibility wears upon you more than the work — and the occupancy of that position by another *for a time* will render you a service." Edgar himself did not have aspirations, but neither did he mention the obvious names in Ontario; he seemed to have followed some of his leader's thinking. Laurier might be the man, yet there were difficulties in the way of that. The trial of Riel had begun and there were danger signs in Quebec. "Northwest matters may take a turn which would render

Laurier an impossibility," and, "If not Laurier what alternative have we?"[12]

He was back to the oldest question, hinting at the usual answer, and Blake brushed it aside. "I can't enter into these subjects on paper."[13] He was still leader; he could not relinquish the thought and he could not escape from the frustrations. "I would be willing to wear out if I were doing good to my country. But I do no good."[14] He was still seething from the resentments of the long session. He was laughed at and yawned at for his speeches seven hours long. But they were that long because there was that much to be said; they were dealing with enormous questions. Who else was there to say it? Everything was left to Blake, everything was loaded on Blake, and he attempted to do what must be done while his friends slept behind him. Or they drifted out of the House, shaking their heads.

"You say I work too hard . . . others have said the same thing but they have not, like you, been willing to do the work themselves. It is impossible to succeed, save by work. The real workings of the tariff can be ascertained and made plain only by *work*. But I have for years called for help — in vain. The jobs and extravagances in the west . . . and elsewhere can be made plain only by work. But I have for years called for help — in vain." Even now there was work to be done; the party should be preparing for battle on the subject of the North-West, the great issue ahead. "We should have people out there to investigate, we should find out from the volunteers — we should now be making ready for the struggle — but I have *not* asked for help because I know it would be in vain."[15]

By mid-August, writing from Murray Bay, he had much the same for Laurier. The North-West would be the issue for next session, but the party would not be prepared. "Effective inquiry involves prior investigation and the painful collection of facts during the recess; and this will not be done . . . I have given up that hope."[16] He had given up many hopes, though there were hopeful signs about him. John Thompson, the Nova Scotia Conservative, already known as able and incorruptible, had been appointed three years earlier to the Supreme Court of his province. He was ripe for wider fields, and he was in Ottawa seeing Macdonald. "I can't think," Blake wrote, "that T. is out here save to discuss the lead."[17] He was to be proved wrong on that, but it seemed for the moment a hint of Macdonald's going. As to his own going he had only casual words, still carefully reserved. Laurier believed that the party was gaining in Quebec. "If this be so it will make easier that which I so much desire, a change which may release me."[18] He was not released yet, even in his own mind, and he was on his way to England. "I leave my country with shrinking and not on my own judgment. But it was thought better that I should get away for a season."[19]

Amid the family pleadings, the advice of doctors and the many claims of the law business, he had hardly thought of Riel. The evidence was in, the sentence was overhanging the Métis leader, but the rope was still far off. For Blake the North-West issue was the blundering of Macdonald's government and in the face of that dismal record the rebel could not die. "Justice is the same everywhere," he had said in his speech to the House, and he sailed for London still firm in the conviction. "I have little doubt that Riel will not be executed," he told Laurier, "and that the Orangemen though grudgingly will yield to that view."[20]

He was still in London in November when Riel was hanged. He had visited Ireland as usual and tried Wales as a new restorer of health, but for the most part he had fretted out life in the city. His Privy Council hearings had had to be postponed by the Lords, and there was enough frustration in that. There was more in the word that came from Ontario and the maritimes, where Liberal losses in by-elections vied with the news of Riel. Recoiling from each mail, yet avidly impatient for the next, he tortured himself in the intervals with the thought of his neglected duties. They outweighed Riel in his mind; they seemed to submerge Riel. The party was drifting leaderless and he was thousands of miles away. He could deal with nothing and escape nothing, nor could he even attempt to escape.

He had a "nervous horror"[21] of discussing the question of the leadership, he wrote Edgar in September. He had not even written to Laurier, "that dear and faithful friend."[22] He was sick, unstrung, incapable of concentration; utterly incapable at the moment of even thinking of the lead. He did not resign, he did not suggest a successor; the question hung in suspense. Yet neither Edgar nor Laurier, in whom he confided, could be blamed for sensing the approach of total collapse.

Under that cloud the party lived through the autumn and the leaders traded their views. Mackenzie, almost voiceless now, had still an acid commentary for his friend, A. G. Jones. "We are making no progress, we lose all elections . . . there is no spring left. The "Young Liberals" are left to the leadership of Edgar!"[23] For all Mackenzie's scorn, Edgar himself seemed much of the same opinion and resigned to the absence of Blake. "I watched him most closely last session," he wrote Laurier, "and nothing seemed to lift him up from his physical and nervous prostration . . . I am inclined to think if he does not feel well enough to lead in the House next session he would be better if he simply stayed in Europe till next spring . . . some committee might be able to run things in a sort of a way . . . what say you?"[24]

For that proposal Laurier had no enthusiasm, though he was quite as gloomy as Edgar about Blake's condition. "I fear very much," he wrote, "that we must lose him as our leader . . . it is the soul which is preying on the body. I believe he is under the opinion that his followers hold him responsible for the lack of progress of the party . . . could he but realize how dear he is to us all . . . how we are all ready to follow him and cheerfully follow him though we should forever remain in opposition his soul would brighten up and his physical health be improved." Yet however brave the words, Laurier dismissed the hope of their realization. He was obsessed with other thoughts. "The North-West troubles concentrate the whole of our attention . . . I rather think that you are right in surmising that the government will hang Riel." If they did, Laurier speculated, they would lose the clergy and much of Conservative Quebec. "In fact very many of the old members of the clergy believe it as actually impossible that Sir John, *l'ami des canadiens-francais* would be guilty of such an odious act."[25]

Against that there was Cartwright, hardening in another mood. On October 23, doubtful of the government's course, he wrote to inquire about Laurier's. "Here in eastern Ontario they are sure to have trouble (and a good deal of it) if they pardon Riel. How will it affect you?"[26] On the other hand, if there were no pardon, he wrote three weeks later, "I hope you will let loose your people right and left . . . here in Ontario our line is simple. We admit that Riel deserved his doom but contend that Sir John is a thousandfold the more guilty of the two. If Riel deserved hanging, drawing and quartering is altogether too good for Sir John. That ought to give us a broad enough platform." On that platform, however, there would have to be different postures. "We must each fight our battle in our own province in our own way. Let Blake in his capacity of Dominion leader rather stand aside and pose as arbitrator in good time . . . I hear he is better and if he will only take a decent amount of exercise and forswear those desperately long speeches he has a very great game before him."[27]

The game began within three days of his writing. On the 16th of November came the execution of Riel. On the 17th almost every newspaper in Quebec wore black bands of mourning. "Henceforth," said *La Presse* of Montreal, "there are no more Conservatives nor Liberals . . . there are only PATRIOTS and TRAITORS — the National Party and the Party of the Rope."[28] By the 18th Edgar was pressing Laurier to direct the battle in Quebec. Demoralized *bleus* were fleeing the party of the rope and they should be gathered in by the Liberals. "I do think that this is a matter which calls for your most earnest attention, and early action. If you give the movement the right direction anything can be accomplished that we desire — but a delay will give Sir John the time he wants to consolidate his broken ranks . . . I hear today that Blake is better, and has taken his passage from Liverpool for New York on 10th December. This is good news — but he is as well away for a few weeks till things settle down to something definite. I feel that by bold and vigorous action the Tory party in Quebec can be split in twain before Blake gets back. What say you, mon frère?"[29]

Three days later, on the 21st of November, Blake wrote to Laurier from London. It must have seemed that he wrote from another world. In Canada the fragmenting parties were becoming English and French, divided around Riel. The Orangemen marched in Ontario and there were Liberals marching with them, while *bleus* deserting wholesale were joined with *rouges* in Quebec. It was Mercier, now the nationalist, who had leaped to the head of the procession, and was swallowing the provincial parties in his *parti national.* He would be either threat or promise to the federal Liberal party. Edgar was in Montreal when Blake wrote, taking the measure of the scene, talking of coalitions. There were *rouges* and *bleus* to be had, there were waverers who no longer wavered, there was a fierce and total resentment that the man who had died was French. It went deep to the roots, it was the single issue for the province, and with discreet support from Ontario it could bring Macdonald down. It was a dangerous issue, certainly, and divisive for many English, but how in the name of politics could that support be withheld?

Chapleau and Langevin in the cabinet, who still supported Macdonald, were being burned in effigy in Quebec. In Montreal, the day after Blake wrote, there were forty thousand people on the Champ de Mars, standing before a dozen platforms, listening to a dozen leaders. They were of all parties and they were all French, speaking for a common anger. "Riel, our brother, is dead,"[30] intoned Mercier, and he was matched from another podium by the voice of Laurier: "Had I been born on the banks of the Saskatchewan I would myself have shouldered a musket against the neglect of government and the shameless greed of speculators!"[34]

Upon all this came the bland voice from London of the man in improved health. "I have often thought of writing you, but a sick heart for Canada and a body not too well deterred me. I sail for home on the 10th." He had friends to visit in

WILL THE "OLD MAN" CONSENT?

New York, there was talk of a banquet in his honour when he reached London, Ontario, and there was not a word of Riel. He looked forward with anxiety to the work of the next session and hoped that his friends would take a leading part. In that work, though he felt himself out of touch, he was sure that the North-West troubles, along with railway matters, would have a prominent place.[32]

It was not Laurier but Mercier who rushed to New York to meet Blake on his arrival, and in that fact alone there was shock and warning. The *parti national* was outgrowing its provincial status; it was threatening to absorb liberalism and even some Ontario Liberals in a united front on Riel. It counted on many *bleus*, and it was counting now on Blake. If he would come by way of Quebec on his way home from Toronto there could be meetings arranged condemning the execution; he could pour his oil on the flames.

As Blake absorbed it all he was abruptly rid of his blandness; he had become the leader again. There would be no visit to Quebec, no progress up the St. Lawrence, he would not even be seen. He had cold comfort for the ruthless politician, burning with genuine anger and eager for party gain. Yet he had learned much from Mercier. This was the man who spoke for the mood of the province, nor was Laurier here to deny it. He could not deny it; he was himself of the same mood. He supported Edgar and he supported Mercier, and he looked for support from Ontario at whatever cost to the party. He could not have it; that was the first decision. There could be no reknitting of liberalism around the single issue of Riel. There could be no support or appearance of support for a party labelled as "French". Blake must divide from Laurier if they could not find common ground, but he would not divide the nation.

He reached home, by way of the American route, and began his work with Laurier. It had all to be at arm's length, all in complete secrecy; each, as Cartwright had predicated, must fight in his own province. Under that imperative the two men groped together, harried by opposing partisans and watched too well by their friends. They could not meet in public, for there could be no appearance of collusion, and even on a talk in private Laurier imposed delay. He could not reach Ottawa till January because of his many meetings, and it was now quite out of the question that Blake appear in Quebec. There could only be long letters, strained, affectionate and never quite in agreement, which seemed to widen the gap.

Blake deplored the musket shouldering, but Laurier was unrepentant. There was a quiet, bitter resentment of the execution of Riel. He had met the man, had no doubt that he was unbalanced, and Riel had not died because of the revolt along the Saskatchewan. He had been hanged to placate the Orangemen for the death of Thomas Scott. The business of the Liberal party, if party it still remained, was to condemn the execution with the causes from which it rose.

It could not be done in Ontario nor in the rest of English Canada. A first few days in Toronto had confirmed the view for Blake. The callers came, the letters flooded in on him, and the sum of all had been given voice by the *Mail.* "The French Canadians are now seeking to compel us to recognize their right to suspend the operation of the law whenever a representative of their race is in the toils. But let us solemnly assure them again that rather than submit to such a yoke Ontario would smash Confederation into its original fragments, preferring that the dream of a united Canada should be shattered forever than that unity should be purchased at the expense of equality."[33]

It was the more impressive and powerful because it was tempered by cold restraint. The anger of Quebec was real but so was this other mood, and it had to be accepted by Blake. "I believe the mind of our party in all the provinces save Quebec," he wrote Laurier, "is very largely satisfied with the execution of Riel."[34] He could not support, as Laurier was inclined to do, the turmoil of shifting loyalties that was taking place in Quebec. The *bleus* gained on the single issue of Riel would merely contribute ultimately to the wreck of the national party. "We can't," he wrote in another letter to Laurier, "make a platform out of a scaffold."[35] Yet neither could the scaffold's shadow be escaped, not by any manoeuvring. "No motion to censure the government for not commuting the sentence would receive the approbation of the bulk of the party from the other provinces" yet "it is not possible nor would it be right to attempt to evade the issue. It must come up and be debated and divided on."[36] To that prospect, by the 31st of December, Laurier was gloomily resigned.

Before the opening of parliament came the banquet arranged for Blake in London, Ontario. He stood up on January 14, 1886, four weeks home in Canada and with the reins again in his hands. He was more than an hour on in his two-hour speech before he even touched Riel. Deliberately, caustically, and incisively he drew the affairs of the country into perspective. It had been misgoverned in many ways, it was suffering from many wrongs, of policy, intention, action. The railway policy had been wrong, fiscal policy had been wrong, the effect of the National Policy was plain to be seen about him in the sufferings of depressed times. There had been waste, corruption, and blundering in the immigration and land policies, and the result of all could be seen in the North-West. Riel could be seen, as one of the results of that.

He approached the issue fortified by a talk with Laurier which had been held in Ottawa on the 8th. As a private meeting it had been all too well-publicized, nor was it quite a meeting of minds. Edgar's work was rejected and Laurier's hopes, so far as they ran with Edgar's, had been finally laid to rest. There could be no unity in the party centring on the issue of Riel, nor was there any prospect of carrying a vote in the House. That must first be accepted. The French voice must be heard, it must be answered by the English voice, and beyond that coming tumult there was only the other hope. It seemed distant and faint enough but Blake had voiced it to Laurier and he voiced it again here. "Let us unite and divide, I say once more, on grounds of reason, argument and opinion, and not of race or creed."[37]

Facing his English audience he returned to the earlier phrase. "I do not propose to construct a political platform out of the Regina scaffold, or to create or cement party ties with the blood of the condemned."[38] He proposed another course; he had set that course for himself. He would wait, he would suspend judgment on the action taken by the government until all its proofs were in, its evidence of fair procedures, its proof of Riel's sanity, its explanations for the last denial of reprieve. He would judge then, and he would judge within the law.

Out of a long, discursive hour little emerged but that, yet it seemed to have served a purpose. "Mr. Blake," said the Essex *Liberal*, "has struck dumb his yelping detractors and sternly reproved those so-called Reformers who preferred office and disgrace to opposition and honour."[39] The *Globe* had got his point. "We of Ontario," it conceded, "must not let our prejudices or preconceptions prevent recognition that Quebec, if Riel was insane, had grounds for crying out against his execution."[40] To the St. Catharines *News*, writing five days after the speech, it "was one of those remarkable arrangements that capture the country and set men thinking. It is estimated that a million people have read it already."[41] Even the vast barrage of hostile comment was somehow oddly diffused, almost in part approving. The "wily Sir Edward" in his "daring balancing act on the Riel question"[42] had been guilty of political clap-trap, hypocrisy and double-dealing. Yet without him, the Ottawa *Journal* speculated, "it is quite possible that the agitation would eventually have resulted in a war of races . . . Mr. Blake has done well."[43] He was, said the Bruce *Herald*, with a sideswipe aimed at Cartwright, Edgar, and friends, "a very different man indeed from the abusive rowdies who have been running the Reform party during his absence."[44]

"We take it," said the Montreal *Gazette*, "he has destroyed the sand castles of his *rouge* allies."[45] From one of these a voice snapped in agreement, "I am not surprised. Englishmen are the same everywhere."[46] Yet Mercier, whatever his real thoughts, pronounced himself as satisfied. "We did not ask Mr. Blake to speak as a French Canadian," said the Liberal *La Patrie*. "We knew he would speak as a loyal Englishman who is without prejudice against our race."[47] Laurier seemed to be encouraged as he took his soundings in Quebec. Blake could have no conception, he wrote on February 10, of what his speech had accomplished. "Its most marked effect has been to inspire the whole community with a sense of security and relief. This, I anticipate, will go far with the thinking men of all classes and must bear its fruit in due time."[48] He was hopeful, and over-hopeful; a cooler judgment came from the place of the scaffold. Blake, said the Regina *Leader*, though "an opportunist . . . a political Micawber, never framing a policy," had nevertheless at London "taken the only course which as a sound lawyer he could take."[49]

It was the least and most to be said. A kind of quiet had been imposed on the stormy country. Riel had been set in frame within the larger frame of the nation and time at least had been gained. Evidence could change little, but the waiting might change much. It might yet establish law, the nearest equivalent to justice, as a guide for the thinking men.

CHAPTER FOUR

LAURIER

On February 25, 1886, Blake sat through the ceremonies of another opening of parliament, shadowed again by death. It was more now than the passing of a well-loved sister; Catherine Blake was gone. The steely Irish gentlewoman who had faced the Canadian bush and come unchanged through fifty years of nation-making had dwindled away with grace, divesting herself of earth. "The personal effects are so small," Sophia Cronyn wrote, "for poor darling always gave away anything nice she had."[1] A book of pious musings had been intended as Edward's portion, but the book could not be found. He hardly needed it, he had no need of remembrances; that mother would walk along with him to the end of his own life.

He faced parliament, he hoped, for the last term of his service as the Liberal leader. He had made that clear in his London speech and emphasized the fact since. Yet he was hemmed in by Riel, as surely as the disrupted parties and the harried party men. Many tempers had cooled, and he had done much to cool them, but it did not remove the issue. It did not avert the danger of a divided nation. Macdonald could not do it; he was fixed in his old positions. Neither could Blake do it; he was the English lawyer from Toronto. It must be a voice that would come from the other side, speaking for French Canada, rising above the angers to express some hope for the future. If Laurier could do that he would become the man of the future. If he could rise to that challenge Blake would be free to go.

It was March 11 when the debate formally began, engineered by Macdonald into the shape he wished it to take. It was to originate from his own side and it was to turn on one point, the execution of a rebel. A Conservative from Montmagny, Auguste-Charles Landry, moved "That this House feels it its duty to express its deep regret that the sentence of death passed upon Louis Riel, convicted of High Treason, was allowed to be put into execution."[2] As he sat down Sir Hector Langevin rose, the senior French Canadian in Macdonald's cabinet. With his motion "That this question be now put"[3] the limits were clamped on the debate, there could now be no amendments. The history of the North-West, the blunderings of the administration, the years of neglect that had brought rebellion on, were not to affect decision. There could be decision only on a hanging for the capital crime of treason, and in neither of the divided parties was there any doubt of the result. The French Canadians who condemned the act would be voted down by the English.

The scaffold had emerged as the issue and there was to be no party platform; it was the manoeuvre Blake had foreseen. He made no attempt to avoid it; he noted it and passed on. While the party grumbled about him he nagged for the production of papers, for the last tittle of evidence that could be wrung from government files. He seemed to his angry English to be a man adrift and floundering, blind to his obvious course. He had two courses, in Cartwright's view, either one of them opening a way to power. He could accept the decision of the courts and fling the gauge to Quebec. Or he could attack Macdonald and his underlings as more guilty than Riel. Actually he did neither; he did not even lead the debate.

It was Laurier who rose before him on the evening of March 16, and when the French Canadian finished there was a new mood in the House. It was a mood welcomed and hoped for by the best on either side, and there were Conservatives as well as Liberals who had sought to give it voice. Laurier had somehow found the common chord, though he had spared the English nothing. "Sir," he said at the end of a long retracing of the many bitter years, "we are a new nation, we are attempting to unite the different conflicting elements which we have into a nation. Shall we ever succeed if the bond of union is to be revenge, if we are to rake up old scores and launch them at the heads of one another?"[4]

When Blake got up at his desk three days later it was heaped higher than usual with masses of books and papers. Macdonald seemed to Cartwright to be strained and very tense. As the speech went on, however, the Prime Minister relaxed, and was soon turning to smile at the colleagues round him. There was to be no attempt to bring a government down; Blake accepted the vote as already lost. He accepted his own diminishment, offering the palm to Laurier. The speech of the other evening, in the party leader's judgment, "merits this compliment, because it is the truth, that it was the finest parliamentary speech ever pronounced in the parliament of Canada since Confederation."[5]

For himself he turned to his documents and the only ground he could hold. There had been "gross, palpable, incredible delay, neglect and mismanagement" in the affairs of the North-West. He would not discuss it now. He had reviewed that history before "at a length variously estimated at from six to seven hours — I hope it was not quite seven, Mr. Speaker." Nor was there anything in that long recital that could be held to justify Riel. "Riel was legally guilty, no matter how great and pressing and long endured the grievances may have been." The government stood condemned but so must treason — if it were the act of a sane man.

Riel's sanity — it was almost the total burden of another seven-hour speech. Blake had demanded evidence and complained that some was withheld, yet the mountain of papers before him was more than enough for the House. It dwindled as he ploughed on, relentless quotation supporting relentless argument, always in a lawyer's monotone and always to the same effect. He had reviewed the work of the alienists who had been sent to examine Riel, and he reviewed it here again. He had ransacked law and history and medical jurisprudence, and he analysed every dogma and expounded every view. He analysed his own motives of fourteen years before, when he had offered a reward for bringing Riel to justice. "I thought then, and I said then, that in my opinion the death of Scott was a cruel murder." There was only one point on which he had come to modify his view. "It is questionable how far the mind of Riel may even at that early day have been thoroughly balanced." It was more the question now at a later day. It was the one question. Rebellion could not be excused, treason could not be pardoned; he would make no plea as Laurier had for the feelings of a wounded people. He would only say what he felt himself convinced of, and it did not exclude doubt. Doubt must always remain; it was the central fact of the tragedy and the key to the great division. Had this government, from mere political expediency, condemned a man who was not responsible for his actions?

He believed it had; he would vote with the Conservative Landry in regretting the execution. Yet he asked for no support, from either side of the House. Cartwright would vote against him, Mackenzie would vote against him; there were many others he valued who would leave him on this issue. He accepted it and let them go. "I know the atmosphere of prejudice and passion which surrounds this case; I know how difficult it will be for years to come to penetrate that dense atmosphere; I know how many people of my own race and of my own creed entertain sentiments and feelings hostile to the conclusions to which I have been driven . . . I blame no one. Each has the right and duty to examine and judge for himself."[6]

It was the oldest platitude of politics, democracy *in excelsis*, and Cartwright heard it with angry incredulity. "Had Mr. Blake done himself justice on this occasion and given us what everyone expected he would do, an impassioned invective of moderate duration, instead of this inordinately prolix dissertation, it was more than possible that it might have turned the scale." Instead there was only quiet and worse than quiet. "Glancing round, I saw that our friends were all, as in duty bound, in solid phalanx in their places, but also, alas, that the majority of them were fast asleep."[7] Yet there was more in that result, and more behind its achieving, than Cartwright was able to see. The scale that might have been turned had deliberately not been turned; there would be no accession to power at the price of racial war.

On June 2 the session came to an end, and it was to be the last for the fourth parliament. Around Riel on the federal scene the clash of division had settled to constrained silence. The parties, at least on the surface, were almost whole again. Macdonald had kept his French-Canadian ministers, and though he was often ill he was not yet ready to depart. Blake, ready to depart, seemed in better health than usual, but disinclined to the raising of dangerous issues. There was trouble brewing with the Americans on the everlasting fisheries question, and it was reviving the cries for trade treaties and measures of reciprocity. They found Blake coldly reserved. He was equally reserved on the National Policy, though he had changed none of his views. He had spoken again on Home Rule for Ireland, and been duly charged with angling for the Irish vote. Beyond that, for the most part, he had been the overhanging presence, always a threat and irritant to the men across the aisle.

"Blake," wrote John Thompson who was a new and imposing figure now as Macdonald's Minister of Justice, "came back last night and was 'awfully clever' for about half an hour and then went up on the back benches and picked his nose and cut his nails for the rest of the night."[8] If it was unkind and inelegant it was the tribute of a formidable man to a formidable man in waiting. The question of the tariffs must wait, the

American question must wait. The CPR was completed and the North-West was quieted; the results and the issues rising from them had not yet taken form. Until they had there could be no new departures, and the only prospect imminent was of another general election.

Blake turned to it throughout the summer with his usual grey distaste, traversing rural Ontario and preparing the party's ground. It was the old ground, harrowed for all his efforts by the angers rising from Riel. He would not make them an issue, yet he was powerless to damp them down. They haunted him in his own constituency; he was not so welcome there. They rose in Quebec in counterpoint where Mercier was now unleashed, dominating every platform in a fierce provincial campaign. In June in Nova Scotia, mobilizing discontent, Liberals had swept the province on an outright cry for secession. Macdonald's capture of Howe seemed to be undone; the National Policy had failed him utterly there. Yet it was hardly to Blake's gain; Blake was a national leader. He could no more build on secession than he was prepared to build on Riel. "What is needed is a new cry," his party followers told him, but they elicited no response. The real issues for Blake were only the old issues, neglect, misgovernment, corruption, and they stared the country in the face. Yet he had not been able to persuade the country to see them; what was needed was a new man.

Edgar in his first enthusiasm, while Blake was still in England, had invited Laurier to Toronto to confront the English on Riel. He had been quickly squelched on that. The musket-shouldering had made it quite unthinkable; Laurier was a marked man. Yet he was also marked by the speech made in the House, that offer to bridge the gulf, that hope to go on together. He had always been liked in parliament and he had risen to new stature; there were essential qualities in him for the politics of a dual nation. They remained, however, to be developed and still more to be revealed. Edgar had been right in his instincts though injudicious in his timing. The Laurier who was now a caricature in most of the English press must be discovered for what he was, or for what Blake hoped he was. If he could face Toronto, and impress Toronto, he would be potentially the party leader.

There could be no thought of the visit through a hot and angry summer, and Blake recoiled from it even in early autumn. Quebec went on with its own election campaign, and there was too much talk of it filling the English newspapers. There was too much talk of Mercier and his *parti national.* The provincial leader had his coalition at last, and it was built on *rouges* and Riel. He was absorbing *bleus* or destroying them, and he was also involving Laurier. For Mercier's federal ally there could be no silence in the campaign, and there was no avoiding the all-pervasive theme. Laurier did not attempt to; he was speaking to his own people, and it seemed in English Canada that he spoke of nothing but Riel.

As the reports of the speeches came to him Blake winced and protested; Laurier was on deadly ground. He must somehow try to reduce "the Regina incident", or at least set it in proportion. There was a general election in prospect and he was being reported in English newspapers. He should turn to the wider issues and view them in a national frame. It was exactly what he had done, Laurier replied, but he had been quoted only on Riel. It was all that Quebec would listen to, and it was all Ontario heard. There was a provincial election to be won before the general election, and it was dominated by this issue. Laurier could not escape it, nor did he seem to wish to escape. He was involved in local expediencies and invading hostile constituencies, and the party was gaining ground. Beyond that, the mood of Quebec was real and must be dealt with. Whatever the national consequences, or the image created of Laurier, it could not be brushed aside. Between the leader watching from Toronto and the leader on the Quebec stumps there seemed at times to be a dialogue of the deaf. Yet it drew at last toward decision. The real man and the real voice, and not the snippets from newspapers, must be made known in Ontario.

"I believe," Blake wrote to Laurier on October 14, "the Young Men's Liberal Club want you to come here and speak on the 29th inst . . . I would also speak."[9] Behind that careful casualness there had been much manoeuvring in the party and there were still doubts and suspense. It was the same day that the polls opened in Quebec, and the result of the long campaign hung in the balance. "The event of today," Blake added, "may be a factor as to the period of the meeting."[10]

What he meant was hardly clear, nor did the event prove clear in itself. Chapleau and Langevin had entered the fight in Quebec, and had held some wavering *bleus*. Mercier had gained immensely but he had no absolute majority; he would be dependent on uncertain votes. It would be months yet before he came to power in the province, vindicating, at least to that extent, the work done by Laurier. Nor would it vindicate the work at all for much of English Canada; Mercier was worse than the musket-shoulderer who would have stood beside Riel. Quebec's state was ambiguous, Laurier's was still worse, and there was much healing and quieting to be done on his own ground. He could not be available in Toronto for October 29th.

For November he had meetings in Quebec and Blake had meetings in Ontario, with the nearest prospect another provincial election. Mowat was going to the polls in late December, and the federal leader was inevitably involved with that. He was neverously watching Macdonald and expecting him to dissolve parliament, opening the national campaign. Blake no more than Laurier could escape the issue of Riel, nor could he bridge the gap that was widening between the provinces. He was rebuffed even in the attempt. He had been advised, he wrote Laurier, that an appearance in Montreal might help the party, or perhaps in the eastern townships where there were many English Liberals. It would be "injudicious" the cool reply came back. As to his own coming to Ontario, though it was now planned for December, Laurier had growing doubts. "I am not sure if I am not to prove more hurtful than useful to our friends."[11]

There were many other Liberals quite of the same mind as the time for the meeting came. The Young Liberals, however, once launched on the adventure, had been determined to spare nothing. There had been every preparation for what was certain to be an immense affair. Well-advertised by friends and well-decried by enemies, Laurier had been for a week the talk of Toronto. The musket had figured largely in every hostile newspaper, and there had been talk of duckings in horse-ponds and dowsings under pumps. Even the arrival at the railway station on the morning of December 10 had provoked its quota of threats. It had passed off without incident under the watchful eyes of police, and Laurier had left with his reception committee to be driven to Blake's home. Yet the quiet surrounding the visitor had been an ambiguous, murmurous quiet, and it persisted into the evening.

The Horticultural Pavilion, the largest hall in the city, was crowded to suffocation on its lower level. There were gusts of chilly air from the packed galleries above, where youths not yet of an age to be Young Liberals were climbing in by the windows. There was abundant British loyalty and there were frequent cries of "Hat!" as gentlemen failed to uncover before a huge portrait of the Queen. Into all this, at eight-thirty in the evening, came Blake and the official party with the guest beside the leader. There was adequate cheering as the speakers moved to their places, but it obviously came from the faithful who were making an unusual effort. From other parts of the hall there was a steady ripple of hisses, and it was followed by the ominous quiet that had reflected the morning's mood. There was little promised by this huge and waiting silence, and among the Liberal dignitaries on the platform there were conspicuous absentees. Cartwright had sent his regrets, so had Mackenzie, and Mowat the Ontario campaigner was not to be seen here.

The Chairman was mercifully brief on general politics, and almost blunt in his presentation of the speaker. There had been charges made against Laurier, perhaps by some in the audience. The man was here now, to answer for himself and be judged.

Two hours later judgment was still suspended, yet something had obviously been done. The tall French Canadian had not been quite at his best. The soft, slurring voice that had risen to such sombre power in the House of Commons had been husky with too much use on Quebec stumps. He had seemed nervous at first, and he had seemed foreign and young. There was still boyishness in the unruly, clustering hair and in the pale, clean-shaven face, though he was a man of forty-five. The full-blown rose in the lapel was all too blatantly *rouge*. Next day there would be newspaper comment on the high, stand-up collar, not of Toronto's fashion, and on the gold horse-shoe tiepin, and the black Prince Albert coat, "his whole appearance presenting at the same time the characteristics of the Londoner and the Parisian."[12] Was there anything here to evoke the sense of leadership, to reknit the strands that were fraying between the peoples?

It had been a spatter of heckling that changed and revealed the man. He was abruptly the politician, taking the measure of his audience and cool and ready. He was more than that; he was the man who had sat by Blake, absorbing the best of Blake. There was much of Blake in his argument for they had worked together on the speech, and the points as Laurier made them were attuned to the English ear. He denied that Quebec had united around Riel, that it had asked more for the criminal than a measure of British justice. There was mercy in that justice and it had been granted to many others; why not to this unsound man? He was no counsellor of rebellion yet he remembered Hampden and Pym, lovers of liberty too. He remembered Burke, he was a disciple of English liberalism, recognizing British rule, loyal to a British Queen. Yet he was also French, linked by blood to the Métis and bound to resent their wrongs. Would a Scot do less if Scottish rights were invaded?

He came to the North-West and dealt with it unsparingly, stamping the guilt on government and on long years of neglect.

He came at last to the musket, which Blake had thought he should attempt to deal with lightly, and here he departed from Blake. There was no lightness and there was no hint of apology, he denied nothing of his anger and withdrew none of his words. Instead he reached out, suddenly the audacious challenger, to strike another chord. "Now, gentlemen of Toronto, men of English blood and descent, let me ask this of every one of you: if you yourselves had been fated to be born on the banks of the Saskatchewan . . . what would you have done?"[13]

The question remained unanswered but it was met with respectful silence. There was no more heckling, and there were even cheers at the end. He had come to speak of differences and he had somehow reduced division, though differences would still remain. He accepted that and he welcomed it, they were the core and burden of his theme; those differences to be retained and reconciled in the hope of a richer union. Over the whole speech as he sat down, transmitted in one great figure, there remained the glow of that hope. "Below the island of Montreal the water that comes from the north, from the Ottawa, unites with the waters that come from the western lakes, but uniting they do not mix. There they run, parallel, separate, distinguishable, and yet are one stream, flowing within the same banks, the mighty St. Lawrence rolling on toward the sea . . . a perfect image of our nation."[14]

The man, it seemed, had been found. When Blake rose that evening, following Laurier, he had never been in better form, never more truculently confident, never more sure in his own mind that he saw the way to release. Yet there were to be other meetings at London, Stratford and Windsor, and after Laurier's departure there were the throes of the provincial campaign. When that ended in the last week of December Mowat had more than trebled his old majority. The Ontarian held the province in the palm of his skillful hand, and it was the heart of English Canada. The French Canadian had been accepted but accepted for what he was; there remained that elegant foreignness, that all too lingering accent, that trailing ghost of Riel.

The leader bound on departure was faced with a general election. It was as immediately and insistently imminent as his own desire to escape. It could not be left to the future nor to any man of the future. He wrote Laurier on the 30th to commend his work in Ontario and to speak of 'immense benefit'. Yet it was a curiously withdrawn and carefully balanced assessment. "I think we calculated with wise boldness in arranging the trip . . . we risked something and have lost something, and are in danger of further losses."[15] He had no doubt that time would recover the losses, but it was the present that governed all.

"What would you say," he wrote to Oliver Mowat a week later, "to taking charge of the Liberal party of Canada?"[16]

CHAPTER FIVE

"THE AMBITION TO RULE A FREE COUNTRY"

IF THERE HAD BEEN any hope of Mowat, fresh from his own election, it collapsed within four days. The old friend was reluctant to say no, but he surrounded possible acceptance with a hedge of anxious conditions. He could only be a nominal leader, and only with Blake beside him. Nor would he attempt to head a government, if the Liberals should come to power, without Blake in the cabinet. He had also, he hinted tactfully, to give some thought to himself.

He was sixty-seven years old, a safely-established premier, and he had always been a cautious man. He was not a rich man. He would have to leave the provincial scene if he embarked on federal politics, and there would be no return to eminence if the larger adventure failed. He would come back as an aging barrister in search of a vanished practice, no doubt straitened for funds.

It all led to futility and concluded the negotiations. Much would be imposed on Mowat, there would be no release for Blake, and it was not the only thought. "The other problem is time, time, time."[1] Time would be required to adjust the party to change, to reconcile leaders' views, above all to absorb the shock of Blake's departure. And there was no time; the announcement of the general election was expected daily. On January 12, 1887, Blake wrote to Mowat again. It would not be right to pursue the matter of the leadership, and he had been in any case too late. "I have again taken up my burden."[2]

He took it up with his own attitude formed, and already confided to Mowat three days earlier. If he could not be replaced, he had written on January 9, he would make one final effort in the approaching general election and accept power if it came. "I feel myself committed to the whole country, in case the Liberals receive its confidence, to remain for a time, at whatever personal sacrifice, in the position of leadership in which I go to the polls. But should the decision be adverse, I shall consider myself free to accept the verdict as absolving me from further service in my present place, from which it is my fixed purpose in that event to withdraw."[3]

On January 14 parliament was dissolved and the election date announced. It was to be February 22; there were to be five weeks of trains and sleighs and snowdrifts, freezing, draughty halls, and campaigning in the dead of winter. Blake faced it all grimly, drawing the party round him, offering the best he had. It was the old best; there was to be no new cry from him. "The general principles and policy of the party have been shaped under my lead by the concurrence of its representatives in parliament. I have already declared them, and I am about to say on them nothing new, but only to repeat and enlarge on my former statements."[4]

He would neither bend nor retreat nor improvise, let the chips fall where they would. He could see no hope at the moment of reciprocity with the Americans, and he was less than ever the free trade doctrinaire. "Our adversaries wish to present to you an issue as between the present tariff and absolute free trade. That is not the true issue. Free trade is, as I have repeatedly explained, for us impossible; and the issue is whether the present tariff is perfect, or defective and unjust . . . I maintain that we should look . . . to the lightening of sectional taxes, to the lightening of taxes upon the prime necessaries of life and upon the raw materials of manufacture, to a more equitable arrangement of the taxes which now bear unfairly upon the poor . . . to a taxation of luxuries . . . to the curbing of monopolies of production . . . and to the effort — a most important point — to promote reciprocal trade with our neighbours to the south. That is a modest programme, you may say, but I believe it to be an extensive programme, representing the full measure practicable of attainment."[5]

The full measure practicable — he would expand trade with the Americans, but he did not look for a treaty. He promised no drastic change. He had opposed the National Policy and opposed the railway policy, and he still felt they had been wrong. Yet they were basic now to the country and the country would have to live with them, mending what little it could. The CPR was a fact. It had enriched the railway barons and overburdened the people, but it remained to be deplored and used. The high tariffs were a fact, more necessary now because of huge expenditures. They must be left largely as they were. "Manufacturers have nothing to fear"[6] — he waved no club at the head of legitimate industry, though he gained few from it as friends. He was bitter on the North-West, he was still stalked by Riel, and the new threat trailed him everywhere of secession in Nova Scotia. For all this and more he had only the old answer, almost in the old terms — neglect, delay, mismanagement by a government essentially corrupt. "They have broken every pledge. They have deceived the people. It is for the people to give them their reward."[7]

He had never been better supported and never more in demand. Nor had he ever been more himself. Quebec for once was fighting a confident battle, but it was Laurier's battle there. Demands came for Blake, particularly from Montreal. He should leave Ontario for a moment and explain to Quebec industrialists where he actually stood on tariffs. He would not go, he had done it all before; let them turn up his old speeches. "Our friends must see that they ought not to propose to move me like a pawn upon a chessboard."[8] He had the same word for Toronto as he swept through the rural ridings. "I can say nothing more than I have said."[9] To the swarm of friends and constituencies in search of election favours he was equally the old Blake."I never give a promise unless I am satisfied that it is right and that I can redeem my word."[10] From the opening speech of the campaign to the final hoarse whispers, he yielded nothing to expediencies and he spared nothing of himself. It was the last fight, and a good fight, and it seemed at first to be won.

With the early returns on February 23 the government's majority was reduced to a hopeless three. By the 24th it seemed to be wiped out; Liberals in Quebec were even proclaiming victory. Then from the distant provinces and the depth of the snowy countryside the late returns came in. There had been ground gained in the Maritimes but it had been lost in Manitoba. Ontario had hardly changed; Quebec had not changed enough. Macdonald's majority was cut to around thirty; but he would sit on where he was.

Neither Blake nor Laurier awaited the final results. For the Ontarian, Ontario was enough; the effort expended in his province had been for a gain of two ridings. "So the fight is lost and won," he wrote to another Ontarian on February 24th. "I expect my duties to terminate with the first day of next session."[11]

"The battle is over, the victory is not complete," Laurier wrote to Blake on the same day, "but . . . I am perfectly cheerful and confident."[12] He had some reason for his confidence in a gain of fifteen seats but he had an overriding reason for expressing it in high terms. The threat that Blake would go had hovered over the election, and Laurier had every reason to fear that it was imminent now. He dwelt valiantly on the temporary nature of the setback, the hope of *bleu* desertions and the problems of the shaken government that would quickly bring it down. They were problems spared the Liberals who would have time to think and plan. Defeat, he urged, was almost better than victory, and he drew a crushing reply.

Blake was unable, he wrote, to accept Laurier's conclusions. "Had we succeeded 20 or even 15 years ago in producing the result just arrived at I should have said with some confidence that it predicted an early defeat; but the case against the Government was so overwhelming, it ought to have so absolutely enlisted the more intelligent and independent and moral parts of the community, it has met with such an inadequate response all over the Dominion, the moral tone is so low, the game of grab is so openly played, that I think it more likely that we shall see a cynical expansion of the iniquitous system of the past than a revulsion against it."[13]

He was completely worn out, he said, and had had neither rest nor relief. In a few days he expected to leave for the south. Before that there would be a circular to party friends, including Laurier, which he would not discuss in advance.

It was despatched on March 3, and as it travelled across the country to the leading Liberals there was a wave of general panic. His present relation to the party, Blake announced, would end with the opening of parliament. There must be another leader to replace him. He was not prepared to serve even if elected; "another choice must be made."[14]

He was in South Carolina when the reaction came, with his address known only to his family. The leaders groped in vacancy, sputtering amongst themselves, with many of their appeals converging at last on Laurier. "All I could say was — Damn," wrote Sydney Fisher of Quebec, "it is simply impossible for him to back out now!"[15] Cartwright's anger crackled in searing phrases. He had written Blake but he had been ignored too often before, Laurier was the man to plead with him. "He is always much more amenable to the influence of men from other provinces . . . But for former escapades I would treat this as a mere temporary aberration . . . as it is I do not know . . . it will be regarded as a cowardly desertion . . . he will be the butt for all sorts of sneers and jibes from the enemy and will get no sympathy from our people, nor will he deserve any."[16] As often, Cartwright was wrong. There was much sympathy in the drift of letters settling on the desk in Toronto, but there was more of utter dismay.

By the 16th Laurier had heard from Blake, and had his address. His letter came down "to the place where you are now seeking rest and where, I hope, you will find it." He was forced, however, to torment his friend with "reference to our miserable politics". There was enough of it and too much and there was also something more, uniquely in Laurier's vein: "I have it on my mind that you are disposed to take the blame on yourself if the party did not obtain a full and complete success in the late struggle . . . you are alone of your mind . . . I am quite sure, my dear Blake, that you do not realize the real position which you occupy in the party, nor the respect, admiration and affection which every one of your followers entertains for your talents and character. You know me too well not to be convinced that in thus speaking I am not flattering you but that I am simply telling you the truth, which I am better situated than you are to learn and to know."[17] There was that from the good friend and there was more from the Quebec leader, flatly assessing the result of Blake's departure. "In this province the effect would be simply disastrous, and we would lose all the ground which we have gained during the last few years."[18]

Mills' and Edgar's pleadings came, forwarded by the family with others selected from the growing pile. Brother Sam wrote, instigated by Cartwright, thoughly hardly in Cartwright's vein. "God has given you a grand position in the conflict and along with it a cross to bear — I would take the position and the Cross." The prophet Elijah, Sam recalled, had also been sorely tried, and supported in his trials by God. "Read this story — it is so good and fits you so well."[19] Whether or not it had been read, by the time Blake left the south there was forceful reading of another sort from disturbed men in Quebec.

Most of them were converted *bleus*, so recently gained for the party, and they were the most direct of all. "We, the new ones, have been elected to fight under your leadership and we are bound to do so. Please excuse my English writing."[20] . . . "It is when I told my people that I wanted to support an honest, intelligent, devoted, patriotic and bright man as the hon. E. Blake that both conservatives and liberals joined together to ensure my success. That immense gathering of voters had confidence in me because I had confidence in you. So you see how guilty you are."[21] . . . "Je ne vous ferai pas de longues phrases. Si vous voulez nous jeter dans un cahot politique, si vous voulez exposer vos amis à l'accusation de trahison, si vous voulez ruiner le parti national et faire la fortune des brigands qui pillent le pays et la conduisent à la ruine, vous n'avez qu'à persister dans cette voie."[22] . . . "Speaking not only for myself but for many other Quebec members, I will state in the most emphatic manner that I will accept no other leader and that any attempt to impose Cartwright or anybody else will drive me out of the party, if not out of public life."[23] Laurier had been quite right; there would be much lost in Quebec. Cartwright had been right too; it would all be blamed on Blake.

On March 28, at home again, he had a long day in his study. Out of it came much writing, the best of which would go to his files unread. He would try, Blake wrote, commencing another circular for the party leaders, to explain himself and his views. When he had taken the Liberal leadership in 1880. "there was then unhappily a general impression that I could work wonders, and I found that the only way was to accept the lead temporarily and try the experiment. . . .

"It is plain now that I have not attracted to our side the neutral mass which turns the scale, and in almost all the provinces the local Liberal popular majority has been reversed in the federal election. The spirit of our country, and the tone of public morality, of which the Liberal opposition are the special guardians, have sunk lower than ever, and the people have twice confirmed the power of men guilty of the gravest delinquencies. No leader ever had a greater opportunity . . . but I have failed. . . .

"It is then fit that some other man and some other methods should at length be tried; and it is no part of my duty to perpetuate our failure. Many kindly tell me that the failure is not due to me . . . but [I believe] it is largely due to my unsuitability for the place. . . . The ambition to rule a free country is a high and honourable ambition. To desire the end is an important, if not essential, element in its attainment. But it unfortunately happens that I am by temperament averse to rule. So far from having any such ambition I shun the idea; and place and power, preeminence and command, controversy and disputation have each year grown to me increasingly repugnant."[24]

There were some who argued that he was in duty bound to remain. "I must respectfully demur to the claim. . . . I am at the moment quite unequal to the work and anxieties of the session. With impaired health, diminished means, vanished business and neglected home affairs, I am tempted to claim the kind indulgence of the claimants, and to beg them to set a limit to their demand . . . for my part I judge this to be the most convenient time for the party . . . I beg you to forgive my shortcomings, and to believe me, Yours faithfully . . ."[25]

He was at the end, but he did not sign. Some of what he had written was distorted by the haze of time; perhaps he was uneasy at that. There was the thought of all those letters, particularly the ones from Quebec. In any case there was more here than was fitting for the public eye, and his previous "secret" circular had found its way to the newspapers. He put the draft aside and began another.

When it was finished he scrawled a private note to Laurier. "To you, as to the rest, I have sent a circular communicating the conclusions to which I have been led after a most anxious reconsideration. You know as much of my mind as anyone, and it is perhaps less necessary to write to you fully than to anyone ele, but still I would have liked to do it, had health allowed."[26]

It had not allowed; the circular must speak for itself. In the second draft, however, there was at least reprieve for the party. "Having regard to the strong opinions expressed, I see no alternative save to yield, as far as possible, to the final determination of my friends."[27]

It was a strictly qualified yielding, and he was not hopeful of the result. "My health will not allow me either to prepare for, or to discharge the work of the session as in former years. It has been suggested that the work should be done largely by a Committee, I retaining a nominal lead. I believe this plan will be unsatisfactory as a makeshift; while as a permanency it would be intolerable. Yet it is only possible alternative." He hoped the friends would reject it; he was sure that in such a position he would try their forebearance more than he had before. But "I shall submit myself for this session to the general judgment."[28]

That much had been wrung from him, but the headaches began again. There could be no doubt what the general judgment would be; he was consigned to the old turmoil. Laurier, for one, knew it, and whatever relief he felt on receipt of the circular was dimmed by the private letter. That had seemed to come, he wrote Edgar, "from one who is acutely suffering both in soul and body".[29] To Blake, on April 2, he was less the politician than the warm, repentant friend. "I am not altogether without remorse for having personally induced you to reconsider your determination to retire . . . if your health and politics cannot go together, I say politics to the dogs."[30]

The sentiment did not help Blake; he was in the hands of the others now. Parliament convened on April 13, and by the end of the next day's caucus he was confirmed as Liberal leader. He was immersed in jubilant loyalty, surrounded by renewed confidence, and the committee that would do his work for him had assumed its nebulous shape. There would be Cartwright, Mills, Laurier, and a few from the other provinces, and they were able, solicitous men. They had been all that before, but they had always depended on Blake, always deferred to Blake, imposed on Blake the weight of the party's problems. It would be the same now; the leader must still lead.

It would be in no new directions; that was clear from the first. He was a sick man and a scarred man, bitter with the sense of failure. It came out in much of its fullness on the day parliament convened, when Joseph Alderic Ouimet was elected Speaker. A Quebec *bleu* who had left Macdonald on Riel, he had since returned to the fold; Riel was to be forgotten now. He had not been forgotten in Blake's case, nor was Blake inclined to forget. "I was insulted in the press, in the pulpit, on the platform. I was called a Rielite, a conspirator against Canadian law, a hypocrite and coward, a knave, a fool, a rebel and a traitor . . . I now extend my hearty congratulations to my fellow-Rielite, to my co-conspirator against Canadian law, to my brother knave and fool, my fellow hypocrite and traitor, my associate in calumny, treason and rebellion, on being about to receive, by the unanimous vote of the Canadian Commons, the position of first commoner of Canada."[31]

For six weeks the drone of parliament went on and his committees bustled about, assisting Blake. He would receive no new proposals and he could propose nothing himself. The party floundered with its head turned to the past. He returned to Home Rule. He returned to the CPR. His statistics were the old statistics, his arguments were the old arguments, and even in his weary sarcasms there was the rank taste of defeat. He noted acidly that the time had come for memorials to "those principal composers of these works of Confederation by which we were deluded into the course we took for the last seven years."[32] In the sea of mountains that he had made all too famous there was a Mount Macdonald now, glowering on the line that pierced them. There was a Mount Tupper and a Mount Stephen and there was also a Mount Sir Donald, obviously far too lofty to be called by the name of Smith. They were not to be removed or diminished by a sardonic, beaten leader. However deplored and ridiculed, they were everlastingly there.

Macdonald seemed equally immoveable when he deigned to rise in reply. "I have a mountain called after myself, but if the honourable gentleman's railway policy had been carried out, no mountain would be called Blake in his time or in the time of the present generation . . . we always like to hear the honourable gentleman, but we would like to hear him say something new."[33]

That, however, Macdonald did not expect. It was May 26th by then, and the condition of the man across from him was too evident. Rumour was abroad in the House, beginning to seep to the newspapers, and the next day it was confirmed.

On the 27th Blake was absent from the Commons, confined to his own house and Margaret Blake had been called to her husband's bedside. For three days there was a coming and going of doctors, and on the fourth of politicians. On June 1, Mills and Burpee were admitted, and emerged a little dazed. They had had no doubt that they were to receive a resignation and advise on a new leader. Cartwright had been suggested, Mills had been willing to allow himself to be considered, and there was always the perennial hope of securing Mowat. "There is only one possible choice," Blake had replied, "Laurier."[34]

He was lying on a sofa that evening when Laurier was ushered in. The visitor's face was drawn, he seemed frailer than usual, and he was a picture of blank dismay. It was real, Blake knew; he was asking too much too soon. He had to ask it; time did not wait on the health of politicians. He could offer nothing as he lay there but what he had won for himself, the sleepless nights and the headaches, the exhausted body and mind, the endless bruises inflicted by a stubborn nation. Yet he pressed it all relentlessly through a long hour and a half, the very strain of the effort adding force to his words. Margaret sat beside him, tense and watching the strain, wiping the sweat from his face. She could tell much herself of the price of politics and she liked this French Canadian and she liked his wife. Yet she leaned forward at the end, reinforcing persuasion. "Yes, Mr. Laurier," she said, "you are the only man."[35]

Laurier left and there was more than a week of waiting, while newspapers bellowed rumour and the sick man lay in his room. Outside the party seethed, the few men who knew of it still incredulous of his choice. Even Edgar was appalled, for all his earlier musings. The man of Quebec had done well in Toronto, but he had not escaped from Riel. He was still the alien and the disturber to many in the Liberal Party, and the dilettante to others. Hardly a man of the group around Blake had seriously thought of Laurier. They had thought of Cartwright, but they had not thought of Quebec which would not have him as leader. He was the rebel-hating Englishman, the apostle of free trade, and he was no longer close to Blake. Mills was close, and he was another sound Ontarian, but he had never warmed to the French nor they to him. Mowat had been much talked of and Edgar sometimes mentioned — always the English names, always the Ontario men. That the time had come to revise such thinking few were prepared to see. Slowly, as the week wore on, they came to see it, or at least to bend to Blake. At a caucus on June 7 Cartwright stood up to propose the name of Laurier and Mills rose to second him. Dubiously, hesitantly, and still hoping it was temporary, the party accepted leadership from the man of the French province.

There was to be a longer wait, however, before the man himself accepted. On June 11 Blake left for Toronto, leaning on Margaret's arm. He needed her support at the railway station where a few friends were gathered, and he had not risked a farewell visit to the House. The tears came all too readily and there was too much cause for them now. He had not seen Laurier again, but he sensed that ordeal too. Laurier was poor and French, he was as often sick as Blake, and he was as well aware of the general mood of the party. "I know that I am not fitted," he wrote on June 10th, "my health is not strong . . . there are other considerations . . . let me say bluntly that all my friends are in the wrong."[36] Even when acceptance came, eight days later, Laurier took up the leadership with little change in his tone. "I know that I have not the aptitude for it, and I have a sad apprehension that it must end in disaster."[37] It was hardly a cause for relief, hardly the gift of release, but that much was done.

"The masses seem to me to fall lower and lower . . . till the heart fails and hope dies within the breast. I suppose it was this, more than all the other things together, which broke me down so that I was obliged to give up the struggle."[38]

It was September 21 by then, and the retired leader was writing to J. D. Carmichael, his old friend in the Maritimes. Blake had passed the summer at Murray Bay, and he was to leave for England in a month. There would be law business in London, but best of all there would be Ireland where this time he planned on a longer stay. He was tired but there were no more headaches, and he would be refreshed by a new interest. His speeches in the Canadian parliament on the subject of Home Rule had impressed the Irish leaders; they had written to him and some had even visited him. He intended to return their visits and to study some of their problems.

As to Laurier's problems and the party problems, he could see trouble ahead. Cartwright was riding hard on reciprocity, and he was drawing Laurier after him. The Ontarian and the free trader had expanded in the absence of Blake, and was half-convinced that he was the actual head of the party. He had half-converted Laurier to some of his own beliefs, and there was a "bold policy" in prospect. To all suggestions of partial reciprocity the Americans had been notably cool. They were to be won now by a larger, grander proposal. All tariffs would be eliminated and reciprocity complete; there would be a total combination, a plan of commercial union.

The idea was hardly new, but there could be no doubt that it had a new appeal for Laurier. The country was in the doldrums and tired of the National Policy; it was ripe for another issue. Laurier, the untried leader at the head of a confused party, was desperate for an issue himself. He apparently saw no danger in that phrase, Commercial Union, nor had he traced the implications of an interlocking of trade. Or if he had he was prepared to accept them and let events take their course.

"The subject of Commercial Union," he had written Blake in July, "has made such progress that it is impossible to ignore it . . . it would be impossible for anyone to appear this day upon any public platform without being prepared to discuss it."[39]

The urgency in the letter was Cartwright's urgency, Blake was convinced of that. He was more convinced of the dangers surrounding the issue. Commercial Union with that vast giant to the south would be attacked by all its enemies as the road to political union. It led that way for Blake; he could see no other direction.

He had hinted as much to Laurier, and he said the same to Carmichael. "As to Commercial Union . . . I think the advocates of it have not faced the difficulties or the questions involved . . . the measure has tendencies which its promoters deny. The tendencies may be right, or inevitable, but ought they to be denied or ignored? I think not."[40]

It was all tired moralizing and it no longer seemed to matter; he was a private member of parliament. The direction of the plodding masses was in the hands of another man. He had invited Laurier to visit him in Murray Bay, but Laurier had not come. The stir in the party went on, the issue was all too obviously taking shape, but it was out of Blake's hands. He could go to England, free.

London in late October was as fascinating as he always found it, and there were high-placed friends and relatives in touch with the world's affairs. It was good to know them and to be a little known. It was better still to be off on the other journey. "I travel light thru Ireland with my handbag and a large roll."[41] His letters home in November seemd to come from another man. He was being received here, he reported, as the revolutionary from Canada, the apostle of Home Rule, welcome in the homes of gentry who were usually Humes or Blakes. "They were very good-natured about my Irish views, Aunt Hume saying I was a nice fellow to come over and help rob them of their last penny."[42] He went on by himself to explore Galway and Athlone, walking for miles in the countryside, drinking in air and change, absorbing other sensations. "I fear I miss much by my stupid aversion to asking questions,"[43] he wrote, but he had his own eyes to see with and he asked questions of some. There were the peat hovels and the desolate tracts of waste, the cattle fatter than the herdsmen who had once been owners of the farms — "the brutality compelling men to work for beasts."[44] There was the Marquis of Hyde with his toll on everything in Westport, and the thousands of acres around the town whose tenants had been driven off. There were the polite and hungry peasants and the scraps of peasant talk, heard by the passing stranger. "Sure, there's no oats at all — what's worse there's no *price* for oats."[45] It was a green land under a pall, held in an alien grip, crying out for redemption.

Justin McCarthy of the Irish party had been a guest of Blake in Canada. He had prepared other of the leaders and they were all to be met now. Blake attended their meetings, was welcomed to long discussions and welcomed as a known man, an admired and desired man. "They have wanted me to speak both in England and Ireland, and there has been some talk about my staying here."[46] Staying here, a servant of this great cause; it was a wide and thrilling prospect. But abruptly that was changed. A rumour came, somehow cabled from Canada and appearing in a Dublin newspaper, that Blake the Home Ruler was pursuing a new ambition. Ireland was to be his stepping-stone to a career in the imperial parliament. There must have been thoughts and dreams of it, for the charge seemed to strike a nerve. It haunted each of his letters from the day he saw it. "This outrageous cable that has laid me so open to misconstruction . . . I have felt tongue-tied . . . I dare say I may not open my mouth again though I had half-promised to do so . . . my pleasure finished by that abominable pin-prick from Canada."[47]

He returned to England with the thought of Ireland spoiled. Beyond that, he was lonely for Margaret now. "I cannot tell you how much I have wished for your company."[48] When she came to join him in December they left to spend the winter on a tour of Italy. He was again in need of "change" and it would not be found at home. With every thought of Canada the headaches seemed to return.

He braved one of them, however, on December 22, to write

a letter from Pisa. It was a wet day, he was not in the mood for sight-seeing, and the new session of parliament was about to open in Ottawa. Among much else that was disturbing in Canadian newspapers, there had been talk that Blake might return to his old position. There had even been talk by Laurier, and it required a word of advice. "It is needful, my dear Laurier, that you should not repeat the too kind suggestion which I see you have made as to my resumption of the lead." Laurier must not regard himself, nor allow himself to be regarded, as a temporary man in his place. It would only weaken the party, and there were already weaknesses enough. "For my own part I have only to say that I see no condition of things within the range of the political horizon which would make me feel it an imperative duty to resume the lead . . . save under *my own personal conviction* that the step was one of imperative duty there is nothing which could induce me to accept a situation so repugnant to my feelings."[49]

It was strong enough but it was lawyer-like, and it was to be read by another lawyer. There was a final qualification. "No wise man, after 54 years of experience, would set up a more absolute bar."[50] How absolute was it? At the heart of all that wordage there remained those personal convictions. There remained imperative duty that might summon the leader back. The work of the rainy day went off to Canada but it changed little there, for the party or the party head. Overhanging Laurier and the Liberals — still as always — was the shadow of the conscience of Blake.

CHAPTER SIX

"ABSENT INVALID"

LAURIER replied in January to the letter written from Pisa. He had warm words of sympathy and understanding and a budget of cheerless news. The Liberal party, having lost a general election, was being further reduced by by-elections and elections contested in the courts. It was witnessing the rise of Mercier as the apostle of a French Quebec, and a counter-rise in Ontario of aggressive English protestantism. Confused, divided, and still stubbornly regarding itself as in the hands of a temporary leader, it was groping about for a policy and was bending Cartwright's way. "We must try to make a new departure," Laurier wrote from Quebec. "In this province I never saw business so dull as it is now. All classes are in more straitened circumstances than they have been within my experience. . . . Commercial union would afford relief and commercial union must be popular. . . . I think it will be wise and politic early in the session to adopt the new platform."[1]

He reflected a general mood of fretful groping. Mercier had done the same, though he had had a good deal more in mind, when he summoned the Dominion's first conference of provincial premiers. Assembled at Quebec in October of 1887, with Conservative British Columbia and Prince Edward Island remaining away, it had been dominated by Mercier and Mowat, loud with the woes of an angry Manitoba, and drastic in all its demands. Few of them would ever be realized — Macdonald would see to that — but it had crystallized discontent that was all too real.

In ten years there had been enormous growth in the capital structure of the country. There was the railway and there were large new industries, of which many were doing well. Both productive resources and the fruits of them had shown a sizeable increase. But it was an increase narrowly concentrated, most of it in the urban centres, and accumulating in too few hands. In Montreal and Toronto the railway barons and the industrialists were building their large mansions, but in the general business of the country there was stagnation or actual decline. There was far more public debt and there was less trade per capita than there had been twenty years before. There was more dissension; with Riel too well-remembered, Nova Scotia secessionist and Manitoba threatening a railway war. The completion of the CPR, instead of promoting settlement, seemed to have turned it the other way; yearly thousands of Canadians were leaving to become Americans. "The United States," said Cartwright, "are becoming literally flesh of our flesh and blood of our blood."[2]

If the process was overdrawn, it seemed to be a natural process. It had seemed so for years to many of the politicians, to southward-looking businessmen and to Canadian intellectuals of the school of Goldwin Smith. In their view the union of the two peoples was a destiny written large on the face of the continent. It was not visible to the peoples nor officially to either party, but under present dismal conditions trade was a different thing. There had been good times before while there was reciprocity with the Americans; why not so again? Amid the never-ending fisheries quarrels the other mood was in the air. It was turning even Macdonald in the direction of negotiations, and Liberals had merely outrun him for a grip on the new issue. But they had run far, and dangerously far, and there was even doubt that Laurier was quite sure of the direction.

Commercial Union, as it had come to be defined by its proponents, was reciprocity *in excelsis*. Instead of partial arrangements affecting specified items, tariffs between Canada and the United States would be completely abolished on "all products of both countries of whatsoever nature, whether of the waters, the soil, the sea and the mine." There would be "an assimilation of the tariffs against all other countries . . . of internal revenue taxes and . . . very probably an arrangement for pooling receipts and customs, and distributing the same. It would be followed by the discontinuance of the services of a strong force of customs house officials on both sides of the boundary line of nearly 4,000 miles between the two countries, which is maintained at a cost to Canada of at least half a million dollars annually."[3]

Around these formidable proposals there had risen formidable questions, which Laurier seemed to ignore. Blake had been asking them now for over two years, in caucus and out of it, in conversations and letters with party leaders, and occasionally on public platforms. Was reciprocity, even in limited form, to be had on acceptable terms? Blake doubted it, and Laurier did not know. There would be a huge reduction in revenue if tariffs were taken off; how was that to be made up? There would be a loss of protection for many established industries; how much of that could be endured? If there were to be complete reciprocity, with the countries trading as a union, every problem entered on a new dimension. There would inevitably be a joint tariff against the goods of the outside world, with the rates set by the Americans. Would England not resent it? Would it not be seen as a step away from the empire? Was it not that in fact? Did it not tend inevitably toward outright political union between Canada and the United States?

Granting that as a goal, though Blake would neither endorse nor disapprove it, the other question remained. Political union, if that was the thing desired, could obviously be better negotiated while Canada was a free agent, in control of her own trade. It would be an enormous step, a change in the orientation and the loyalties of a whole people. How could it then be presented to them as a mere commercial question? It could be offered only in its fullness with the long view clear to the end, and were the Canadian people yet ready to accept it?

To that Blake's answer had been no. Laurier's appeared to be yes. Or rather, it seemed, he was prepared to beg the question. If he saw the dangers, even in the matter of nomenclature, there was no hint in his letter. Yet even a man far off, reading the Canadian newspapers, could see that he had had warnings enough.

There was Cartwright's speech, made at Ingersoll, Ontario, on October 12, and reported at length in the *Globe*. Obviously with Laurier's assent, Cartwright had dwelt on the virtues of reciprocity, on "free intercourse with the United States, the most Unrestricted Reciprocity", and gone on to make his point. "I am as averse as any man can be to Annexation or to resign our political independence, but I cannot shut my eyes to the facts. We have greatly misused our advantages. We have been foolish and wasteful in our expenditures. We have no means of satisfying the just demands of large portions of the Dominion except through such an arrangement as Commercial Union."[4]

The speech had been judicious in tone, had not once mentioned Blake, and had been presented only as Cartwright's personal opinion. Yet Cartwright could not speak without half-committing the party, and there had been almost instant retreat from the fatal phrase. By November, in a series of letters to the *Globe*, Edgar was involved in a scramble of explanations. He favoured freedom of trade, but with no connotations of union. He was for keeping Canadian customs houses, though he was not sure what they would do. He was for an independent tariff structure, though it would change jointly with the American. "The extensive remission of duties upon manufactured goods should not be made suddenly, but only after ample notice, and even when the reduction begins it must be gradual."[5] With these reservations, whatever they were intended to accomplish, the movement proposed by Cartwright became Unrestricted Reciprocity.

It was apparently to be presented now, in the view of the Ontario Liberals, merely as an adjustment in trade. The customs houses would remain, the visible symbol of Canadian independence. Canada and the United States, each as a free agent, would reduce the tariffs between them to the point of zero. They would set up, by joint consent, a common tariff structure against the goods of other nations. Yet neither the semantics nor the machinery could conceal the actual results. Under either plan and by whatever name, Canada would be commercially united as the junior partner of the Americans. The fact was being disputed now by battalions of Liberal lawyers, but there were no differences for Blake and apparently none for Laurier. He was prepared to commit himself to Commercial Union.

One sensed disaster in the prospect and desperation in the man. "Our friends have become impatient of repeated defeats" — he was being driven by party pressures and he was sick and tired of his place. He accepted, or seemed to accept, the finality of Blake's departure "yet a secret hope always was lurking that some day, when your health was restored, you would again resume your post . . . since your mind is made up in the direction which you have just told me, I must at an early day ask our friends to relieve me and make another choice."[6] The choice would probably be Cartwright and it was a catastrophic thought, but for a month Blake thrust it away. His health was not restored, the party must look to itself. Margaret was with him now, they were seeing Italy together, and the correspondence with Canada was confined to the family at home.

It seemed to tell for a while of release and freedom. "We went in the morning to look at the Pompeiian and Herculanean remains . . . we spent five hours about the museum where we might spend weeks . . . this morning we left Naples for Capri . . . there was a good view of the highlands of Ischia, something of Vesuvius and a fine view of the cape or mainland three miles off . . . the glorious sea beneath and the sky above and the balmy air made all lovely to look at as we sat by the ruins of the scene of Tiberius' revelries and crimes." Here where the Emperors had summered and the sirens called to Ulysses there was a touch of healing magic. The Canadian tariffs slept, gratefully consigned to Lethe, and the eye of the tireless sight-seer was becoming quick and amused. "We passed through the open air market, very large, full of vegetables and fruit . . . crowded with buyers and sellers jabbering, gesticulating, eating at tables in the open air . . . I ordered a horse for myself and a donkey for your mother, but was provided with two donkeys. I mounted with doubt . . . but there were soon signs of failure and I slipped off and went the rest of the way afoot. On our return the driver said if I was not too *satisfied* he hoped I would pay something extra. I said that I had to walk both ways, which he seemed to think an irrelevant objection! . . . we visited a very large orange orchard and citron garden . . . we also visited a macaroni factory . . . we went to the shops . . . we bought a lot . . . your mother who has been hankering after tortoise shell goods and dickering with a young individual who infests the hotel at last made her bargain. . . ."[7]

Some of the scenes reported must have been trying for the frail Margaret, and the Blake of southern Italy seemed hardly the Blake of Canada. "Figure to yourself, as the French say, your mother on a dejected looking horse with the waterproof before her on the pommel, and guided and attended by the proprietor, making her way up the steep steps . . . the horses go zig-zag so as to make it easier for them, tho' not for the rider. Figure then to yourself me, leading the way on another horse with a large black lunch bag slung over my shoulder and in all respects regardless of appearances . . . so we wended our way at a footpace till at last we reached the spot . . . it would amuse you could I describe to you our adventures with the cabmen and drivers . . . and our means to keep them down to a reasonable and moderate limit of extortion. But I can't attempt the humours of it."[8]

By March 6, however, even the desire for humour seemed to have left him. He had arrived in Florence with the weather turning bad, and it was time to reply to Laurier. "The desire to return home in early summer," he wrote, "has caused us to visit most places in Italy at unseasonable times . . . and I fear the rest of our journey will be under the same conditions." As to the affairs of the troubled party, "these things prey on my mind and I cannot shake them off now, tho' for some months I was able to keep my thoughts in other channels." He had sympathy for the entrapped leader but there was no intention to free him, though he touched the *status quo* with a shade of caution. "It has seemed to me for long that the public interests would be best served by a change; and the change having come at last I think it not unreasonable that it should be regarded as permanent, in the sense which I stated in my letter to you. I cannot discern the least indication of my being able to *effect substantial good* as a leader . . . I no longer possess, if I ever had at command, the elements of success."[9]

There was with that a vaguely ominous addendum, hinting at other service. "As to the trade question . . . I have not seen that either the Country or our party was prepared to deal with it, and therefore it has seemed to me that it was best for some independent liberal to take the bull by the horns, most likely getting gored in the attempt." Yet the spectre of Blake as toreador, rampant and independent, seemed to be dismissed even as it rose. "Into the discussion of these matters I don't feel able to enter as headache ensues on the attempt to concentrate thought on them. I can only hope and pray that you may be wisely guided."[10]

The hope was dashed in a little over a month. By early April in London there was another letter from Laurier. "We have adopted unrestricted reciprocity. We are still engaged in the debate."[11] He had been persuaded to remain as leader, Cartwright had had his way, and Laurier seemed optimistic as to the success of the new departure. Yet his major theme was the cry of a harried man, distracted by money troubles and determined on his own release. "The fact is that I have not the financial means . . . I have to work for my living, and I can give neither to my profession or my position the time which either would require." He did not ask outright for Blake's return to the leadership, yet every word was a call. "I have often told you that you do not realize the unbounded affection which every one in our ranks feels for you . . . Remember this well: there is one man only in the reform party who does not believe that you are a born leader of men, and that man is yourself."[12]

The hyperbole changed nothing. The new direction of the party led directly away from Blake. He had polite words for Laurier's financial difficulties and few useful suggestions. "A man not only has the right but he is bound to preserve his independence and to avoid degenerating into a political hack dependent on office for maintenance. But is there not an alternative? Can you not . . . explain frankly the impossibility of your giving all your time to the lead?" If Laurier did that, what could it possibly mean but a return to the committee system which Blake had found intolerable? The suggestion was not pursued, there was cool reserve on the other points in the letter, yet once again the addendum with its hint of forming cloud. "I say nothing about current politics, the intrusions of an absent invalid being worse than worthless. But there are several things I want to talk over with you when we next meet."[13]

As he wrote to Laurier he was a man alone in London, detained there while Margaret left for Canada. Whatever his state of invalidism he was not to be left idle nor was he to be alone for long; in another week Oliver Mowat was arriving. D'Alton McCarthy, the hard-riding, hard-fighting Conservative squire of Simcoe County, Ontario, would be coming at the same time, quite possibly by the same ship. The five-year-old dispute which Blake always referred to as "The Ontario Lands Case", and which was officially known as "The St. Catharines Milling and Lumber Company *vs* The Queen", was to be heard before the Judicial Committee of the Privy Council, with Mowat opposing McCarthy. Mowat, on behalf of the Province of Ontario, and for a fee of £6,000, had engaged Blake to assist him.

It was once again a Dominion-Provincial quarrel, with the federal government behind the St. Catharines Milling Company and "The Queen" standing for Ontario.[14] In April of 1883 the milling company had obtained from the Dominion government a license to cut timber on a large tract of pinewood lying in the Algoma District to the north-east of Lake Superior. At that time, with the boundary award in suspense, the actual ownership of the territory was still unsettled. During 1884 the award was finally made by the Privy Council, and the Algoma District became a part of Ontario. In October of that year the Ontario government entered suit against the St. Catharines Milling Company, charging them with trespass on provincial lands. The defence, ignoring the boundary award, brought up the question of a prior Indian title. It asserted that its grant, lying in northern Ontario above the height of land, was "until recently claimed by the tribes of Indians who inhabited that part of the Dominion of Canada . . . and that such Indian claims are, as to the lands in question herein, paramount." The Dominion of Canada, "in consideration of a large expenditure of money made for the benefit of the said Indian tribes, and of payments made to them from time to time, and for divers other considerations, have acquired the said Indian title . . . and still have full power and authority to confer upon the defendants the rights, powers and privileges . . . under which the said pine timber was cut."

The case had been heard by the Chancery Division of the High Court of Justice for Ontario, the Court of Appeal for Ontario, and the Supreme Court of Canada. Each court had dismissed the claim of the milling company and accepted the provincial position. Mowat arrived in London to face a final appeal with three verdicts supporting him. He was anxious, nevertheless, and he was showing the signs of age. It was obvious by July 12, when the hearings finally began, that the second counsel would be doing most of the work.

Blake commenced his argument, after a month of preparation, on July 20, 1888. Before him, in the unpretentious quiet of the room in Downing Street, sat the Earl of Selborne, Lord Watson, Lord Hobhouse, Sir Montagu Smith, Sir Barnes Peacock, and Sir Richard Couch, the presiding Lords of the council. They were unwigged and ungowned, ordinary gentlemen in morning clothes sitting at a long table. But they were a court of last resort, and Blake loved the atmosphere. There was nothing in this room of the "ignorant impatience" of parliaments. There were sharp and spacious minds, there were enormous stores of learning, there was a view as wide as the empire and as long as the long past. It was here without ostentation, but with huge and lasting consequences, that the lawmaking of the centuries was applied to great affairs.

The second counsel for Ontario was only moderately pleased with his first day's work. He was less pleased with the work that had gone before it. Mowat and McCarthy had each laid out their cases, and McCarthy had had the best of it. The argument Blake was faced with, and the arguments he used to meet it, all pivoted around three sections of the British North America Act. He began as usual well back of the beginning with an exposition of the aim and purpose of its makers.

"First the Act is an attempt — perhaps a somewhat ambitious attempt — to create in one short document a very complicated written constitution . . . thus its very nature requires a large, comprehensive and liberal spirit of interpretation . . . in truth the Act is in many points little more than a skeleton which is to be clothed with flesh and muscle, nerve and sinew, into which the breath of life is to be breathed by interpretation."

What was its general scheme? It was to create "a union composed of several existing and continued entities. It was not the intention of Parliament to mutilate, confound and destroy the provinces mentioned in the preamble and, having done so, from their mangled remains stewed up in some legislative caldron, to evoke by some legislative incantation absolutely new provinces into an absolutely new existence . . . it was the design . . . to preserve the vital breath and continue the political existence of the old provinces . . . they were being made, as has been well said, not fractions of a unit but units of a multiple."

That was the intent, to be exactly understood. "From one word or phrase we must sometimes construct or develop a system. For instance, you find a single phrase, as I conceive, the governing phrase in this Act, appearing only in the preamble but operating on the whole structure — the phrase 'federally united'. The word 'federal' is the key which unlocks the clauses and reveals their contents. It is the glass which enables us to discern what is written. By its light the Act must be construed. So again we have a description of the constitution: 'similar in principle to that of the United Kingdom' — where a single line imports into the system that mighty and complex and somewhat indefinite aggregate called the British Constitution. So further a few words in other cases comprehend vast and complicated subjects" and "upon a sound and comprehensive interpretation of these meagre phrases the most important interests depend."

He turned then to the meagre phrase and the single word upon which his own case depended. The British North America Act, in subsection 24 of section 91, allotted to the Dominion government the power to make laws for "Indians and Lands reserved for Indians". The Dominion now, speaking through the mouth of counsel for the St. Catharines Milling Company, claimed that the word "lands" referred to all territory on which the Indian title had not yet been extinguished. If that were so, said Blake, then it comprised the entire northern half of the Province of Ontario, all of which had been used by the nomad tribes and little of which had yet been formally ceded. The possession of all Indian lands, according to the Dominion's contention, was implied by the power to legislate.

That Blake flatly denied; there was no such implication. The Act had no such meaning. The word "lands" as it was used had reference only to specific Indian reserves, set apart by agreement for the use of specific tribes.

There was no doubt of the right of the Dominion government to make the laws for Indians. That was its responsibility. It was in all provinces their tutelary, guide, and arbiter. But it did not have, and it had not been conceded by the Act, the ownership of Indian lands within the provinces.

What had it actually done at the time of Confederation? It had appropriated from the various provinces, for specific national purposes such as the control of waterways, coastal navigation, etc., certain specific properties. It had named and described each of them in exact and painful detail, and they were all set out in the schedule accompanying section 108 of the British North America Act. "We turn to 108, which supplements 91 . . . and we find no mention of lands reserved for the Indians, any more than we find mention of the Indians themselves. But we are asked to imply it, forsooth! I say you might as well imply a proprietary right in the Indians themselves and turn them into slaves. . . . Barren, worthless Sable Island, that little mass of sand which is diminishing year by year until it is about half a mile wide and twenty miles long — that is expressly transferred because the property was to go. Buoys and beacons, boats and dredges, firelocks and soldiers' breeches — these are expressly transferred, they are thought worthy to be expressly granted; implication does not suffice for them. But at the same instant, under the same Act, half Ontario is left to be transferred by an implication from the grant of legislative power! . . . I submit, my Lords . . . that it was not intended to effect any transfer to Canada of the proprietary interest in these lands.

"My second proposition is that it is expressly vested in Ontario by section 109. By that section, with which your Lordships are painfully familiar, 'all lands, mines, minerals and royalties belonging to the provinces at the union . . . shall belong to the several provinces in which the same are situate or arise, subject to any trusts existing in respect thereof.' Possession of the land, therefore, remained with each of the provinces, 'subject to the Indian burthen, whatever it may be.' "

That much Blake had established, or at least attempted to establish, by the end of the afternoon. Ontario owned the land subject to its Indian trust, "burthened with a servitude, with a right of tribal occupation for the accustomed purposes, so long as the tribe either subsists or chooses to remain." But the right was not absolute; it was slender, precarious, and vague, subject to the lord of the soil. Beyond the problems of Ontario the Indian problem remained, still consigned to the future.

There was an interval of three days, during which the preoccupied barrister shopped and fretted. "I yesterday received your letter," he wrote Margaret, "and this morning have bought the night dresses. I am glad you will wear them . . . I am in the middle of my argument which began on Friday . . . poor dear Mr. Mowat made the most lamentable failure; no judgment, no capacity for answering questions, no facility for meeting difficulties and a persistent presentation of minor, unimportant and untenable points against the mind of the court. They were very kind and patient . . . but the case is distinctly worse still than it was before he spoke, and is still in danger . . . it makes me dreadfully nervous — *a more pitiable exhibition I never saw* . . . if we fail I shall never hear the end of the £6,000! . . . you see my mind is so full of the case that I can think of nothing else. . . ."[15]

As he resumed on the 24th, however, he was soon in better heart. The atmosphere of the court seemed better. Discussion turned to the old grim facts of conquest, and of what was left the conquered. "In the earliest days," said Blake, "it was the Pope who claimed the right to grant away the kingdoms of this world as well as of the world to come . . . it became the recognized doctrine of the Christian states that the discovery of the heathen lands gave the discoverer, being a Christian state, the soil absolutely — "

Lord Selborne interjected. "The argument about the Pope is a very extravagant one. The pope's authority can hardly be made an argument at this time of day."

Nevertheless, Lord Watson thought, it established the pattern of the past. "A pretext has never been wanted for taking land."

"Respect was to be paid," said Blake, "to the discovery and occupation by other Christian states in America, to the absolute disregard, the ignoring altogether of rights or interests on the part of Pagan inhabitants."

"I think," said Selborne, "the word Christian should be left out."

"I quite agree."

"We know," Lord Watson added, "what has been done in the name of Christianity in the taking possession of land."

With that, too, the counsel for Ontario agreed. "My contention, however, is that founded upon whatever fantastic, and I might almost say revolting notions — "

Lord Watson cut him off. "I do not dispute the good title of the power who has taken possession."

No one disputed that. The facts of history stood, sustained by law. France had been the possessing power, and it had been superseded through conquest by the power of the British Crown. The title to the lands in question had devolved from the British Crown onto the old Province of Canada, then on Upper Canada, and Ontario had retained the title at the time of Confederation. It was the whole of Blake's case. Indians, in Watson's view, "have recognized right of occupancy or enjoyment, tribal in character, perhaps limited to hunting and fishing, capable not of transfer but only of extinguishment or surrender to the owner." Blake concurred; the Indian claim existed. But Ontario owned the soil, Ontario was the lord paramount.

"Even so," he concluded, "upon the highest ground to which the rights of the Indian can be elevated . . . this was clearly land which passed to Ontario under the 109th section of the British North America Act."

The next day he reported to Margaret again. "I spoke for 3¼ hours on Tuesday, thus making nearly six hours in all . . . our chances of success are distinctly improved and poor Mowat who thought the case absolutely lost has recovered spirits and we both think we shall win . . . my argument has made a sensation . . . my *opponents* said it was the most brilliant piece of eloquence they had ever heard . . . so that I have, I hope, done my duty . . . nevertheless the case hangs by a thread, and if it be lost I will have seriously to consider about the attitude to the fee . . . I have hardly slept a wink for some days and am worn out. . . ."[16]

He was already packed and had booked his passage for Canada. It would be six months before he knew that he had won his case, but he felt victory in his bones. He had appeared before the Lords previously, and there would be many future appearances, but this was perhaps the greatest of all the occasions. He could claim to have rescued half the Province of Ontario from the potential grip of Macdonald and the federal government. He could claim more, though it was almost an afterthought. "I contend that possibly, nay probably, the Indian position is by our construction of the Act materially improved."

The Dominion government by its legislative power was "the superintendant or guardian of the Indians, and the protector and vindicator of Indian rights". It would be more and less if it also owned his lands. It would bargain for its own advantage, "attempting to consider the interest of the Indians by one mental process while it is advancing its own interests by another." There would be no such dichotomy with Ontario owning the lands. In the long future, when the time came for the extinguishment of the Indian title, the province would bargain with the natives, and perhaps for its own advantage. But over it there would be a third party, a disinterested federal government, as guardian of Indian interests and a watchful referee.

It was not a first purpose, it was hardly a recognized purpose, in the course of his six-hour argument. Yet it was the effect of sound law, the law he loved and believed in. It was more flesh on the bones of the constitution, and it is breath breathing in the body of the nation today. From the case of the Nishga Indians in British Columbia to the case of the native peoples in James Bay, the precedents of the Ontario Lands Case are still of force and value.

CHAPTER SEVEN

"HE IS HIMSELF AGAIN"

BY EARLY AUGUST the retired leader of the Liberals was again in Murray Bay. Laurier came down to join him, and it was a reunion of good friends. It was overhung, however, by the question of Commercial Union, and it was not a meeting of minds. Laurier was as worried as ever, as unhappy in his own position, and he was already becoming dubious of the new policy of the party. Yet he had brought it to this point, he was responsible to his own supporters, and his hopes were centred as always on the return of a converted Blake. Blake, as leader again, would release Laurier. Blake, leader or not, if he would support the party line, would be a vast infusion of strength.

The wrestlings in the Privy Council seemed to have improved the invalid's health. But he had not changed in his view of Liberal policy. He would not think of the leadership, and he thought less of the party in its present posture. It had changed nothing and solved nothing by the adoption of Unrestricted Reciprocity. It was offering the same goods; it had merely juggled names. The policy under any title was Commercial Union in fact. If it were going to be offered to the public it should be presented as what it was.

Yet that, as Laurier had learned too well, was to invite complete disaster. He had Joseph Chamberlain to think of, the high priest and prophet of an Imperial Federation. If Canada,

Chamberlain had said, speaking with all the authority of a cabinet minister in England, should choose to involve herself in Commercial Union "she must be made to know that it means political separation from Britain."[1]

Also much to be thought of was Blake's recent opponent in the hearings of the Privy Council. D'Alton McCarthy was more than a rising barrister and Conservative politician. He was a local prophet of empire who was promoting Chamberlain's ideas. There was no difference for McCarthy, or indeed for any Tory, between Commercial Union and Unrestricted Reciprocity; either policy for them was the road to annexation by the United States. They proposed to block that road and reknit the bonds of empire by a structure of tariff preferences in favour of Great Britain. Beyond that, moreover, the greater goal stood up. Imperial Federation, with McCarthy now at its head, was again a lively issue. A wave of British loyalism had risen from this question of trade and it was all the more essential, as it was always a little more difficult, to maintain Liberal distinctions. Neither Mowat nor Edgar would support Commercial Union. Neither would William Mulock, another of the Toronto barristers who were powers in the Ontario party. They inclined toward reciprocity, they had been argued along to approve of it unrestricted, but at that brink they stopped. They would not be Commercial Unionists on the way to become Americans.

Why not, Blake asked suavely, if that was what they really were? Was it not the question actually facing the country? Laurier had many answers but they seemed to be no answer, and at that point effective debate stopped. For the moment, Blake said as the conversations dwindled and became casual farewells, he would neither support nor condemn the Liberal program; he would remain the observant sphinx. He could provide no further comfort for the leader taking his departure but he had, at least, reserved a crumb for himself. This ill-begotten policy with its swarming implications was hardly out of the egg. It had emerged in parliament as a resolution by Cartwright, and the resolution had been lost. Perhaps like other fantasies it would be somehow lost for good.

That prospect seemed to be a reasonable one as August wore away. Laurier was beset with complications and afterthoughts, and the doubts of British Ontario were troubling some of his men. Reciprocity, in any case, depended on the views of Americans who had not revealed their mood. Since they were now in the throes of a presidential election there would be delay for that. The Canadian scene was shifting with the onset of a new quarrel. Trade had awakened the question of loyalty to the empire; Mercier was rousing the old fears of the Pope. The Jesuits' Estates question was about to rear its head.

The lands and buildings of the Jesuit Order had been taken over at the capitulation of Canada. They had been held since Confederation as the property of the Province of Quebec. The rents and revenues had been administered as a fund for education, yet no rights had been extinguished and the ownership was not clear. Both the Jesuit Order itself and competing parties in the church had maintained for years that they were entitled to compensation. Since there was legal substance in the claims and a settlement would remove confusion, Mercier had decided to assent. He had passed in the Quebec legislature a bill which appropriated the sum of $460,000 to be distributed among the various claimants. Of this, $60,000 was to go to Protestant schools, which had been partly supported by the revenues. The balance was to be paid over to the ecclesiastical authorities of the province, and was to be shared in due proportion by the Jesuit Order and the Church.

It was a thoroughly reasonable arrangement, with some seeds of potential trouble. Both Macdonald and Laurier were convinced that Mercier had deliberately sown them. The division of the money allotted to Church and Order was a matter for arbitration, and Mercier's selection as arbitrator was His Holiness Pope Leo XIII. A voluminous correspondence between Quebec and the Holy See was reproduced at length in the bill's

MISS CANADA VACCINATED.

DR. JOHN A.—"AH, MADAM, IT IS TAKING SPLENDIDLY!"
DR. BLAKE.—"YES, LOOKS AS THOUGH IT WOULD END *FATALLY*. MADAM, DISMISS THAT QUACK, AND TAKE ME ON."
MISS CANADA.—"AND WHAT WOULD YOU DO IN THE CASE?"
DR. BLAKE.—"I WOULD—UM—ER—OCCUPY HIS POSITION."

Once the CPR charter had passed into law, many people found little that was positive or different in Liberal policies, a fact seized on by J. W. Bengough for this cartoon that appeared in *Grip*, February 25, 1882.

Oliver Mowat, the Liberal premier of Ontario from 1872 to 1896

The young Wilfrid Laurier, who succeeded Blake as leader of the federal Liberal Party in 1887

The Blake family at Murray Bay, about 1884

Margaret Cronyn Blake and her children, (*seated*) Sophia and Sammy, (*standing*) Hume and Ned, about 1885

(*Right*) Sir Richard Cartwright had been Minister of Finance in the Mackenzie administration and was opposition financial critic in the 1880s. (*Below*) Honoré Mercier became premier of Quebec in 1886.

The trial of Louis Riel (shown standing in the dock) and his subsequent execution created bitterly divisive forces within the nation, forces that were further stirred by the activities of D'Alton McCarthy, (*left*), a founder of the Equal Rights Association.

A composite portrait of the leading fig

.e Liberal Party of Canada, about 1886

G.F. SPROULE
IMPORTER,
WHOLESALE
& RETAIL.
BRITISH AMERICAN
BUSINESS
COLLEGE
LONDON
FURNITURE
COMPANY
CHINA
BAZAR
HATS

HATS

The cities where Blake lived and worked were changing and growing; (*left*) Yonge Street, and King Street West from the corner of Yonge Street, Toronto, in 1888, and (*above*) the York Street market in Ottawa at a slightly later date.

BLAINE, IF THESE FELLERS GIT INTO OFFICE, CANADY IS OURS!
DIGNIFIED ATTITUDE OF THE "LIBERALS."
ANNEXATION
GIVE US RECIPROCITY
PLEASE ACCEPT OUR COUNTRY

(*Opposite, top*) Blake reluctantly stayed silent about his disagreement with the Liberal Party's policy of Unrestricted Reciprocity in the election of 1891, but cartoonists for Conservative newspapers had a field day. (*Opposite*) Samuel Hume Blake, about 1911. (*Above*) Margaret Cronyn Blake and Edward Blake, about 1892

Spy

(*Opposite*) The member for South Longford, as portrayed in *Vanity Fair*, 1894. (*Above*) Mr. and Mrs. Edward Blake crossed the Atlantic innumerable times over the years. Here they are shown aboard the S.S. *Parisian*, August 17, 1900.

Edward Blake in 1906

preamble. In the Quebec House, with its few English and fewer Protestant members, both the correspondence and the arbiter had raised some mild questions. Had Mercier not been negotiating with a foreign power, inviting interventon in Canadian affairs? He had not, Mercier replied; this was a Quebec affair. Nor was it actually even that. His Holiness had merely been requested to superintend the division of the fund after it had passed into the hands of the Church. He was the natural and proper authority. If it was an acceptable answer in Quebec it was hardly so in Ontario, and Mercier's Jesuits' Estates Bill was already a *cause célèbre*. The burgeoning D'Alton McCarthy had widened his field of action. To his Imperial Federationists he had added alarmed Protestantism, and was bent on curbing Jesuits by the disallowance of the bill. When Blake returned to Toronto there were war drums throbbing again.

He had not come back, however, as a working politician. He was a lawyer with much to do and with a new zest in his practice. The firm prospered as always with Sam at his right hand, and he had sons about him now. Edward Hume, his eldest, had been a partner for three years. In the early autumn Edward Francis joined him. "I fancy," Cartwright wrote, after the cancellation of an appointment by an all too busy Blake, "his mind is set on making a fortune in the next three years and putting his sons in the way to do the same and he is pretty certain to do it."[2]

Times were changing, prophecies were being borne out, new men were appearing. The CPR, still in financial difficulties, had had to call on government for another guarantee. More than that, with Van Horne now its president in place of Stephen, it was involved in a dispute with government and had called on Edward Blake.

Its claim was that on sections of line constructed in British Columbia the work done by the government had not been up to standard. There would have to be much rebuilding and there would have to be compensation. It was a question solely of contract and the interpretation of law; politics could be consigned to the past. The railway wanted the best lawyer in Canada, and for the laying of grounds for such a case the best lawyer was available. On October 15, retained by the CPR, Blake left for the Pacific coast.

Whatever he thought of his mission or of his reception in British Columbia, he came back much refreshed. Neither old causes nor new causes seemed able to compete with his zest for present business. There was an invitation awaiting him, from Ingersoll, Ontario, where Cartwright the year before had launched Commercial Union. It appeared now that an antidote was desired. Blake had spoken once for Imperial Federation; would he be willing to speak again? He declined politely, "being at the present unable to take an active part in political affairs."[3] It was in any case too late; he was as far from the views of Aurora now as he was from the views of Cartwright, and apparently serene in freedom. "He is himself again," Edgar reported to Laurier, "himself of his best and brightest days . . . I would not ask him to return to what he felt to be a state of bondage in the leadership."[4]

Cartwright was of the same mind, though for other and different reasons. Imperialists or not, Jesuits or not, he was bent on reciprocity. His new policy, he thought, had pulled the party together, though every day brought signs that it was a frail unity. Blake might smash it at a stroke with one major pronouncement, and Cartwright bombarded Laurier with appeals to plead for silence. Yet even that would be precarious; absence would be better still. "I saw Blake," Cartwright reported to his leader on December 10, "and found him rather pessimistic and critical . . . it may be just as well that he should not be at the first caucuses."[5]

They were beginning to be thought of now; the new session of parliament was to open at the end of January. It would be dangerous for Liberal unity, since there was a growing ripple of cross currents and a horde of questions troubling the party mind. Cartwright had never answered them and he had dissuaded Laurier from attempting them, but he had his fears of

Blake. "I would not like to guarantee he might not deliver himself (without altogether meaning to do so) of a very judicial review of the difficulties . . . and I am not anxious that he should, either in the House or caucus. We know them well enough and we don't want to fortify our enemies with *his* summation of them."[6]

Of all this the busy Toronto barrister seemed to be oblivious. He corresponded with Laurier about joining the Quebec bar, and the prospect of an examination. "My dear Blake," came the reply, "the only examination that you would undergo would be a general handshaking with the examiners."[7] The friendship was still unchanged, but so were the friends' positions. On December 24 a circular from Laurier heralded the coming session, and it was amplified by a personal letter four days later. For all the months of debate, the party policy remained. "I am greatly impressed with the objections which you put before me at Murray Bay, but . . . I think we ought to adhere to it unless we are prepared to offer something better."[8]

Nothing better emerged, and Blake had nothing to say. In the session which opened on January 31, 1889, and closed on May 2, he spoke in total less than a hundred words. "If I can't help I shall at any rate not hurt," he had promised Laurier. "I am laying my plans for an *idle session*, saying nothing, doing little and a good deal away from Ottawa."[9]

All this he faithfully performed. He was not present at the pre-session caucuses when the waverers of the party were once more shepherded through the hoop of Unrestricted Reciprocity. He had nothing to say himself, nor did Laurier say anything, as a second resolution in support of the policy was limply proposed by Liberals and duly voted down. The truth was that reciprocity slept, barely breathing. It was not a rejected idea, even by Macdonald himself. He had often spoken of the National Policy as a means of forcing reciprocal concessions from the Americans. He had hoped that agreements on fisheries problems might lead to agreements on trade. Yet he could not hope for it now, and there was less hope for the wider goals of the Liberals. The American elections in November had returned high-tariff Republicans. They were stiffer than ever on the fisheries questions and as stubbornly devoted to protection as the National Policy itself. There was no forcing them, there was no coaxing them, and parliament and the Canadian public had become indisposed to try. It was the other question that was filling the newspapers now.

On March 1 Colonel William Edward O'Brien, member for Muskoka, Ontario, gave notice in the House that he intended to move for the disallowance of the Jesuits' Estates Act. On March 26, obviously inspired by McCarthy and prefaced by large demonstrations of Protestants and Orangemen in Ontario, the debate itself commenced. Quebec, the argument ran, was diverting money from public education. It was subsidizing the Jesuit Order and enriching the Catholic Church. It was involving the Pope as an authority in the affairs of Canada; it was in effect reversing the conquest.

It was not an impressive argument for the great majority of the House. When the vote came two days later it was supported by thirteen men. Eight were Conservative, five Liberal, and none of them except McCarthy was of much importance by himself. Yet McCarthy made the difference. He was already regarded by many as Macdonald's presumptive heir. He was hard, narrow and able, and he was no parochial bigot. He was as imperial as Joseph Chamberlain in his vision of Anglo-Saxondom, and he was a central Ontario Protestant determined on a British Canada. He would survive this vote in parliament and he would soon outgrow his province; he offered the promise of new religious war.

Macdonald had voted against him. He saw no grounds for the disallowance of the bill, and beyond that there were earthy politics involved. He had intervened before in provincial affairs, and had had his fingers burned. He was prepared to risk an incipient split in the party rather than provide Mercier with

a grievance to exploit in Quebec. Laurier had voted with Macdonald and for most of the same reasons. Yet both men, speaking with rare eloquence, had dealt with the larger question. They were concerned here, and for once concerned together, with the new rift of dissension that was threatening to tear the country.

Blake, though he said nothing, had sat through much of the debate. He had recorded his "nay" on division. Whatever his private feelings or his suspicion of Mercier's motives, he was at one with Macdonald and Laurier in rejecting disallowance. The bill had been framed to inflame but it had been properly framed in law; it was within the powers of the province. He had turned fiercely on the *Globe*, a week before the debate, when its dislike of Jesuits and Mercier had led it to prejudge decision. Content with its own authorities it had announced itself as "entirely and absolutely dissociated" from any member who should vote against disallowance. "I do not remember," wrote Blake, dissociating himself from the *Globe*, "even in the old days when the Browns were said to control the course of the party line . . . any instance approaching the insolent, dictatorial, over-bearing character of this language."[10]

He had driven the *Globe* into fuddled and confused retreat. With his vote recorded in Ottawa he had done his minimal duty. Yet it was not enough; the thought haunted him for a month. The voice of parliament was not quieting the country; Ontario was growing louder and there were louder answers from Quebec. The federal government, in considering a provincial bill, had a year by law to decide on disallowance. There were still five months remaining and the decision might be reversed; Macdonald might yet weaken. If he did that the dreary tumult of bigots and politicians would only be thrice renewed.

There was one prop, however, that Macdonald had not yet used. There was one voice still unheard that had spoken with effect before. It might do so again and it might dampen even McCarthy, not only on the Jesuit question but on some of his future plans. To Blake, now, the ideal imperial relationship was less and more than Imperial Federation. If it involved autonomy in decision-making it also involved sharing, a draft on the stores of wisdom that had built up British law. The Jesuits' Estates question, stripped of the rags of prejudice, was essentially a question of law. It was another question for that room in Downing Street. On April 26 Blake telegraphed directly to

Macdonald, urging that the Jesuits' Estates Act he referred to the Privy Council.

He was leaping the gulf of party, and for the moment at least he was superseding his leader. But Laurier was to be shown the telegram and a letter to Laurier followed which he was free to show to Macdonald. There was to be no jockeying of parties, there were to be three concerned leaders, united by imperative duty and acting for the public good. For a moment the great ideal rose again. The public mind, wrote Blake, "that tribunal so highly inflamed, and at the same time so imperfectly informed",[11] was being confused by many agitators. It had been set at rest before by the cool voice of the Lords, speaking in the Judicial Committee. The precedent should be re-established; it was more than ever necessary, and not with an eye alone to present troubles. The question of the Jesuit Estates was as yet a minor symptom, foretelling greater malaise. "There are difficulties great enough in our future, difficulties which we must meet, not shirk . . . For the moment, it seems to me, the best we can do for our country is to grapple with that part of the present problem capable of solution by the machinery we can set in motion."[12]

The machinery did not move; only Macdonald could act, and he chose not to. He wrote to Tupper in England asking him to obtain an expression of opinion from British law officers, but there was to be no argument at length before the Lords. The session came to an end, the agitation went on, and Cartwright feared a new pronouncement from Toronto. "I hope you keep up a pretty steady correspondence with Blake," he wrote Laurier. "I rather think he is meditating a deliverance on the Jesuit question and to say truth would rather he did not. He is a 'bête noir' with the Orangemen already and I do not believe it will do the Liberal party in Ontario one atom of good to discuss the matter on its merits — constitutional or other. If you find he has any such intentions and can persuade him to keep quiet it would be well."[13]

By July, it seemed, Cartwright's hopes had been realized. Blake, with his suggestions ignored, was publicly keeping quiet. He hoped as usual for a rest in Murray Bay, and as usual for a visit from Laurier. But he was doubtful now, he wrote in a letter to his leader, that he would face an election again. Even in West Durham he was becoming an alien figure, with his stand on Riel and Orangemen and his latest vote on the Jesuit question all recorded against him. There was the trade question too, he added unforgetfully, "which for me complicates the situation."

"So you see I view it rather from the philosophic standpoint of a bystander than from that of a combatant; though I do not pretend to say that I have no regrets . . . we have, I fear, fallen upon evil times, and much which some of us have dreaded appears likely to develop in an aggravated form. God grant that my forecasts may be gloomier than the event."[14]

In Murray Bay, in August, he saw the time pass for the disallowance of the Jesuits' Estates Act. It was established in law and a running sore in the country, spreading its venom elsewhere. Ontario was loud in its fears of a Catholic Quebec, and Mercier, flamboyant as always, was engaged in feeding the fears. McCarthy had carried them westward to the Territories and Manitoba, where there were Frenchness and Catholic schools. He was vocal and open now on more than the Jesuit question; it was the French question as a whole.

On July 12, speaking in Stayner, Ontario, on the great day of Orangemen commemorating the Battle of the Boyne, he had put a hard point to his thought. The "bastard nationality" must be redeemed in spite of itself for the sake of the nation. "This is a British country, and the sooner we take in hand our French Canadians and make them British in sentiment and teach them the English language, the less trouble we shall have to prevent. Now is the time when the ballot box will decide this great question; and if that does not supply the remedy in this generation bayonets will supply it in the next."[15]

The answer, if there could be an answer, was soon to be attempted. Blake learned of the fact from a newspaper report while he was still at Murray Bay. "I see you are to be in Toronto at the end of the month," he wrote Laurier on September 13. "We hope you will be able to stay with us."[16] The careful graciousness overrode the sense of rebuff, and he refrained from comment on the venture. It was a decision of younger Liberals that was bringing Laurier to speak, and it would certainly be an act of courage by the party leader. But the Horticultural Pavilion, in the present mood of the province, would not be promising ground.

On the night of Sepember 30 Laurier came. The man who had not been consulted was not present on the platform, but he read the speech next day. He was reassured by the words and more by the account of the reception. Laurier had had no apologies for the Jesuits' Estates Act, but neither had he praised the author. Mercier, he clearly intimated, had made mischief out of justice. There had been words for McCarthy also, though most of them remained unheard; Laurier had been drowned at that point by steady and deliberate applause. Yet there had been other applause too, for the French Canadian who respected English law, who would not be ruled by the Church, who quoted Shakespeare here.

"No Italian priest
Shall tithe or toll in our Dominion."

It seemed that once more Toronto had accepted the man. One could feel again that there was a leader wisely chosen, that there was a nation broad enough to contain its Lauriers and McCarthys. The imperialist had had his answer; it was not to be a British country. Mercier and Mercier's nationalists had been given their answer too. "If there are any amongst my fellow countrymen of French origin who have ever dreamed of forming themselves into a small community on the banks of the St. Lawrence, I am not one of them."[17]

Yet there was no tour of Ontario to follow the single speech. If Laurier had been bravely welcomed by a majority of the party leaders, he was seen off with relief. They returned to their own constituents to find them reading of the west. The government of Manitoba was considering the abolition of separate schools, most of them Catholic and French. In October, from the North-West Territories, where French was an official language in the courts and legislature, came a petition to the Dominion Government to withdraw the right to its use.

The political parties were approaching a new session, each of them adrift and floundering in a medley of clashing currents. Schools, languages, Jesuits, and reciprocity all inter-acted together to confuse each separate issue. While Laurier struggled to contain Mercier in Quebec, Cartwright surveyed Ontario with his worries always widening. Though his own major policy seemed to be obscured by new conflicts he was still determined to pursue it and he was obsessed by the thought of Blake. It would be "triply inexpedient" he had written Laurier in August," that Blake should in any way throw cold waters on the movement for reciprocity."[18] McCarthy's work in the west gave cause for new anxieties, and he feared a deliverance on that. "I am strongly of opinion . . . that if at all possible, you had better persuade Blake to keep silent . . . I think it is very undesirable that Blake should speak at all at present and I hope he will keep in his present frame of mind."[19]

By the end of the year, however, Cartwright had other thoughts. He had discussed some of them with Blake, and he imparted the gist to Laurier. The question of trade was involved with imperial relations, and even vaguely involved with the question of race. It was after all a French-Canadian Catholic who was leading the party's march toward the Americans. It might be well to delay the march; to impose a truce of silence. Better even than that, there might be a policy of diversion. There might be other issues, or issues to be made up, and Blake had seemed to concur. He had at any rate been enlivened, in the course of "a very long chat", by the thought of a session free of reciprocity. He might again be active in the House.

Cartwright had changed the prospect, perhaps more than he wished to, but he had decided by December 30 to make the best of it. "Write Blake," he instructed Laurier in his usual peremptory fashion as the guiding senior, "and try to get him to put his views on paper as to the Separate Schools question here and in the Nor. West. I think he will do it if you make a strong personal request and it will be of consequence.

"He will be in Ottawa," he added, in a mood and tone familiar to him since the old days of Mackenzie, "but I don't know what he means to do."[20]

CHAPTER EIGHT

"MR. LAURIER KNOWS MY VIEWS"

ON ONE POINT doubts were quickly resolved. In the session that convened on January 16, 1890, Blake sat for the last time as a member of the Canadian parliament. Determinedly self-relegated to his position on a back bench, he saw ahead of him Laurier sitting as the party leader, Cartwright beside Laurier, and across the aisle Macdonald, still in the highest place. There was enough in that tableau, after twenty-three years of politics, to tell of failure and frustration. He felt it, he often spoke of it, yet there was a kind of freedom too. It was here now, if ever, and with all its ambiguities, that he realized his image of himself as a public man. Bestriding the divisions of politics, the ruthless foe of expediencies, he was a leader only of citizens and a friend of the common good.

It did not necessarily advance friendship in the party. Within two weeks of opening day the high tacticians of Liberalism were engaged in evasive manoeuvres. Cartwright, unofficially, was making hay with the Americans. He was to be seen in New York in February under the auspices of Erastus Wiman, the Canadian-born businessman who had gone to the United States to make his fortune, and who was now the great proponent of Commercial Union. Presented by his host at a banquet of the New York Board of Trade, he had been eloquent on his own ideas and in obvious accord with Wiman. From there he had gone to Washington to confer with James G. Blaine, the American Secretary of State, who was a powerful factor in policy-making and at least politely receptive.

At the same time, on the home front, Mulock, Edgar and others of the leading Liberals were fending off Tory attacks. Every American gesture, when a gesture was made at all, seemed somehow directed to the acquisition of Canada, and whenever an American spoke there was a new outcry from the Imperial Federationists. It was forcing Liberals into a condition of battered stalemate. On the issue of reciprocity they were not prepared to advance, they could not publicly retreat, and their only recourse at the moment was to avoid its implications. The resourceful Mulock, strongly supported by Edgar and most of the Ontario caucus, had proposed as one measure an address of loyalty to the Queen. It would reassure Canadians, defy the plotting Americans, and diminish reciprocity to an innocent hope for trade. Impatiently agreed to by Laurier and proposed in parliament by Mulock, the resolution emerged as a thing of such vacuous and pious irrelevance that even Macdonald gave it tongue-in-cheek support. Blake, however, got up and walked from the House before the vote. He would not, he declared in the corridor, for once indifferent to newspaper men around him, be made a party to a sham.

It was an augury of much of the session. He would be of no help on the trade question while it was camouflaged or obscured. He was remote from party leadership, unconcerned with strategy, and totally immune from discipline. Always unpredictable, he was often absent on business, and the back bench when vacant was frequently a welcome sight. Yet he was there to rise beside it, and to rise ahead of his leader, when the issue came that Laurier had most feared.

It entered parliament in the form of a resolution proposed by D'Alton McCarthy. Blake read the words to the House on February 14. "Whereas it is expedient in the interest of the national comity of the Dominion that there should be community of language among the people of Canada . . . the enactment in the North-West Territories Act allowing the use of the French language should be expunged therefrom."[1] He questioned the word "comity" and McCarthy rose to correct it; "unity" was the word intended. That, said Blake acidly, at least removed his puzzlement in regard to the sense of the text. "Comity" meant kindliness or courtesy or friendly consideration, which were not to be discovered here.

He had had a part himself, fifteen years earlier, in framing the Act that governed the North-West Territories. It had provided rights for an expected coming of peoples, of whom he had hoped many would be French. He was forced to admit that much of that hope had failed. There had been little migration from Quebec and there were obvious reasons for that, the Riel troubles among them. The language of the vast majority was now English, and French was hardly used in the courts or legislature. Perhaps there was little wish for it except by a small minority, which might in time accede to the general will. But that was a question for the territories and not for the Dominion parliament. It should not be decided here, it should not be decided now, and certainly not in the spirit of McCarthy's motion.

That spirit breathed in the preamble. The French language was to be "expunged". Where? Among the few scattered thousands who inhabited the North-West Territories? That would be the immediate effect, but it was not the whole of the intent. It was expedient, the preamble said, "that there should be community of language among the people of Canada." The principle here to be established, the purpose here to be declared was the elimination of French throughout the Dominion.

It had been expressed in exuberant amplitude by the speaker preceding Blake. John Charlton of North Norfolk riding in Ontario was a sixty-year-old lumbering magnate and a leader in the Liberal party. There were still the remains of a Yankee twang in his voice, for he had been born in New York state and had only come to Canada at the age of twenty. He had made his money on both sides of the line, and had hopes of making more through reciprocity. He was, nevertheless, the most prominent of the five Liberals who had gone with McCarthy in the matter of the Jesuits' Estates. Still sore on that point, he had gone with him here again, and his speech had preceded Blake's. As the old leader of Liberals stood up before the House, the glow of Charlton's oratory was still warming the air.

Trafalgar and Waterloo, the Battle of the Nile, and the battle of the Plains of Abraham had all been duly recalled to the memory of the French. For all Charlton's ancestry there had been a thoroughly British lecture on the pride of empire, and there had been more than that in his conclusion. "I hope that the French members will forgive, if they deem it necessary to forgive . . . our purpose, our avowed purpose to make this a Saxon state. The avowed purpose of the Anglo-Saxon is to make the Anglo-Saxon race the greatest race on earth, and the hope of the Anglo-Saxon is that the day will come, and come before many decades have elapsed, when the English language will be the common means of intercommunication between all the races of the world, so that the Anglo-Saxon will fulfill the destiny which God has evidently designed he shall fulfill in this world."[2]

There had been all that, and it was the worse for the American twang. It evoked the thought of millions below the border, Anglo-Saxon too, sharers of the same hope. It came here, after twenty-three years of politics, twenty-three years of life for the young Dominion, addressed from the side of Liberalism and addressed from the Province of Ontario to a Canadian parliament. Quebec would answer it, but Quebec could never silence it. It could be silenced only by the voice of another Ontario, speaking from the same side, schooled by the same years, and in words which told of a different hope for Canada. Charlton, said Blake, beginning with deadly mildness, had formed the habit of speaking much in the plural. He used "we" and he used "our" when speaking of views and intentions that should be presented solely as his own. He could not speak for the House, he could not speak for his party, and he did not speak for Blake.

"I knew well that . . . there were great masses of prejudice and suspicion, of ancient hates and misconceptions and bitter memories of former conflicts lying ready to the hand of the incendiary, easy to be kindled, difficult to be extinguished, and that the proportions of the conflict they might excite were impossible to be calculated in advance." He knew now that the conflict was under way. "This Bill . . . is only the beginning of the campaign." There was an attack directed here, not at the French minority in the North-West Territories, but at all the French in Canada.

Why? There was discontent with Quebec. There had been provocation by Mercier. There seemed to be a turning-inward and a turning away from the English on the part of the whole people. Was there anything surprising in that? Had it not been provoked too? There had been the tumult over Riel, there had been the magnification of the Jesuit question and now there was McCarthy's bill. It foreshadowed even more, and it would have the inevitable effect.

"Sir, at all times and in all countries minorities are inclined to be susceptible, jealous, apprehensive, exacting — such is the condition of human nature. Those who are in minorities feel it; and those who happen to be in majorities, though they may complain of it, ought to understand it too. Minorities are apt to believe that they must unite in order to protect themselves against aggression; and such union amongst themselves, and such consequent isolation from their fellow-countrymen is, wherever it occurs and just in proportion to the extent of its occurrence, a serious danger to the state . . . I am speaking this day mainly in the hope to avert it . . .

"On what conditions, circumstanced as we are, can we live and thrive and grow in Canada? Certainly not on the lines which are being laid down by those engaged in this agitation. I would ask them to put themselves in the French Canadian's place. You may selfishly wish that he had agreed to be suppressed . . . you may earnestly desire for all men the inestimable boons of British birth, of English speech, of Protestant religion. But still, after all, cannot you put yourself in his place? And can you not, must you not, admire the courage, the fidelity and the determination with which, at great odds, he fought in all fields . . . for what to him was as dear as what you call your birthright is to you? Fought, aye, and conquered too! Cannot you recognize that his was, after all, a victory for humanity? And that if, as is the case, it has imposed greater difficulties and more arduous efforts and toils on those who are engaged in making a nation of Canada, it yet by that very circumstance, gave the chance for more exalted triumphs, gave an opening for the exhibition of still higher and deeper and broader feelings of justice and liberality and tolerance than are permitted to a wholly homogeneous people? Can you not at least see — if that much you cannot see — that he has in fact conquered? Do you seriously hope to prevail today in a conflict in which, under infinitely greater disadvantages, he obtained the victory long ago?"

He rejected McCarthy's preamble and proposed his own amendment. "That, on the contrary, this House declares its inviolable adherence to the covenants in respect to the use of the French language in Quebec and Canada . . . that the expunging of the provisions allowing the use of the French language in the Territories is not required to remedy any practical grievances at this time . . . that it is expedient to leave those provisions undisturbed . . . until time shall have further developed the conditions of North-West settlement." The flow of peoples should decide the fate of the French language in the Territories; it should not be pronounced on here. Nor anywhere, in the spirit of the present bill. He did not insist on the terms of his own amendment, but "on these lines, or on lines like these, I would invite this House to act. . . . This, I feel, is for Canada a turning point. I see but dimly; I may not see aright; but if I at all discern the signs of the times, until Canadians on such lines agree, there will be for Canada neither progress, prosperity nor peace."[3]

Three days later Laurier spoke, and he was an angry, admiring echo. The next day Thompson rose, the Catholic Minister of Justice on McCarthy's side of the House. He held the text that was to be the final resolution, and his views were coldly clear. A man's right to be heard in "the tongue that suits him best" should be conceded at least in courtesy by any Canadian legislature. It was so in his own province, without law or guarantee. "The man who would object to an Acadian in Nova Scotia speaking his own tongue in the legislature of his own province would be laughed to scorn."

The assembly of the North-West Territories, the resolution declared, should itself decide on the language used by its members. The Dominion parliament, however, "having regard to the long-continued use of the French language in old Canada, and to the covenants on that subject embodied in the British North America Act . . . declares its adherence to the said covenants and its determination to resist any attempt to impair the same." It would change little in the west, to be governed by its coming peoples, but it had drawn the venom of McCarthy. Thompson did not look at him as he raised his eyes from the text. "I need hardly say to the House that a portion of that resolution is taken from the one that was suggested by the honourable member for West Durham."[4]

For once the ideal of leadership, of good men working in common, had spanned the carpeted aisle.

It was the high point of the session but there also had to be a low point, and it again centred on Blake coupled with Charlton. Prompted as he claimed by the taunts of hostile newspapers, Charlton moved in April to revive the Jesuit quarrel. He could change nothing in the settlement since the Act had passed into law, but he could refresh some fading memories and encourage some useful rancours. What he proposed in effect was a vote of censure on the government for not referring the question to the Privy Council.

It was an act of pure mischief-making and as such was deplored by Laurier, who had tried for months to prevent it. It was also deplored by Blake, but he himself had created complications. There was the telegram of the year before and the letter sent to Laurier, both of them urging reference to the Privy Council. There was his often-stated opinion, which was not shared by Laurier, that there could be an alternative reference to the Supreme Court of Canada. Earlier in this same session, with Macdonald's warm approval, Blake had moved that "on solemn occasions touching the exercise of the power of disallowance or of the appelate power as to educational legislation, important questions of law or fact may be referred by the Executive to a high judicial tribunal."[5] He had been looking forward in this case to the approach of trouble over the schools of Manitoba, but he could not refuse to look back. If he had wanted reference before he must approve of reference now; he would have to support Charlton.

He did so with reserved frigidity, and with considerable contempt for Charlton's view of law. Yet he had magnified Charlton's nuisance value by entering the debate at all, and he proceeded to enhance division. The Blake who opposed the government spent much of his time in defending the inaction of government, and its almost-valid reasons for declining to refer the bill. He considered them strong but hardly strong enough; he restated his own positions. He could not agree with Laurier over reference to the Supreme Court; he still thought it would have been useful in calming the uninformed. It did not calm Laurier who was already ruffled enough. How so, he asked, if Quebec had refused to present her case to the Court? If she considered the matter settled, as Mercier certainly did, what could a reference mean but more commotion? "I cannot censure the government on the present occasion."

James Trow, the resentful Liberal whip, got up to glare at Charlton. Why had he saved this question, if he had to broach it at all, till the last weeks of the session? He had not, Laurier replied, glaring in turn at Trow; Charlton had held his motion at Laurier's own request. It should have been dropped completely, it could do no possible good, but whatever Charlton was blamed for it did not include delay. As the party bickered in public with the family wash on the line, Charlton's motion was lost. Laurier voted with Macdonald, Blake voted to censure him, and Liberals retired to the smoking rooms profanely censuring Blake.[6]

By May the session was over but the party problems remained, and they were still not lessened by Blake. For all its recent setbacks McCarthy's work went on, widening the rifts in the country with every advancing phase. In Manitoba, where a Liberal provincial government was abolishing separate schools, a national issue was building. Blake saw it, and saw all sides of it, and sometimes wrote to Laurier at troublingly discursive length. He had fears, platitudes, and alternatives but they cancelled each other out. He had done his duty by parliament, he was immersed again in the law, he had not determined an actual line of policy. Nor, even if he had, "should I for a moment dream of presenting it myself. Recent events have strengthened my conviction that my political career is practically ended; and I look on this and other subjects more as a bystander than as one expecting to be in the thick of the fight. But perhaps this may not be without its advantages."[7]

They were not apparent to Laurier, who was again threatening to resign. He had even thoughts, it seemed, of giving way to Cartwright. That much he confided in a letter to the young John Willison, the hyper-active Liberal who was now an editor of the *Globe*. Frayed by the past session, Laurier could see ahead of him only more and worse. The schools of Manitoba were becoming the final straw. It would be a question of provincial rights, the dearest cause of Quebec. But it would be French rights and Catholic rights that would be extinguished by a provincial legislature; only to be restored by federal intervention. To propose that or oppose it would be equally to invite a storm, and it would certainly be the more disastrous because Laurier himself was French. He saw that fact as the root of the party's difficulties and the heart of all division. He could never succeed in Ontario while it remained in its present mood. He was opposed by the Church in Quebec. He was ill at ease with Mercier and yet eternally involved, and his very provincial necessities were the bane of the federal leader. It would not be so with the bystander, and Laurier wanted him back. He wanted him back as leader, though he had invoked the prospect of Cartwright to serve as a useful threat. The everlasting trade question still lurked in the underbrush, but it must be somehow walked around. From all necessities and involvements there was only escape through Blake.

Yet the prospect dimmed with every exchange of letters. The two men could never arrange to meet, they were manoeuvring at arm's length, and a new, unheard-of difficulty soon began to intrude. Even in West Durham, Riel and the Jesuit question and French in the North-West Territories had had their fatal effect; Blake was no longer safe. "In truth," he wrote Laurier, "the question for me is whether I shall be returned again, not whether I shall be called to lead again. It was thought best I should not go into my riding, and I do not choose to go elsewhere."[8] He offered the improbable prospect of Sam running in his place, partly at least "because of his well-known Protestantism", which was becoming a valuable asset. Throughout Ontario the party was tainted with bigotry, Orangeism was on the rise, and the Protestant clergy was defecting en masse from the Liberals. "We shall have a bad quarter of an hour," Blake predicted. Yet he hoped with remote optimism that conditions might one day mend, and he was firm in leaving it at that. "Let us come into a compact, my dear Laurier . . . neither of us shall press the other on this subject of the leadership."[9]

He was not to be changed even by the thought of Cartwright

taking the succession. Willison showed him the letter written by Laurier, and newspaper talk continued with a steady barrage of hints. They drew nothing from Blake but one disclaimer, published in the columns of the *Globe.* He begged space to deny that he had any thought of ever resuming the leadership. "My only wish is that the confidence and affection of Liberals of all shades may induce Mr. Laurier to hold the place which he so admirably fills."[10]

It was July by then, and he was writing from Murray Bay. He hoped for a visit from Laurier and he had promised Laurier that he would stop at Arthabaska when he returned up river in the autumn. But the summer waned, the visit did not materialize and the nation went its way. Provincially the scene was bright. Both Manitoba and New Brunswick were now in the Liberal camp. By the end of July, Fielding, Mowat, and Mercier had all been returned to power in new elections. Faced with the hostile provinces and visibly aged himself, Macdonald seemed to be losing his grip on government. Yet his major worry was also a Liberal worry; the problem of tariffs was back on stage again.

It was a question now of the response to an urgent threat. Maturing in the United States under the hands of Congressman William McKinley was a new Republican tariff bill that would probably appall the world. It was already frightening Democrats and certainly it alarmed Canada. The new duties proposed would not only affect industry; they might well wipe out the export trade in agricultural products. For Canadian butter, eggs, barley, hay, and livestock the prospect was that they would be barred from the American market.

Under that threat negotiation of a fisheries treaty between Canada and the United States became all the more imperative. It might be combined with negotiations on trade. It might lead to reciprocity if the Americans could be made to think of it and induced to lay down their club. In Newfoundland, which was much concerned for her fish, there were actually negotiations under way, encouraged by a British government that was also nudging Canada. As the pressure built on Macdonald he seemed to be inclined to yield. It was a reluctant yielding and a tentative one, but it posed an enormous question. If Macdonald went to Washington where would the Liberals go?

They must obviously go there too, and endeavour to get there first with the most to offer. If reciprocity was good, it was better unrestricted. The thought was reviving policy and creating its own momentum. There were hints in the air that Macdonald was preparing to move, that he intended to call an election, that it might be based on a new accord with the Americans. There was a new accord of Liberals in the face of the awakening issue, and the intimations came down to Murray Bay. Laurier himself supported and reinforced them in a letter on September 9. "Do you not now believe," he wrote, "that the idea of reciprocity is making headway?"[11]

The answer came from Toronto four days later. Blake had returned in haste, and it had not been possible to stop at Arthabaska. "Continuous nausea and nervous prostration have beset me, and . . . I suddenly decided it would be better to come up here and try the effect of a change." Otherwise nothing had changed, except that the attitude of the bystander seemed to be slightly stiffened. "I will not attempt to enter into any detail in the political question you suggest . . . nor have I yet any solution of the difficulties I have stated to you . . . I still keep groping for some light."[12]

While he groped the darkness thickened. The McKinley tariffs came into force in October, precipitating a world-wide slump. Canada was standing still, Macdonald had made no move that was yet visible, and the mood of the Liberal party was hardening in resentful gloom. If there was to be no light from the old leader it would have to come from the new. Or perhaps it would come from Cartwright. There was a thought in the air, wrote Laurier, in a careful letter to Blake on December 5, that the Ontario members should hold a party convention. There would be a trade policy enunciated, and he felt regretfully that Blake might disapprove. Had he a better policy to suggest?[13]

Blake had not. There were suggestions about him, however, conveyed to Laurier in private. "As far as I can judge," wrote Cartwright on December 13, "we had better have a convention. As to Blake he had most decidedly better not attend. He can do us very little good but per contra he may do much harm." Also, in Cartwright's view, what applied to the planned convention would be true of the next parliament. "The very best thing that could happen would be to induce him to go to England during the session."[14]

There was no one prepared to attempt to induce Blake, and the wheels of government were turning on higher levels. On the same day that Cartwright wrote to Laurier, a letter went from Macdonald to the British ambassador in Washington. Forwarded through the official channel, for the eyes of James G. Blaine, the American Secretary of State, were Canadian proposals to open discussions on trade.

Macdonald had been spurred by London, driven by political necessity, and tempted by Washington itself. In the hands of the Colonial Office, awaiting ratification, was the draft of a trade convention between Newfoundland and the United States. It was not yet signed but it might be, and in that case the consequences would be portentous. The second British dominion in North America would have forged a link with the Americans, and Canada would be left in dangerous isolation. Macdonald could not face that, yet neither did he dare discourage the hope for trade. London was anxious as usual for improved relations with Washington, and Washington for once seemed rather more responsive. High-tariff Republicanism had been damped by Congressional elections held in November. Even William McKinley had been defeated, and Democrats were now the controlling majority in Congress. Since they were traditionally for low tariffs, they might be prepared to deal with Canada, and there were even hopes for a change of heart in Blaine. He was a *bête noire* with Macdonald, and on every count the Prime Minister was sceptical, but he had decided glumly and warily to make a tentative approach. Blaine was invited, as he had often been invited before, to consider limited and reciprocal reductions of tariffs, mainly confined to the agricultural and other natural products of the two countries.

By the end of the year, as rumours filled the newspapers, the cautious gesture had nourished huge forebodings. Liberals doubted the reports and derided Macdonald's sincerity, while they fought with their secret fears. Cartwright's doubts about Blake became mixed with more pressing worries, though the old continued to grow. There would probably be no next session of the present parliament. There might instead be a treaty of reciprocity, fashioned by Tory hands. There might be a general election, with the treaty a major issue. There might be a new Macdonald preaching trade with the Americans, posturing in Liberal clothes. It all should have been incredible but it was all too clearly possible, and for the party in opposition there was only one thing sure. It was to hold a Convention in Ontario with which Blake would have nothing to do.

Nor was even that to remain long a certainty. By the first weeks of January, 1891, a ripple of dubious afterthoughts was troubling the Liberal leaders. The prudent Oliver Mowat, whatever he lacked as a lawyer pleading in London, was as closely in touch as any man with the grass roots of Ontario. He emerged from one of his cabinet meetings to draft a letter to Laurier, intending also to send a copy to Cartwright. As to "the Convention which is called in your name, all or nearly all of my colleagues feel great doubts as to the expediency of it in view of Mr. Blake's difficulties in regard to Unrestricted Reciprocity." If Blake attended he would certainly speak his mind, and that would invite disaster. If he stayed away, as he seemed determined to do, his tacit disapproval would have almost the same effect. Worse still, for Mowat and most of his colleagues, the afterthoughts extended to party policy. "Nearly all of us were willing to take the plunge under the hope that a way out of darkness would be discovered afterwards."[15] It now seemed all too obvious that a way had not been found.

Laurier and Cartwright were both spared the letter, since it was first submitted to Blake. He saw no point in sending it and was ominous as to his own mood. Why write Laurier, he snapped, when the convention had now been called? "The wine is poured and must be drunk, as the French proverb says." He had been represented, said Blake, as "sole obstructionist and marplot" and he did not relish the position. He was growing tired, moreover, of his silence on reciprocity. "Personally, my opinion is that the longer I wait the worse the effect when the time comes, and but for the wish of Laurier I would have spoken long ago."[16]

It was as yet only a warning, but there was an intervening event. Edward Farrer was an associate of John Willison as one of the editors of the *Globe*, and the *Globe*, to say the least, was a friend of Liberals. There was much made of the connection when despatches datelined Washington appeared in the *Globe* on January 28. James G. Blaine, in an interview granted Farrer, had discussed relations with Canada at large and leisurely length. He had gone further than that. In a letter to an American congressman written the same day he had brushed away Macdonald's tentative proposals. There were, he said, "no negotiations whatever on foot for a Reciprocity Treaty with Canada, and you may be assured no such scheme for reciprocity with the Dominion confined to natural products will be entertained by this Government."[17]

To Macdonald it was a flat lie, and confirmed his view of the Republic's leading statesmen. To Liberals it seemed a godsend and a burst of illumining truth. The real truth, however, lay somewhere on middle ground. There had been proposals and exchanges of letters but there had also been much foot-dragging, and no one had yet sat down to discuss a treaty. There would not have been much point to it while limited reciprocity "confined to natural products" was all Canadians offered. Yet it was all Macdonald would give, and he had been given his final answer. The only reciprocity would be total and unrestricted; if Washington listened to any plan it would be to the one that Liberals offered.

There could be no doubt thereafter that an election was in the wind. Nor were there any doubts for Macdonald as he composed his election cry. The long-to-be-remembered phrases began to go down on paper. He would oppose with his last breath the veiled treason and the hopes of annexation that were hidden in the Liberal version of reciprocity. He had been born a British subject and a British subject he would die. "I appeal . . . to the men who have trusted me . . . to the young hope of the country . . . in this, my last effort, for the unity of the Empire and the preservation of our commercial and political freedom."[18]

It must have been a lively period for the *Globe*'s editors and directors. When Farrer returned from his Liberal coup in Washington the seeds of a Liberal disaster were sprouting in Willison's files. They were carefully locked away, but there was no security in that. A letter from Edward Blake, intended for publication, must somehow find the light.

In mid-January, as he smouldered over the thought of the approaching convention, the Liberals of West Durham had tilted the scales for Blake. In Bowmanville, the heart of his constituency, the scene of the first and so many later triumphs, the party faithful had met. They were now diminished in numbers but the fewer seemed more fervent, and they had renewed their loyalty to him. A resolution of confidence, more welcome now than it had ever been before, had confirmed and reaffirmed him in the capacity of voice and guide.

It had turned his mind to the election that lay beyond the convention, and it had sharpened the prick of duty. In spite of Riel and Orangemen and of all McCarthy's work, there was still trust in Blake. There was faith in his views of policy, yet how was that faith returned? The chosen voice was silent, the guide gave no direction, the sheep milled in confusion while the shepherd stayed away. By the 28th of January, in spite of the news from Washington or perhaps even because of it, he could no longer bear the thought.

He sat down that day to address himself to D. Burke Simpson, a leading barrister of Bowmanville and President of the West Durham Reform Association. He was touched, Blake wrote, by the confidence again reposed in him and firmly resolved to keep it. There had been many difficult decisions "in the agitated past" which he hoped soon to be allowed to explain to the electors. "But there is one vast and complex subject which I have not been able hitherto to discuss, my views on which I feel it right now to state to the Association. I refer to the Trade Policy."[19]

The views came then in full, vast and complex as his subject, ripened by years to brooding ambiguity. They marched down his pages negating each other as they went, devastating Liberal arguments, arriving at one conclusion. There had been no solution proposed, there was no solution visible; Blake still groped for the light.

"A moderate revenue tariff, approximating to free trade with all the world, and containing liberal provisions for reciprocal free trade with the States, would be, if practicable, our best arrangement." But the best was not feasible; the arrangement would not be made.

Every reasonable effort should be made to enlarge trade with the United Kingdom, "yet the results of all such efforts must be small compared with those which would flow from a free market throughout our own continent . . . unrestricted trade with the States . . . would greatly advance our most material interests; it would help our natural, our largest and most substantial industries; it would create an influx of population and capital and promote a vast development of forces and materials now dormant; in three words it would give us men, money and markets . . .

"But, after all, it would be taken in bad part by important classes in Britain; and would seriously change their present tone in regard to the Colonial relation.

"Of this we must run the risk.

"The tendency of unrestricted free trade with the States, high duties being maintained against the United Kingdom, would be rather toward ultimate political union with the States . . . our hopes and our fears alike would draw one way.

"Of this too we must run the risk."

Yet even if the risk were accepted, "it is quite uncertain whether the States would, under existing conditions, agree to the plan . . . it is only our neighbour's northern fringe that actually realizes the existence of a material interest in free trade with Canada . . . over fifty millions of the population know little and care less about it."

In the United States the governing factor would not be economic. It would be "the underlying national sentiment . . . that some day the political unification of the continent should take place. This sentiment it is which will colour opinion as to the plan. If it be thought that its adoption would advance the cause of political union the plan will be favored. If it be thought that political union would be advanced by refusing commercial union, it may be declined."

The latter contingency could not be disregarded, nor could other and different questions. If free trade came, how to make up the gaps in Canadian revenue? "Of the financial question I have seen no solution which would leave us without a great deficit."

The other questions rose, also without an answer. There could be nothing of a temporary nature in an arrangement for free trade. "Permanence in the new relation would be important to secure a full development of great interests, to prevent disaster to important industries, and to realize many of the material advantages of the plan." Yet "it would be impossible for either country to fix its tariff for a long term . . . changes in the stipulated tariff must therefore be provided for." Yet in that event "it would be necessary to concede to the States, if not a formal, at any rate a practical preponderance in respect of changes." There would have to be a clause in the treaty providing that in case of differences either party might terminate it, "a stipulation which would probably result in concession by Canada to the States; while its existence would deprive the treaty of that assured permanency whose importance I have stated.

"I have not seen any satisfactory plan for combining the two elements of permanency of the treaty and variability of the tariff."

With which conclusion arrived at, "I have now fulfilled, as best I could, my difficult task." He had opened his mind to his constituents and deposited his doubts with them, for "dispassionate consideration". He now respectfully informed them "that, while voting with great heartiness in favor of negotiations for the most enlarged trade relations practicable between the two countries, I must, in the absence of further light, do so subject to these views; and must therefore request to be allowed a free hand in the treatment of the plan."[20]

Signed and sealed that evening the letter went off to Simpson, already accompanied by the first ripples of dismay. James Young, publisher of the Galt *Reformer*, was a good friend of Blake, a leading Liberal in parliament, and he had somehow seen the work in the course of drafting. He had gone home to compose an anguished protest which was back in the next day's mail. "I am so deeply impressed with the consequences certain to follow your manifesto that I cannot forbear sending you this hurried note . . . whatever chance the party has at the coming elections . . . your statement will, I fear, completely destroy . . . all our friends in the House committed to U.R. will feel aggrieved . . . Sir John will see that our position is hopeless."[21] The arguments had had no effect; the letter was on its way, nor had it left for Bowmanville alone. On the night of January 28, close to the stroke of midnight and in time for the morning press run, a copy had arrived at the *Globe* for John Willison.

Willison read it, shuddered, and took it to one of his confrères, whose reaction was instantaneous. There was a chance here "to produce one of the greatest sensations in the political history of Canada."[22] So there was, and there was also the certainty of disrupting the Liberal party, for which Willison was unprepared. Robert Jaffray, the president, with the other directors of the *Globe*, must see the letter first, and they were all peacefully asleep. There could be at least one night's delay.

There was even, perhaps, a slender hope of evasion. When the squire of Humewood looked in the *Globe* next morning there was no epistle from Blake. Instead, arriving by messenger, there was a note from Willison bearing the marks of haste. The editor assumed, it said, that since Mr. Blake had marked his letter "personal" is was not for publication. He was disabused of that idea by a prompt and frigid reply. The letter was intended to be published and it had better be done soon.

The *Globe*'s directors met in the afternoon, prepared to bow to the inevitable. They had the rival *Mail* to think of, which would receive a copy of the letter and quite certainly publish it if they appeared to refuse. They could not reach Laurier and neither could they reach Cartwright. The one was on his way to New York and the other already in Boston, the scheduled guests at banquets of American Boards of Trade. They were there to enthuse Americans on the program Blake was damning. They would be striking while the iron was hot, as it cooled to ice behind them. The letter went into print but it did not go into the paper; Willison was not yet beaten. With the type and galleys locked in his safe that evening, he sought out David Mills. The next morning, fortified by new arguments and tired from a late night session, he went out to beard Blake.

He was met in the study at Humewood with a grey and glowering welcome. Jaffray had been before him and had accomplished nothing. Even Sam Blake had come to protest in vain. If the *Globe*'s columns were closed, Willison was reminded grimly, the letter would appear from Bowmanville as a despatch to the Toronto *Mail*. The plea for time and consultation with Laurier set off a final explosion. Had there been time to consult Blake on the matter of Cartwright's convention? Was Blake now to be ostracized and gagged? If there was to be a convention held in spite of him it would not be held without him, for he had made up his mind to be there. And he would be there to speak, exactly in the letter's terms.

Willison left with that word, but there was one more card to be played. Laurier was in Montreal by then, just returned from New York. By the next morning he was in the *Globe*'s office in Toronto. He had had two sleepless nights on a jolting train. He was recovering from the shock of his banquet meeting where the American Secretary of the Treasury, the principal guest of honour, had dropped dead. He was expecting and dreading the call for a general election and he had been summoned by an urgent telegram to absorb Willison's news. On the last cold day of January, with all that to rejoice him, he went off to confront Blake.

"Much of what was said cannot be disclosed."[23] Twenty-nine years afterward, in the matter of Laurier's remarks as he returned from that interview, Willison was still discreet. On one point, however — and to Cartwright's black resentment — there had been total capitulation. The convention of Ontario Liberals would not now be held. On the other side there had been at least partial concession; the *Globe* might return unpublished its copy of Blake's letter. But it was not the original letter; that had been sent to Bowmanville, and in the midst of a rumbling secrecy was creating its own storm there. He would recall it, Blake had agreed, he would reconsider his methods, but the electors of West Durham must be informed of their member's views. That threat remained, hovering and still imminent, as Laurier went home from Toronto to resume the debate by mail.

"I was placed in this dilemma," he wrote on February 2, still endeavouring to salve the wound of the convention: "Since you could not speak in accordance with the voice of the party, the interest of the party demanded that you should not speak at all, and I saw that in consequence I would have to ask you not to attend." That Laurier had done, yet he had done it with a sore heart, and in any case the Convention was now abandoned. The primary grievance was disposed of, but there remained the question of the letter.

"My dear Blake, listen to the voice of a true friend. You should never publish such a document."

Laurier had never denied, nor would he ever deny, Blake's right to speak for himself. He went as far as Blake in considering it a public duty. But what, in right and duty, was Blake proposing to say?

"The weak point of your position is that while showing all the objections to every system and to every policy, you conclude with nothing at all . . . if you have no policy of your own to offer, if you simply remain in the negative, why should you sever from your friends, and why should you strike at them such a blow at such a moment? . . . I have no hesitation, for your sake, for my sake, for the sake of the party, to ask you not to let this manifesto go to the public."[24]

The next day Macdonald called the election. It was to be held on March 5, it accentuated all urgencies, and it showed already the touch of a master hand. Macdonald, girding for battle, had condensed a confusion of issues into one that was sharply clear. He had negotiated for trade with the Americans on fair and reasonable terms, and he had been repudiated and betrayed. There remained now the totality of Commercial Union, control and absorption by the Americans, the Liberal program stripped of all disguises. Or there remained Macdonald, defending the British birthright. The old man, for his last fight, was to be wrapped in the old flag.

He would not find Blake in the Liberal ranks opposing him; that decision was taken. The national figure, condemned to national silence, would not now be a candidate for the constituency of West Durham. The letter sent to the *Globe* was safely home. The original recalled from Simpson was unaccountably delayed, but it would certainly be arriving from Bowmanville by one of the early mails. In either case, however, recall meant only revision; the letter was to become an address of explication. Why was the guide and counsellor to be absent from this campaign? Duty was still inflexible, and the friends had a right to know. The nominations for Durham were to be on Thursday, February 12, presided over by all the local leaders. There in familiar Bowmanville, delivered to friends in confidence, they would have the truth from Blake.

By February 5 the text of his speech was ready, and on the 9th he wrote to Laurier. The newspapers blared around him spouting rumour; Blake was at odds with his party, Blake was soon to retire. The mail came and the doorbell rang with a daily stream of entreaties, but he had worked through it all unmoved. He had expanded, altered, and clarified, and he had hardened in all his views. He had not agreed to delay, except in part. "I have prepared," he informed Laurier, "the last dying speech and confession of a decayed politician, to be delivered in confidence on Thursday and published in the *Ides of March*."[25] That phrase, with its ominous evocations, conveyed the one concession. By the Ides of March, when the general public received the truth of Blake, the general election would be over. If there were still dismay at the thought of the Thursday meeting he could offer no help for that. Those oldest friends of the old and trusted leader must know his inmost heart.

The next day, however, came the expected letter from Bowmanville, hardly in the expected terms. D. Burke Simpson, obviously and unsuccessfully, was attempting to restrain his fury. "I regret that you had to write again in reference to your letter of the 28th ultimo; I remedy the omission by personally seeing to the enclosing of it on this occasion." Being rid of that, he turned to the personal appearance and the matter of the planned address. "I can only say that in my judgment . . . it is unfair to me and to us all . . . what good can be effected by such a course I cannot conceive, if you wish to place yourself on record surely you cannot add to what you have done, you have made your views known to all the leaders of the party . . . you have withdrawn from the contest, what can you gain by now embarrassing us in the Riding?"[26] From that point Simpson went on for another page and cited other opinions, some of them stronger than his own. But this was strong enough, and there could be only the one answer.

Silenced by his national leader, and now shut out from his constituency, Blake sat down to compose it. It was to be read that Thursday in Bowmanville to the friends who would not hear him, and it came to bury Caesar. "My object was to ask that my name should be withdrawn as I found it impossible to accept the honor of a nomination, to give my reasons for this conclusion, to return my heartfelt thanks for the unbounded kindness of four-and-twenty years, and to bid my faithful friends an affectionate farewell.

"With this view I had prepared a paper for communication to them."[27]

It had now been intimated, however, that his appearance was not desired, and the result was the present letter. "I will only add that the writing of it is the most painful event in the political life of which it is the close."[28]

On February 17, three days after the obsequies at Bowmanville, a new spectre rose to confront the Liberals. The ambiguous Farrer of the *Globe*, though he was Willison's close associate, was neither confined to newspaper work nor bound by party ties. A figure of delightful mystery so far as his background went, he knew everyone, was liked by everyone, and wrote whatever he pleased. "It is literally true," said Willison, "that his left hand did not always know what his right hand was doing."[29] His left hand, since his recent trip to Washington, had been subsidized by an American congressman to indulge in some speculation. If the United States wished for it, and the Canadian people opposed it, what were some means of pressure that might bring on annexation?

It was an intriguing question to the mind of the ingenious Farrer, who was usually straitened for money and only amused by politics. He had worked out some answers in a pamphlet of a few pages that were as yet only in proof. There were many obvious means of forcing the Dominion's hand. A tax on Canadian fish could be aimed at Nova Scotia to cripple her export trade. In spite of the CPR, and in spite of the national Policy, there were bonding privileges and railway connections that carried Canadian goods through American territory. They were all essential and they could all be suspended or cut, with ultimately disastrous effect. Trade with England could be stifled by the manipulation of tariffs. Finally, it seemed to Farrer, Macdonald himself was the bar to manifest destiny. With his going a movement toward annexation would become inevitable in Canada.

Still lying in the print shop, destined only for the congressman and a few of his American friends, Farrer's musings were quite unknown to Liberals. But they had been seen by a thieving proof-reader and they had found their way to Macdonald. On the evening of the 17th, at the Academy of Music in Toronto, the Prime Minister got up before a great Conservative rally, waving the sheets in his hand, making his fatal point. Farrer was of the *Globe*, the *Globe* spoke for Liberals; here were the Liberal plans. At one stroke that night, and for all the ensuing storm of protesting innocence, the campaign was anchored securely to the ground of the non-issue. Was Canada to be betrayed by Liberals or saved by the Grand Old Man?

Laurier groped, with increasing desperation, for a coherent line of attack. What was Commercial Union but a name that Liberals had abandoned? What was Unrestricted, as applied to

Reciprocity, but a little more than Tories had sought themselves? There was no question of loyalty, it was a question of building trade, and free of the shackling National Policy, Liberals could do it better. He would negotiate not betray, and he would negotiate in good faith, as Macdonald had never done. But he would offer nothing to the Americans and he would yield nothing of sovereignty that a free and British Canadian would not be prepared to grant.

None of it had much effect, either in his hands or Cartwright's. "Negotiate" was a wide word, but it had a vague sound on a platform. It was vague enough even to the leading Liberals, for they were divided and dividing hourly on the scope of their own proposals. For all their talks with Americans, they had no key yet to the official American mind. The British mind in Canada they were beginning to learn too well. In Ontario they wilted and waffled before the charge of the loyal hosts. Mowat was becoming reticent, Edgar was becoming difficult, and there was everywhere a nervous sharpness that was hardly a fighting edge. It was a waiting on the great silence, a premonition of the thunderbolt that was still held back by Blake.

It grew with every rumour, suspended over the campaign. Newspapers all knew of it and hostile newspapers talked of it, guessing its size and shape. Blake wrote only to his friends, deepening every mystery, magnifying mystification. He had decided to "die dumb",[30] he had accepted "political extinction", but public duty remained. So did pride of authorship, asserting rights to be fulfilled in due season. The message denied to Bowmanville would not be denied to the nation, but the time was not quite yet. Nor could there be any revealing hint, lessening its import. It could hardly have been better advertised, hardly more damaging to Liberals, but it was done with the anguished fortitude of a man betrayed by his friends. Blake could no longer help them but he was determined to refrain from hurting them; it was the sum of every answer. "Mr. Laurier knows my views"[31] was the sole response to the inquirer seeking guidance. "As to my speaking in the riding, if you get Mr. Laurier's request that I should go down and tell what I think, I will consider it. But as I am silent with his approval I don't imagine he will call on me."[32] Everything hinged on Laurier, everything was blamed on Laurier, with heavily grieving emphasis and wholly pious intent. "For more than three years I have maintained and he has agreed . . . that it was necessary for me when I spoke to say what I thought. The error was in the early request that I should refrain from speaking."[33]

The campaign swirled around Blake and he bore the weight on his shoulders. Atlas coped with the wounds and wars of the world. Friends gave up with him, enemies teased and slandered him, and even his faithful brother joined the doubters. They could change nothing for Blake; he was still locked on his course, suffering and single-minded. "It adds greatly to a pain which I did not think could be keener," he wrote to his old law partner, Wells, "to find that you and Sam also, pronounce me to be failing in my duty. But I will try to bear it all."[34] It was as grievous a sacrifice now to relinquish public office as it had usually been to hold it, yet "those for whom it is made will all believe that I am sacrificing not myself but them. This also must be borne."[35]

The bathos deepened daily as the mail flowed in and out. March 5 neared, the day of judgment at the polls. It would only confirm misjudgment on the course of Edward Blake, "isolated in opinion and without any ground to expect a return to public life."[36] Yet beyond burial and extinction lay the flinty gleam of promise. There would not only be a March 5, there would also be a March 6. "Suspend your judgment of what my attitude is till you see it stated fully in a paper which has been sometime prepared, but which is not to see the light till after the election[37] . . . what is to be known will be known very soon."[38]

It had been known to Willison for over ten days, and the word from him had long since gone to Laurier. On February

12, with the act of abdication despatched to Bowmanville, Blake had summoned Willison to a private reading at Humewood. The editor had heard the last farewell to the electors, and the longer speech the leaders had been deprived of. Much of it was too familiar, for the undelivered address was a newly-eloquent expansion of the suppressed letter to the *Globe*. In any case there had been nothing to cheer Willison nor to lessen Laurier's dismay, though neither man had received a text from the author. "For obvious reasons it is written by and retained in my own hand."[39] But it was bound as surely as ever for the unwelcoming columns of the *Globe*, and on February 27 the instructions came.

They were from Blake to Willison, and they were crisp. "It is my intention as I intimated to you some time ago to release on the morning of March 6 public documents as to my retirement, with the nature of which you are acquainted. They will take about 6 pages of the size of the enclosed pamphlet. If you desire to publish them in the *Globe* on the morning of the 6th March I will supply you with them confidentially on the 4th . . . if you do not wish to publish them as above, please let me know by Monday next, March 2nd at the latest, that I may make other arrangements."[40]

From Laurier, on March 3, there was a letter to Blake that was no longer quite an appeal. So far as the election was concerned, the harm was done. "I have no intention of attempting to interfere with what I understand is your settled determination." If he was coolly reserved on the act, however, he had a final word on the effect. "Undoubtedly your utterance, coming when the bitterness of the campaign will just be at its highest pitch, will not be received with the calm temper, by either side, which the public welfare would require . . . do you not believe that even from that point of view it would be preferable to be heard by a less prejudiced public in a less excitable moment?"[41]

The word next day was no, and it would be the last between Blake and Laurier for over four months. There would never again be a word exchanged with Cartwright. To a campaign venomous enough there had been a new venom added by talk at a Liberal meeting of Blake and the CPR, the silent Blake who was now the railway's counsel, and of huge sums in retainers that had been given to shut his mouth.[42] It had not risen with Cartwright but it had been voiced by Cartwright's son, never to be forgotten or forgiven. It was not forgotten in the letter that went to Laurier but it was brushed aside with contempt; there was matter enough without it. His only doubt, Blake wrote, "is whether my patience has not degenerated into weakness and my loyalty to friends into indifference to the public interest. God only knows what I have suffered in these last days. I do not expect now any such results as you seem to think I might anticipate from publishing my views. But that is not because the publication will come too soon, but because it is already too late. My feeling is that the sooner the last painful stage is over the better for all concerned."[43]

The next day the nation went to the polls, speaking its mind as always above the hubub of politicians. Even the silence of one seemed to have had an ambiguous effect. Ontario and Quebec, the greatest prizes, had almost gone to the Liberals; putting the two together they could claim a majority of one. Only the Maritimes and the West had saved Macdonald, and it might not be for long. There would be recounts and by-elections and the usual contested elections and there was the hovering threat of a great Conservative scandal. There was the frailness of the old man. The master of all strategies and the heart and soul of Torydom, he had collapsed during the campaign. There was healing hope for the Liberals and even a scent of victory, till the morning papers came.

In the *Globe* first, and in the others a day later, were the letters of Edward Blake to the electors of West Durham. There was the farewell of February 11 in its wounded magnanimity and there was the address he had not delivered, which was dated February 6. The dates made plain that they had been written weeks before, and suppressed by a designing party.

The words did more than that. They enhanced and elaborated on everything that he had first expressed to Simpson. They revealed the martyrdom of Blake, they rattled the chains that had bound him, and the Liberal platform crumbled as each of the links snapped. There was the petty, juvenile, sanctimonious egoism of the son of Catherine Blake. There were arguments of unanswerable power that have not been answered yet. And they still came out to nothing. Laurier had hoped to negotiate,

GRIP

VOL. XXXVI. | *TORONTO, MARCH 14, 1891.* | No. 11. Whole No. 926.

THE LOGIC OF THE SITUATION.

BLAKE—"I am convinced that both your policies lead alike to Annexation; therefore I retire from public life."
CANADA—"Nay, Edward, as my greatest statesman, *therefore* you should remain and show us the way out!"

to seek out ways and means, to grope along with the Americans in the hope of a new beginning. Blake would have no beginnings because he could not see through to the end.

With the final arguments expounded, there remained the question of himself. What, he asked his electors, would be left for Blake now? "This only. Since I cannot help, to hurt as little as I may . . . to go down with my own little ship, in silence." Yet before the silence, straight at Laurier and Cartwright, came the crash of the final broadside: "Assuming that absolute free trade with the States, best described as Commercial Union, may and ought to come, I believe that it can and should come only as an incident, or at any rate as a well understood precursor of Political Union; for which indeed we should be able to make better terms before than after the surrender of our Commercial Independence. Then so believing — believing that the decision of the Trade question involves that of the Constitutional issue, for which you are unprepared, and with which you do not even conceive yourselves to be dealing — how can I properly recommend to you now to decide on Commercial Union?"[44]

CHAPTER NINE

"THE ATTITUDE OF MY FORMER FRIENDS"

"WELL, we were defeated," Willison wrote to Laurier on March 11, 1891, "but we did not do so badly. What effect is Mr. Blake's letter having?"[1]

For Laurier there was one answer, from one of his lesser stalwarts, arriving the next day. "I want you to understand," wrote George E. Casey of Bruce, "that we of the 'Peninsula' have our own views and are utter mules in sticking to them . . . it makes no difference to any voter in this region what E. Blake thinks about the situation. We are exactly where we were on polling day . . . I can only echo the words of Cartwright, received tonight, 'I am sorry for Blake — but I suppose he was built so.' "[2]

So far as it expressed sympathy it was hardly the general mind; there was little of that in Liberals. The party had been badly hurt, and was also bitterly resentful. Tories and Tory newspapers were jubilantly exploiting division, and the author of it all had taken to print again. On March 10, as a dwarfed appendage and supplement to all that had gone before it, another letter from Blake appeared in the *Globe*. "The contradictory inferences to which a sentence in my Durham letter, detached from its context, has in several quarters unexpectedly given rise, conquer my reluctance to trespass again so soon upon your columns; and I crave space to say that I think political union with the States, though becoming our probable, is by no means our ideal, or as yet our inevitable future."[3]

He was answering, if he was answering anything, some speculations in the newspapers. From the quarters that meant most to him there was only an oppressive silence. The mail dwindled, the door-bell rang less often, and there were none of the looked-for callers. Country and party seemed to have absorbed their lecture and be going along without him. He had snubbed Edgar during the late days of the campaign, and there was now no word from Edgar. That friend was writing instead to Laurier, and it was to Edgar that Laurier replied. Both men were agreed that there should be no unkind words. "Blake," Laurier wrote, "will neither lead nor be led . . . yet at the same time, strange as it is, I am sure that he wishes us well." However that might be, the party would hold to its line, with or without Blake. "I must and will leave him free to come in or to go out according to his own inclinations."[4]

It was a dismissal worse than the predicted isolation. Neither opposed nor appeased, Blake was to be ignored. Through April, May and June, except for one tentative and exploratory note from Mills, there was not a line from any of the party leaders. By April 29, when the new parliament convened, there had been no pleadings to Blake, nor talk of a seat for Blake. Laurier's line of action had been deflected far from its course. Both the West Durham letter and reciprocity itself had been pushed aside by the affairs of Thomas McGreevy. There was to be the greatest scandal session since the time of the Pacific Railway, and the greatest of Liberal prosecutors was to be far away from the scene. Yet even that, it appeared, was now accepted. "This is where we miss Blake's hand," Edgar wrote to Laurier, "but let us see what can be done without him."[5]

He was more optimistic than Laurier, who was in possession of more of the facts and glumly dreaded the inquiry. Nevertheless it began, early in May. J. Israel Tarte, as journalist, provincial *bleu* and federal Conservative henchman, had been at the heart of every political feud in Quebec. He had fled some of the latest to arrive in the Dominion House, a small, quick-moving warrior who had "spoiled too many soups". A federal Liberal now, determined to spoil more, he had brought his materials with him in a sizeable black bag. Out of that bag, document by deadly document, the underside of politics crawled into the public view. Thomas McGreevy was the intimate friend of Langevin, Macdonald's Quebec lieutenant and Minister of Public Works. Successful on a large scale as railway builder and contractor, he was also federal organizer for the Conservative party in Quebec. Over a period of ten years, as the inquiry soon brought out, he had been the controlling hand in the awarding of federal contracts. Quite naturally he had taken the best for his firm, but he had exacted a cut on all. With the same deliberate system, through a web of aides and affiliates, he had administered the graft as a Conservative party fund. Some $800,000 was said to have passed through his hands.

Even in this hardened House it was an awesome record of corruption, and it was to end Langevin's career. It was to send McGreevy to jail. Yet it did not elate Laurier whose official friend was Mercier. Laurier had known much and suspected a good deal more of his friend's relations with McGreevy. In the matter of Quebec contracts and the building of Quebec railways the federal Tory organizer had been a loyal provincial Liberal, and as useful in buying votes. He had hardly gone down with Langevin before scandal broke in Quebec, destroying Mercier too. The mud lapped over other friends to the very feet of Laurier, and though it stopped before it reached him it had washed away his case. Among competing parties in Ottawa there was no monopoly on dirt; Macdonald's government was safe. But it had become by then a government without Macdonald.

There had been a warning on May 12, when a brief symptom of paralysis had troubled the old man's speech. Few knew of it in Ottawa and Blake had been in Vancouver, on business for the CPR. A non-political lawyer, he had been a guest at a banquet there, with much of the past forgiven. He had spoken with appropriate irony of the phrase he had made his own, and the "sea of mountains" had passed away in laughter. Much of his own bitterness had passed away in acceptance as he travelled home by the railway that would always recall Macdonald. Then, on June 6, Macdonald himself was gone, and in the midst of an emptied landscape there was a new emptiness for Blake.

He had stood for a quarter-century as the alternative to this man, and he viewed the past through his own tortured perspective. Yet he had stepped aside for Mackenzie and he had given way to Laurier. He had attempted to guide Laurier, and his guidance had been repelled. In a last and greatest giving he had relinquished a seat in parliament, and the cost of that magnanimity was now being driven home. There was no strength in Conservatism without the hand of Macdonald, and there was no virtue in Liberalism while it held to its wrong way. Now, if ever, with parties crumbling and squabbling in a dismal interregnum, was the hour for the return of Blake.

Yet it was not to be allowed to be. With determined wrong-headedness the Liberal leaders refused it. They had just lost an election and they were putting the blame on Blake. They resented the vow of silence imposed through their own fault, made at such heavy sacrifice, and kept throughout the campaign. They resented still more the breaking of the long silence, as though Blake could withhold truth from the country. Unthanked for past favours and abused for present convictions, he was being brutally thrust aside. With every hour of brooding the thought took shape in his mind, unsoftened by resignation and unchanged by haunting words. Even Sam, his brother, and Wells, the old law partner had considered Blake in the wrong during the election. "Pray what have you done," Wells had written "that you should perform hari-kari? When you resigned the leadership to Mr. Mackenzie you did an act for which nobody thanked you and to which I trace all the misgovernment of the past twelve years. You made a mistake. Don't make another."[6] The letter was five months old now, but it was still Wells who was wrong. It had not been hari-kari, it had not been Blake's mistake; nothing would convince him of that. The mistakes had been made by others.

He was at Murray Bay in July, a man condemned to tranquillity, when the first of the coming overtures began to ripple the surface. Mills wrote again, and again tentatively, hinting at party difficulties on which he would welcome advice. The reply could not have warmed him. "With the exception of a former note from yourself, this is the first communication I have had from any prominent member of the Liberal party since the elections at which I made for it the greatest sacrifice in my power . . . I do not now write with the idea of preferring through you any remonstrance or complaint. To do so would be neither dignified nor useful. Good will cannot be constrained . . . I was sensible indeed that I was by my withdrawal creating a vast void in my life; but I will confess to you that I did not expect its shadows to be deepened by the further deprivation which I have suffered. Having decided to accept the attitude of my former friends, I do not feel that my anxiety for the future of our country and for the triumph of old liberal principles, absorbing though it be, calls on me under present circumstances to obtrude opinions or engage in confidential discussions on party plans and prospects . . . the wound is still too green."[7]

Five days later Laurier wrote, with his pretext a minor legal question on which he would be glad of Blake's advice. As a deft attempt to diminish the "apparent estrangement" it did not seem a success. The answer bristled with fortitude, enclosed a copy of the previous reply to Mills, and left no doubt whatever as to who were the parties at fault. "I should feel constrained wholly to repudiate any attempt which might be made by anyone to put on me the least responsibility for a condition to which I have found it difficult to reconcile my mind."[8]

Yet Laurier's request for advice, however obvious its purpose, was answered with thoughtful care. And beyond that came a poignant cry from the depths.

"Not being the brute devoid of natural affections which some politicians have made me out, but a man perhaps more than ordinarily dependent for my happiness on my friendships, I am not ashamed to say that I have suffered heavily . . . but time will make life tolerable or end it; and meanwhile I am, with a heart which has never beat otherwise than warmly and kindly towards you, and which must love you still, Yours faithfully, Edward Blake."[9]

It was more than enough to signal an approaching thaw, and Laurier himself was moved. Another letter came from him by almost the next mail. "Of all the things which are the cause of pain to me, in this position which I now occupy, the most painful is to find myself not in perfect accord with such a friend as you have always been to me from the first day that I knew you."[10] The tone persisted through two more lengthy exchanges, as the recent past was reviewed. There could be no doubt of Laurier's distressed sincerity, and there was even less of his need. Defeated in the last election and defending a riddled policy, he had led or been pushed by his party into a windowless cul-de-sac. His one hope of deliverance seemed to lie with the old leader, and to himself apart from his politics he evoked a lyric response. "Thank God," wrote Blake, "all is now clear between us from a personal point of view, and I do not think that anything can again cloud our perfect friendship."[11] The old warmth had returned, warming the world again, yet the cold breath of the trade question still blew through it all.

It was renewed in every discussion and returned to the same point. "The party cannot go back; it must go forward";[12] Laurier was pinned to that. Yet where, Blake asked, with grave and grieving persistency, was the party heading now? It was for promoting trade with the Americans — unrestricted trade — and the price eventually might be political union. Was the party ready to accept that risk? Could it ask the country to accept it? Laurier was prepared to try. He would advance the program to outright Commercial Union, he would pursue trade where it led, and he would deal with the results later. Yet most Liberals would not, and Blake certainly would not. He was even less prepared to go forward by indirection, to sell policy by halves, to create a web of obscurities around the bald truth of the goal. The country must be shown the light, the whole way to the end. He had done that, or had tried to, in the letter to West Durham, and Laurier complained that the results had been disastrous. Perhaps they had, but only to the policy itself. If it was not feasible politically, and Blake believed it was not, then policy would have to change. There was no way to go forward; the only way was back.

By the first week of August they had arrived at amicable stalemate. It was darkened by a hint from Blake that public duty might demand another pronouncement, but it was lighted by a pale hope. Reciprocity was ailing but it was not to be allowed to die, even at Tory hands. The new government, which was now the government of Sir John Joseph Abbott, was turning again to Washington and preparing revised proposals. There was a meeting planned for October and there would at least be a period of suspense; something might yet turn up. "The negotiation at Washington," Laurier wrote, "will clear up what is now obscure as to what we have to expect from our neighbours . . . whatever takes place, the whole situation will have to be considered anew, and then I hope that we may wipe away the unhappy differences that now sever us upon that one, and that one question alone."[13]

Blake was less a Micawber, but for the time being he would wait; he would delay his public statement. "You propose to see what the fall brings forth at Washington . . . so be it . . . I will endeavour, after what you have written, to maintain till fall 'an attitude of observation'."[14]

Yet the fall came and Washington was its old self, brusquely postponing the conference till after the turn of the year. Policy stood still, anchored in indecision, yet pointing in wrong directions. Government without Macdonald groped and fumbled; scandal smeared the parties with a lavishly impartial hand. In the attitude of observation there was little good to be seen, and there was lean cheer in Laurier's new year message. "I have not heard from you for a long time . . . I do not know how you feel, but I ask myself if sometimes you do not thank your stars that you are not in the inner circle of party politics." Yet, sick, disgusted, and despairing for himself, the party and the country, he returned single-mindedly to the familiar question. "And now, my dear Blake have you made up your mind to re-enter public life?"[15]

The reply, on January 2, 1892, had only an edge of irony for the postponed Washington negotiations "from which you expected so much light as to the future of the party . . . I daresay from your silence in respect of them that you share my notion that we cannot expect much help in that way." Nor had Blake hopes for himself. "As I feel that every month of absence from parliament renders me less capable of useful service, I look forward to being able at an early day to dismiss from my mind all idea of the possibility of my return."[16]

He was as busy as ever with the law, and he was newly busy as Chancellor with the troubled affairs of the University of Toronto. He had, as always, more than enough to do. Yet he was still the public figure, looming over party plans. He was lonely out of the arena, he was nagged at for his opinions, he was resented, feared, and besought in equal measure. If he had formally forgiven his friends he had forgotten none of his injuries, and whatever his changed position he had altered none of his ways. Newspapers probed and speculated, forever ruffling his surface. The banked fires of duty smouldered beneath. In his attitude of observation he obviously disapproved of much he saw. In parliament or out of it, he remained a potential threat to nervous Liberals. He might yet be impelled to speak, or worse still to write. The prospect of another Durham letter, threatened since last August, still lurked in the offing.

By February there was more than that. As the opening of parliament approached he was toying with and recoiling from the offers of possible constituencies. There was none from West Durham; that was forever lost, and it would remain an unhealed wound. In Welland there were Liberals asking for him but it was one of the border regions with most of the voters inclined to reciprocity. East York was a constituency where a replacement would have to be thought of, for Alexander Mackenzie was now dying. Blake would not consider it while Mackenzie was still alive, and in any case it would be another difficult riding. He had to think of that now; there were few safe seats for Blake. Beyond the place in parliament there was still the question of the leadership, and that continued to be raised. He answered with the old refusals, qualified with the old care, but also now with a specific note of warning. "I think it is only as an Independent Leader that there is the smallest chance of my re-entering Parliament."[17]

Cartwright dreaded the thought of a second coming, and harped on his fears to Laurier. There must be no concessions to Blake; he would be the "secret enemy" in the camp. Laurier himself, prepared for every concession, was blocked by the one essential. Unrestricted Reciprocity, somehow or other to be divorced from Commercial Union, must remain an article of faith. He did not believe in the divorce, any more than Blake himself, but he did believe in the program. However labelled, it was at least a tool to work with. That one item of policy, however diluted and disguised, had become the great issue for Liberals, and it seemed to be all they had. Pursuing Conservative scandals, attempting to diminish their own, and steadily losing by-elections, they clung to the single plank. It could not now be abandoned, even to recover Blake. On February 25, when Parliament opened without him, it seemed that nothing had changed.

By early March there had been change rather for the worse. As Liberals pursued scandal, Laurier pursued Blake, and a lesser Tory boodler seemed to offer a mode of approach. He was to answer charges of graft before a parliamentary committee, and the Liberal party as accuser would speak through legal counsel. For that role the greatest of absent Liberals seemed obviously a strategic choice. Blake as the party lawyer might renew communion with his friends, and Edgar was the friend selected to convey an offer of the commission. The reply, direct to Laurier, was freezing in new hauteur.

"I did not choose to give Mr. Edgar the reason for my necessary refusal. But I owe it to you as leader of the Liberal party, and to myself, to say to you that the circumstances under which I have been excluded from my seat in parliament did not in my opinion warrant the Liberal party in asking me further to accentuate the change in my relations to Parliament and the public life of the country by appearing to plead as counsel before the great tribunal of which I was for so long, and but for these circumstances, still would be myself a member . . . I hope that you have quite recovered from your illness . . . I don't expect any answer."[18]

He received one, nevertheless, but it was from a tired man whose health he had not improved. "You persist in believing that your friends have been ungenerous toward you. It may be so; if so, on my part it was unintentional."[19]

It was March 9 by then, with portentous change in the wind. The reciprocity discussions, postponed since fall by the Americans, had finally been held in February. On March 22 the results were announced to the House in the budget speech of George Eulas Foster, the dry, precise, and professorial Maritimer who was Conservative Minister of Finance. He had gone to Washington with other members of the cabinet, rather expecting the worst. In the view of Liberals he had gone deliberately to arrange for it, hoping to destroy their program as a live political issue. If he had he had certainly succeeded, with the generous cooperation of the American Secretary of State.

Blaine, who had given the Liberals the impression that he might be softening, appeared to have hardened instead. If there were to be reciprocity at all, Foster reported, it could be nothing less than complete Commercial Union. Canadian and American tariffs would have to be totally assimilated while British tariffs remained, practically excluding the mother country as a rival of the United States.

Laurier's hopes of August had been all too well-realized. He could be in no doubt now "as to what we have to expect from our neighbours." Nor could there be any doubt as to the effect on Liberal policy; it was reduced to a complete shambles. Commercial Union, in the form acceptable to Blaine, was totally unacceptable either to the Liberal party or the nation. Yet reciprocity without it could not be had at all, if Blaine had been correctly reported. There were only two courses, each as dubious as the other, that would leave the party holding a patch of ground. It could be denied that Blaine had really meant what he said, or it could be claimed that the Liberal party had means to change his mind.

The dilemma was one day old when there was other change at Humewood. The attitude of observation became suddenly one of action. On March 23 a letter descended on Mills. It was in the form of a draft from Blake, addressed to the party leaders, and was to be sent if Mills concurred. "The report of the Budget speech induces me to take the liberty of pressing once again on you, and, if you choose, through you on other leaders . . . the necessity of early party action in regard to the policy of Unrestricted Reciprocity."[20]

The draft recited Foster on the result of the talks with Blaine and was to be accompanied, if sent to the leaders, by a copy of the West Durham letter. Everything Blake had said and everything that Liberal policy had sought to veil and obscure was now confirmed by the American government itself. "Is it not time . . . when both governments declare that they can find no solution of the problem of Unrestricted Free Trade which shall not involve a common tariff practically controlled by the

United States, that the Liberal party should reconsider its position? . . . Can you expect to succeed as 'men of mystery', the possessors of some charm or recipe of wondrous virtue not to be disclosed to the common herd? . . . if you cannot, then should you not, taking advantage of the U.S. government's declaration, acknowledge the fact, and take new ground . . .?[21]

"I do not pretend," the draft concluded cheerily, "to be able to offer a satisfactory solution of your difficulties. I believe them to be almost as serious as can be conceived . . . But if time, reflection and late events here and on the other side of the line have changed your opinion, is it not your duty to reconsider the situation, however difficult, and to take the first step toward getting on the right track, however unpleasant?"[22]

Imperative duty had once more raised her voice. Blake's last offensive had opened with a clarion call for retreat. It appeared to pivot on Mills, with Laurier left aside; and it was ominously reminiscent of the move that had deposed Mackenzie. Certainly and still more obviously it recalled the mood and intentions of the recent manoeuvres in Durham. But Blake was fifty-eight now, he was repeating old patterns, and times and men had changed.

The first sign was in Mills' reception of the draft of the intended circular. He acknowledged it promptly and coolly and reserved comment, pending discussion with Laurier. He would also discuss it with Davies, the Liberal leader from the Maritimes, though he carefully omitted any mention of Cartwright. He was angrily sceptical of Foster and of the views attributed to the Americans, and the budget speech in his view was "a thoroughly dishonest performance".[23] Old and loyal friend though he certainly was, he echoed the smoky voice of the Liberal caucus. He was writing as a man on the inside to the one who remained out. "I wish it were possible," said Mills, "to have you meet our old Committee, or at all events the most of them."[24] What he obviously did not wish for was private discussion and decision with his old leader alone.

Since this was what was desired there was instant chill in the rejoinder. Mills had revealed to others what had been intended only for himself. "But let the affair pass; it cannot now be helped."[25] To Blake, with his initiative rebuffed, the alternative suggestion was totally unacceptable. "The utter failure to agree . . . the unfortunate results of the silence to which I was, during that period, condemned, and the present feeling as I gather from your note, all, I am sorry to say, point in my view to the uselessness of any such meeting."[26]

Yet the next day came Mills' cry from the heart, authentic and newly warming. "I want to see you in your place in the House with your old friends." Much more than that, he opened the glint of a prospect. "As to the trade question let me say this much," he wrote. "Unrestricted Reciprocity with me means a large measure of reciprocity — negotiations not confined to natural products — not restricted to any particular articles of commerce. I believe that with Blaine you can have a treaty which will embrace a large list of scheduled articles, leaving many things still subject of taxation."[27]

It appeared that "unrestricted", if Mills reflected the evolving mind of the party, had suddenly a new meaning. It defied the uses of language, but it made political sense. One's hopes could be wide as the heavens but one took what one could get, giving it another name. "I confess," Blake replied with a shading of incredulity, "I do not see how it is possible to interpret 'unrestricted reciprocity' in the limited sense which you propound." Yet if that feat could be accomplished all differences were resolved; they had never in fact existed. "If this be the party view, then, while I cannot blame myself for my error, and must blame the name for the result . . . I would never have objected, on the contrary I would have given such a proposal my hearty support."[28]

The statement came, embedded in a long reply, bristling as usual with wary qualifications. Yet it was a definite hint from the prodigal that he would accept the family back. That one word "unrestricted" seemed the bar to reunion now and the only need was open renunciation. The party must avow its aim and return to the proper name, which was Limited Reciprocity. Yet Foster had wanted that, or professed to want it, and so had Macdonald before him; it was the age-old pious hope. It deprived the issue of all political bite, it stripped away the aura of advancing Liberalism, and on that the leaders stuck. Their goals were limited, their hopes slender and diminishing, but their slogan remained unchanged.

"I am delighted to find that there is a hope of your early returning to public life."[29] The letter came from Laurier on April 9. Yet he had taken a week to write it, and there was cool significance in that. Officially he had seen no circular, nor even the draft of a circular, and the sessional work and the policy-making remained in the leader's hands. He was still responsible for the party, still of the mind of the party, and he did not hide the bare bones of the decision. Unrestricted Reciprocity was to remain at the Liberal masthead. He had the same attitude as Mills toward the manoeuvrings of the Conservative government and the reported views of the Americans. "I would have no hesitation to advise a change of front, if any honest effort had been made to obtain any kind of reciprocity, limited or unlimited, but I confess to you that I for one would not be disposed to make a change under compulsion, as it were, from Mr. Foster."

Nor, inferentially, under compulsion from his friend, Blake. He was anxious as always for Blake's views in full, for any means that could lead to an accommodation. "To facilitate your re-entrance in public life I would be disposed to do almost anything," but, "I may say beforehand that, in so far as I am concerned, a change of front means a movement forward."[30]

He received by return mail some eighteen pages of typescript, thirteen of them the draft of a public statement. It was required now, as it had been required before at Durham, "because the situation in which I have been placed forbids my keeping silence longer."[31] It was to be published without delay, possibly without warning; a recalcitrant Liberal party must submit to the rod once more.

It was now nearly five years, the draft of the statement began, since the Liberal party had launched the "trial balloon" of Commercial Union. It had quickly abandoned that for the more innocent-seeming Unrestricted Reciprocity, and it had been change only for the worse. Under either policy and any name the tendency remained the same: "impairment of Canadian autonomy, severance from the United Kingdom, and political union with the States."

The tendency had not been admitted. It had rather been disguised and denied, and there had been equal confusion and deception as to how the policy would work. "It has always seemed to me that its proposers were bound to show the practicability of Unrestricted Reciprocity." That they had never done; yet everything they claimed or hoped for depended on the United States.

"Among the inconveniences of a national policy resting on a plank, one end of which must be propped up by another nation, is the circumstance that the consent of that nation is essential to success." Had that consent been obtained? To anything short of complete commercial union it had just been flatly denied. In Blake's view, moreover, and however Liberals protested, Blaine had meant what he said. For their hopes of reciprocity, as embodied in present policy, the prop had been knocked away.

Where, then, did they stand? What should be their true course? They had been bound for years, whether they were prepared to admit it or not, in the direction of political union. They might openly proclaim it now, and attempt to convert the country. Laurier was prepared for that, and it was a course Blake could respect, but he was not disposed to adopt it. "I have never been blind to the importance of Reciprocity," but it was presently unobtainable at any price he would pay. "No new plan can in my view be devised"; the issue, presented honestly, had come to a dead end. "I repeat then that my attempt must be to recall what is old, rather than to display what is new."

That he did with a vengeance. Point by point, for three and a half pages, he quoted the Liberal platform of 1887 — the policy made by Blake. "Allow me to suggest to you . . . not to consign to the flames nor even to the lumber room any of those planks." They must all now be returned to and the party must take them up, resuming the onward journey where Blake had left it off.

From that, in his final pages, he rose to another argument, previously left untouched. "My Durham letter, for stated reasons, expressly declined all speculations on our political future." He had disclaimed them supplementally in his brief epistle to the *Globe*. Now, however, the time for speech had come.

"It has seemed to me that, by the courses which of late years Canadian politics have taken, we have been drifting ever nearer to political union with the States . . . to join them on fair and equal terms would be for any province of this Dependency no ignoble lot. Nevertheless this is not the goal at which I aim. I cling to the hope of a higher though more arduous destiny for the great Dominion. I look for the regeneration of my own country. I cling to the hope that — sooner or later, and rather soon that late — there may be born into the world an independent Canadian Commonwealth; nerving itself to solve, after its own fashion, the many racial and religious, moral and political, economic and material problems which confront us; united by enduring links of kinship and sympathy, hope and aspiration with three of the leading nations of the world; advancing more effectually than now our own varied interests and also the true welfare of the old land, the proud mother of free nations as well as free Parliaments; and enjoying, under arrangements which a wise and liberal statesmanship on both sides of the line and of the Atlantic may mature, bright prospects of unbroken peace and absolute security, together with the fullest freedom of trade and the widest measure of intercourse compatible with the provision of our revenue and the preservation of our autonomy. May these things be!"[32]

With all he had dragged from the lumber room he had also produced this, and the dream of liberal nationalism would outlast political platforms.

The note from Laurier arrived two days later, more deflating than a storm of protest. One read it blankly, doubting the uses of eloquence and even the meaning of words. "There are many things in your letter which with all my heart I approve, and as to the other parts to which I might be disposed to take some exception, there would be nothing to gain by carrying the controversy further." The core of the argument was dismissed; could Laurier even have read it? "On the whole," he added incredibly, "I am very glad to find that we are yet so near each other. I am sure we must before long be in complete accord." Worse still, the impending threat conveyed with the draft of the statement was simply waved away. "I and the two friends to whom I have shown your letter, can find no fault with your publishing your views as you intend to do."[33]

There was that, and there was a bulky envelope from Mills. He had received a copy of the draft and he had not found time to comment on it, at least by way of a letter. He had merely scribbled some notes along the margins, usually wry and resigned. If this was actually to be published, then published it must be.

There was no longer a beseeching party begging the help of Blake, or even begging his silence. There were only regretful friends, going their way. It was the wrong way, he was so passionately convinced of that, and the friends as they grew more distant seemed only to grow more dear. "What are the views of Blake?" — the old question, so vital for so many years, seemed now to have lost all meaning. So had the hope of leadership and so had the lust for parliament, though public duty remained. Yet there was also duty to Laurier, holding that curious hope. "I note with pleasure," Blake wrote to him once again on April 16, "the remark in your letter that we are yet so near each other . . . it is the strongest reason which influences me in seeking to defer as long as I can any public announcement. . . . As I wrote you, my letter was subject to reconsideration on my part . . . will you kindly therefore return it to me at once, and I will send it back to you when completed in final form."[34]

Better than that, Laurier came himself, and for a few hours in Toronto the two met face to face. "This miserable trade question", in the warmth of that encounter, became a generous sharing of minds, almost a joining. The old friendship, the mutual need, the trials of the man in Ottawa and the loneliness of the man in Toronto melted differences away. Or almost so, or so it seemed to Blake. "Thanks," he wrote, after Laurier had gone back to Ottawa, "for the draft of my letter returned. I retain it for a time, pending this correspondence, which furnishes me a prospect far more agreeable than any public letter."[35]

The correspondence, resumed at Laurier's request, was to be a setting down of the views formed at the discussion, the essential terms of agreement. Blake gave them now, in hope, with their basis underscored: "*The policy of this party as at present understood and expressed is impracticable, and therefore must be revised.*" There were large and surrounding arguments which came to a blunt point. "Every month during which you persevere in the attempt to hold your present false position will render your extrication more difficult. I think now, when the fortunes of the party are at the lowest ebb . . . is the time to act."[36]

They were stronger words on paper than they had seemed in cordial talk, but they had nevertheless to be said. They had been asked for, they had almost seemed to be agreed to, and glimmering beyond agreement was the hope of a restored party. It warmed the writer at Humewood and led him beyond the first intent of his letter. He attempted before he finished to "chalk out", as he said, a basis for Liberal policy. It was a rare glimpse, too late and near the end, of how this man might have viewed his work if he had ever sat in power.

"Insisting upon the right of the Canadian people to that measure of freedom in the control of their affairs which is necessary for their prosperity . . . you might indulge the speculation that, Imperial Federation being a thing impracticable, the nearest realization of its spirit would be achieved by the creation of an Independent Canadian Commonwealth . . . really strengthening, by relieving it from responsibilities and jealousies and complications, the position of the United Kingdom. You might contend that this settlement of the Canadian question, together with a solution in the sense of Home Rule of the Irish question, would create an entirely changed sentiment in the United States, making them much more than now, really cordial friends of their English speaking kin on both sides of the Atlantic . . . you might aver that this prospect would produce such an improved feeling on the part of the U.S. as to render extremely likely their assent to the most favorable arrangements for the adjustment of the relations between the two countries which we could in fairness ask."[37]

They were seminal words, but like so many thousands of his others they would grow anonymously. The fruit borne of them would be harvested by other men. Laurier was one, to his own advantage and the country's, but they could not change him now. Six days passed and his reply came back to Blake. He had talked again and at length with Mills and Davies. "No one of us three feels convinced that, as you state, our policy is impracticable." The rest was the old arguments and the old pleadings. "You cannot deprive the country of your great services . . . if you cannot see eye to eye with us, come out with your own views."[38] To what purpose? There was no heart left for that. The drafts and sheaves of paper went to the files, with a copy of the closing letter.

It went from Blake to Laurier on May 2. "I have to express my deep regret to you, and through you to Mills and Davies, for having added to your sessional labors by opening the discussion; and to give you and them the only amends I can by promising never to do so any more. It only remains for me to say and to beg you to let them know that my quack medicine was prescribed for immediate consumption; and I think it very likely that conditions may so change shortly that I would neither prescribe it for the patient nor take it for myself. Therefore I am not to be understood as recommending it for use at any future time, or as being committed to it under any changed conditions."[39]

A year and a month later the Liberal party would swallow his quack medicine, and be relieved and freed by the dose. Yet if there was vindication in that there was also condemnation. Stripped of its political bedevilments the aim of Laurier and Cartwright, and for that matter of Macdonald, had been to make a bargain they could live with on the continent of North America. Trade with the Americans was essential, and the wider it could be the better. A reciprocal arrangement was possible, whatever the degree or form. It might have involved the predominance of the United States, it might have led to the political absorption of Canada, yet no one was sure of that and no one actually wished for it. There had been *Zollvereins* or customs unions between several states of Europe, and they had not been found to compel political union. They had certainly created the tendency and they might have done so here; it might have been irresistible. But no one knew, no one had been allowed to learn, no one had been allowed to measure the effects and place them before the people. Instead of haggling and bargainers there had been slogans, charges, and oracles. Macdonald had stood on Britishness, Liberals had sought to evade the unavoidable, and Blake had stood on a name. "They have built for themselves a stone wall," he said of his friends in Ottawa, "against which they have knocked their heads."[40] It was quite true; and it was quite as true of Blake.

CHAPTER TEN

"THE OPPORTUNITY OF SERVICE"

THE POLITICAL CAREER in Canada had come to an end. Blake had said so before, many times. Luxuriant despondency was the too-familiar habit; he had proclaimed more than he believed and more than he meant to be believed. In the depths of his mind he hardly believed it now, but he had made it fact at last. He had grown in his own image; the death-wish had been fulfilled.

Among the scraps and oddities of youth, still preserved in trunks and boxes at his home, were several well-thumbed exercise books containing samples of verse. Much of it is easily identifiable as copyings from Victorian favourites but two pieces are not, at least to the present writer. They tempt to the speculation that the man who was fond of poetry, the man so eminently Victorian, had tried in some lamp-lit musings to discover himself with his pen. Or that he had tried at least to find what he ought to find:

> He loved his friends, forgave his foes,
> And, if his words were harsh at times,
> He spared his fellow-men; his blows
> Fell only on their crimes.
> What'er his neighbours might endure
> Of pain or grief his own became;
> For all the ills he could not cure
> He held *himself* to blame
> His good was mainly an intent,

His evil not of forethought done,
No work he wrought was meanly meant,
Or finished as begun.[1]

Certainly there, as in the second sample, whether or not his own, are familiar claims and griefs and a familiar wounded acceptance.

I who have spoken for freedom at the cost
Of some weak friendships or some paltry prize
Of name or place, and more than I have lost
Have gained in wider reach of sympathies
And for communion with the good and wise,
May God forbid that I should ever boast
Such easy self-denial, or repine
That the strong prize of health no more is mine.
Now overborne at noon-day I must yield
To other hands the gleaning of the field,
. . . the days decline,
For blest beyond deserving still, and knowing
That kindly Providence its care is showing
In the withdrawal as in the bestowing,
Scarcely I dare for more or less to pray.[2]

As often, and at all periods of his life, the writing begins in a firm, clear hand, and deteriorates little by little into the sprawl of haste or exhaustion. It is a poor clue as to dating. The verses, if they are his own, might have been in the mood of a dozen periods of his life — defeated moments at the hands of Sandfield Macdonald, or John A. Macdonald, or Mackenzie, or Cartwright, or Laurier — any one of the times when he saw the truth turned back, the dispenser of truth slighted, and resignation and departure the only course. Certainly, in May of 1892, they reflected much of his attitude in faintly ludicrous pathos. There was justification for their ring of final defeat. Yet they were premature as the epitaph of a politician, and they belied the reach of the man. Even then, immersed in his own gloom, bewildering as always to his contemporaries, he was towering and indispensable in the work of another sphere.

With all he had given to politics and all he gave to the law, he still had time for his first love, the University of Toronto.

He had been a member of its Senate for nearly thirty years, and Chancellor since 1873. From the beginning, like William Hume before him, he had been a powerful and dominant figure. During the 1880s however, while he was leader of the Liberal party, he had had much less time than usual for the university's concerns. He had prepared a report on its requirements in 1882, but the implementation had been largely in other hands.

William Mulock, the Vice-Chancellor, though a fellow Toronto lawyer and Liberal member of parliament, was not much liked by Blake. Shrewd, drivingly ambitious, and an inveterate politician, he could be "Farmer Bill" on the hustings, while still maintaining his eminence in the best circles of Toronto. He could be brilliant and witty, ruthless and intriguing, and as foul-mouthed on occasion as any carter beating a lagging horse. There could be no doubt of his ability or of his formidable appetite for power, and he was soon directing affairs. Neither Daniel Wilson, the President, nor James Loudon, the physics professor destined to be a future president, was at ease under his rule. The university progressed, but it progressed in Mulock's way. Blake, absorbed in politics, was said to have become a figurehead and to be allowing affairs to drift.

If it was true at all it was true to a limited extent, and it was abruptly changed by tragedy. On the evening of February 14, 1890, Blake rose in the House of Commons after the dinner recess to continue the speech he had begun in the afternoon on the use of the French language in the North-West Territories. He had warned movingly of the dangers of lighting the fires of racial conflict, and he was the more moving now. "Sir," he said, "we have just heard of an event which we must all deeply deplore. The great institution, the crown and glory, I may be permitted to say, of the educational institutions of our country, is at this moment in flames; and we know how small a spark may have kindled the great fire which is consuming that ornament to the whole community of Canada, the University of Toronto. That ornament, a great material ornament, and a still greater exhibition of the triumphs of the principles of toleration and of our advance in higher education, a university where we have gathered together the youth of all denominations, Protestant and Catholic, under the sanction even of the Catholic Church — a State institution of non-sectarian principles, where all were gathered together as fellow-subjects to acquire the highest training that the land afforded is now, so far as its material fabric goes, a ruin tottering to the ground."[3]

Early that Friday evening a servant carrying a tray of lighted oil lamps had tripped on the east staircase of University College. Within half an hour the building was a mass of flames, and by morning it was totally gutted. The books of its library, the priceless specimens of its museum, all the equipment and treasures of its years of life were strewn about in a desolation of blackened timbers, melted snow, and re-congealing water. The great bell, falling at last from its tower with a mighty clang, seemed to have sounded a final requiem.

Yet for all that was gone and irretrievable in the loss, the way had been opened to reform and to a new future. On Saturday, while Blake was in Ottawa, he received a telegram. It had been sent by H. H. Langton, who was then the assistant registrar of the University, and considerably closer to Wilson and Loudon than to Mulock. There was to be an emergency meeting of the Senate held on Sunday, and Blake's presence was essential. On that day, as the members prepared to sit down with Mulock as chairman, Blake walked quietly in.

The surprised Vice-Chancellor rose to offer him the chair. Blake refused, and took the place to his right. It was another return in crisis, another abrupt response to imperative duty, and it had its abrasive undertones. For Mulock, the university had tended to become an extension of his own career. He had sought growth and he had achieved it, but he had played much politics to get it, and he had often clashed with the other directing heads. His political methods were repugnant to Daniel Wilson, the Scottish dominie from Edinburgh devoted to pure learning. They were equally repugnant to Loudon, though he was a native Canadian and a scientist and a man of the newer day. Both men, when overridden by Mulock, had frequently turned to Blake, and they would certainly turn to him now. With the Chancellor back, and the Vice-Chancellor determined to retain control, the stage was obviously set for conflict on a high level.

It was a conflict in the midst of disaster, however, with the wrestlings devoted to recovery. The questions were immediately of methods, and beneath them of principles. In much that Mulock had done during his twelve years as Vice-Chancellor he had had the support and approval of Blake. But he had also accumulated power, antagonized much of the faculty and set some dangerous courses. By establishing a Board of Trustees to oversee the endowment he had gradually stripped the Senate of its power to control finances. Blake disapproved of that; he would not have the Senate reduced and thrust aside. With large plans of expansion for which he did not consider the university's endowment to be sufficient, Mulock had begun a campaign to secure provincial grants. In Blake's eyes direct grants by the province would be another wrong step. Provincial money would mean extension of provincial control, and the eventual loss of the university's autonomy. He meant to live on the endowment and to adhere to first principles.

From the days of Sandfield Macdonald and the old conflicts with Ryerson, Blake's ideas had gradually emerged and prevailed. He had always had the support of Mowat and of George W. Ross, the Minister of Education. There had been inspiration for him in a group of brilliant men, and he was himself the inspirer of men like James Loudon. Determined as his father had been on a university free of religious entanglements, he had still been sympathetic to the claims of the various colleges.

Always open-handed where the university was concerned, he had been a particularly generous contributor to Wycliffe College, the home of Low Church Anglicanism. He had been more closely bound to the college since 1886, when Sophia, his daughter, had married the young George M. Wrong, who was lecturer on history and Dean. He had been proud of St. Michael's, the Catholic college, because it seemed to him a symbol of the broad and tolerant atmosphere that he and Mowat had created. He was equally welcoming to the colleges of other denominations which were affiliated with the University. They were exponents of Christian thought, developing in linked freedom, but the freedom of higher learning must be dominant over all. The colleges must be self-supporting, with no claim on the endowment; that was the sacred trust of all the people.

Apart from the religious issues his quarrels with Ryerson had been many, but they had had one general basis. Education must not divide, nor create a class structure; it must lead to common advancement, toward the equal opening of every man's horizon. Instruction on the lower levels must conform to the goals of the higher, and must tend in that direction. Ryerson, controlling the high schools and primary education, had endeavoured to set curricula and establish his own patterns. Blake would have none of that; he had fought it at every turn. If lower education were to pursue a separate course it would produce separated men, divided from the higher spheres, condemned to inferiority. The lower school must lead to the university, pave the way to its door. "I have looked upon our system of public instruction as in theory what it ought to be, namely one harmonious whole . . . let us take care that our whole course of instruction leads up to the university at its highest level . . . let us not isolate it from the popular mind, and thus sap the foundation on which alone it can and ought to rest."[4] As the "ladder concept" it would come to be disputed later, when the practical necessities of thousands required an earlier branching off. For his day, however, where the few were usually envisioned as the trained leaders of the many, he had had a generous enough ideal.

He had kept a sharp and fascinated eye on the growth of science and technology, and it had drawn him close to Loudon. Both men at first had opposed the movement for a separate College of Technology, because they believed its basis wrong. If it were separate from the university and the faculty of science it could only result in the production of glorified tradesmen. If it were expanded to include science it would only dilute or duplicate the resources of the university. In either case it would be a school without the arts, deprived of the influence and stimulus of university life. The need was once again for the "harmonious whole", and it was finally achieved in part. In 1878, when the red brick building of the School of Practical Science went up on the university campus, it was an unimposing monument to an almost complete marriage.

The report of revenues and requirements, which Blake had prepared with Loudon in 1882, had brought many improvements and changes. The library and museum had grown, graduate work and research had developed, the fields of instruction had widened and co-education had come. At the same time, and partly because of Mulock, there had been simmering discontent. Faculties seethed with politics, grievances had been accumulating, and there was confusion and aggravation over ranks and salaries. All this, swept over and obliterated by the great disaster of the fire, was waiting to perplex the work of reconstruction.

At the first emergency meeting Blake was a silent listener. He had little to say at later meetings, but he was becoming a familiar presence. Through most of 1890, as plans for rebuilding developed, his hand was felt in support of Wilson and Loudon. Mulock favoured the building of a new convocation hall; Loudon opposed it. What was more immediately required, he thought, was a students' union and gymnasium which could be used on a temporary basis as a convocation hall.

Blake, the unathletic, familiarized himself with the details of gymnasium design and was to be seen on some occasions considering the site of an outdoor running track. It was January of 1891, however, before he was ready to move.

In that month, and on Blake's motion, the Senate appointed himself, Mulock and Wilson as a committee "to inquire into and report upon the present and prospective requirements of the University of Toronto and of University College, and as to the time, mode and order in which these requirements should be dealt with." It was quite obvious that in that work Blake's would be the master hand; the Chancellor had taken control.

In the world of outside politics, during January, February, and March, the general election passed with its storms and silences. The West Durham letter was written and published, and the aftermath closed round Blake. Through all of it he worked on the report, compiling results in the surly gloom of his study. He demanded exhaustive submissions from every faculty and department, and exhausted his aides in the process. The university staff, according to Loudon, worked as it never had before or since. For six weeks, as the facts and figures came, Blake studied them and put them together. Sore, bruised, and absorbed, in the depths of political exile, he finished the work in April. The report on the revenues and requirements of the university, actually the guide for its next ten years of life, had been completed. It was tossed down before Loudon, who had been summoned to Humewood to receive it. "There it is at last, and it has cost me six thousand dollars."[5]

Mulock, who had been much occupied elsewhere during the lively political months, disputed some of the report before the committee. There was short shrift for him there. He had no right to criticize, the Chancellor commented acidly, since it was Blake who had done the work. The committee was firmly with Blake, the faculty was relieved and elated, and Mowat and the provincial authorities were all of the same mind. The report stood as it had been written.

It laid out in magisterial form the assets of the university, the annual revenues to be expected, and the order in which its projected requirements should be met. The new buildings, with priorities established for their construction, were to be an anatomy building, a gymnasium, a building for mineralogy and geology and a convocation hall. A plan of finance was laid out, recommending debentures to be issued by the university on a provincial guarantee. Except for the guarantee, there was no request for special grants from the province. Blake's earlier conviction had been reinforced by new analysis. The university's endowment, if the funds were wisely used, would enable it to live and grow in independence.

The staff questions and the questions of ranks and salaries had come to be a perplexing shambles. There were quarrels over titles and duties and over the nature of the work done. Lecturers in modern languages had claimed the rank of professors, and had been denied that by the entrenched older disciplines. There was little established relationship between work and rank and rate of remuneration, and certainly at least in the lower ranks there were men inadequately paid. The report dealt with it all, and prescribed reform with a hard and even hand. There was to be a set gradation of ranks, Professor, Associate Professor, Lecturer, Demonstrator, and Fellow. All were to be paid at a fixed and rising scale, which provided in future for regular yearly increases, but there would be no increases now. The recovering university was still in financial straits, salaries must wait until that time had passed. As conditions improved the first increases would go to the lower ranks, with the others following in order. There were hard times still for everyone, but everyone knew his prospects.

For several months more, as the work resulting from the report got under way, Blake kept a watchful eye on its implementation. There were other difficulties, however, and he was soon involved with them. This time they concerned the faculty of medicine, which had moved in its own orbit and accumulated its own troubles. There was confusion, disaffection, and inefficiency, and with that the cry for another investigation.

The Chancellor was once more called on, and once again responded.

He had, as always, to know everything of his subject. With his usual painful industry he mastered the details of medical schools, the routines of hospital procedures, and the ways of medical staffs and medical teachers. What he found in the university was an old, entrenched clique, fiercely jealous of its position, and squarely in the path of progress. Younger members of the staff were securely under its thumb, held down by threats of dismissal, discouraged by lack of promotion, and, for the most part, miserably paid. When the report appeared it was a prelude to drastic change. Here once more there was to be an orderly assignment of duties and there were to be clearly recognized ranks, commanding adequate salaries. There were to be appointments of new professors, some easing out of the old, and there was to be a thoroughly organized staff in each department. The way was cleared for the development of a great faculty.

By May of 1892, as he closed his correspondence with Laurier and Mills, Blake had also completed this other work. It had not exhausted and defeated him as politics always did; it had lifted him up with success. He had set the university on the way to recovery, he had redirected its energies and he had also refreshed its spirit. There was a new morale with Blake at the head of affairs, and the sense of it refreshed him. In this sphere he was at home, freely granted pre-eminence; and in the great plans he had fostered there was work for a lifetime yet. There were to be new reorganizations, there were new buildings to be planned and there was to be re-financing to support them. Beyond that, justifying it all, there was the greater challenge of the opening of a nation's mind. "I am ready and anxious," said the Chancellor, writing to George Ross, on June 13, 1892, "to continue to devote the leisure which my enforced retirement from public life has placed at my disposal to the advancement of University interests, and will therefore heartily respond to your request to cooperate with you in the preparation of any measure tending that way."[6]

He was secure as always in his great place at the bar. He had rediscovered the sphere of the University, the most satisfying he would ever know. Yet the same day the cablegram came from Ireland, changing everything: "Irish party unanimously invites you to accept Irish seat at general election."[7]

He would always claim that it had been totally unexpected, as indeed at the time it was. He had left Ireland in 1888, embarrassed to the point of agony by a mere hint in a newspaper. He could not bear the thought — or bear that the thought be known — that he might have hopes for a place in the imperial parliament. Yet he had been prepared to speak in Ireland, and he had studied affairs in Ireland. There had been "some talk about my staying here", and it had come from the leaders of the Irish Nationalist party. He had sat at a banquet in London by the side of the greatest leader, Charles Stewart Parnell. All this he had faithfully reported in his letters home from abroad, and it could not have been forgotten on return.

Through the next four years, he said, his correspondence had lapsed with the Irish leaders. Yet he had not been blind to developments, and he could not have been free of his thoughts. He had seen Parnell pulled down by the scandal of Kitty O'Shea, and dead a year later. The Nationalist party, split by the scandal, quite unhealed by the death, had divided into bitter factions. The leaders now, pro-Parnell or anti-Parnell, were quarrelling over his memory, quarrelling over his policies, and quarrelling still more fiercely over the remains of a party fund. Yet Home Rule itself, even as Parnell died, seemed more alive than ever. It was rising in the imperial parliament, again in the hands of Gladstone, as a great and hopeful issue.

It was a time of tragedy and challenge, and it was a time of opportunity. The Nationalist party was tearing itself on the brink of its greatest moment. A man free of quarrels, respected by both factions, might perhaps assist in healing. A fresh voice and a known voice, coming from across the Atlantic, might be heard with new effect. One could not help but think of it, one could not help but dream of it as a relief from the thoughts in Canada. Yet it was more than a mere dream; it was a practical possibility. One was not so remote from Ireland as to be unaware of that. The Irish Nationalists on their own ground had many ridings at their disposal, impregnably loyal constituencies that would return the man they named. All this Blake had known, and kept in the back of his mind and put away from him. Now it was all here, on a sheet of yellow paper.

These far-off, casual friends, distracted by many difficulties, were involved in a great cause. They had remembered and turned to him. Their voice was a cry to the new world to redress the balance of the old. To the son of Catherine Blake it was the command of a greater Voice, justifying the pains of a lifetime and demanding a single answer. The reply went back to Ireland after a sleepless night. "Deeply sensible high honor. Fear too old and unfamiliar for service. But if thought anyway useful to great cause would accept safe seat . . . cable essential points."[8]

On June 26 he sailed from Quebec for Ireland. Only Samuel, his youngest son, went with him. He had bade farewell to Humewood and he had had a glimpse of Murray Bay. He was leaving Margaret, he was leaving his brother and the firm, he was to be deprived for a precious summer of the joys of family life. It had been a wider and richer life in recent years as three of his children married. Now, dear as his own, there was Sophia's George Wrong, a man close to his heart. There was the beloved "Georgie" Manning who had married Edward Hume, and Ethel Benson, equally dear, as the wife of Edward Francis. There were the first of his children's children, for he had become a grandfather now. The ashy taste of politics was still dry in his mouth and in the forsaken university there was a sense of greater loss, almost a sense of guilt. But Sam, the ever faithful, would carry a part of that work, and the rest must be left to others. There was no time to lose, hardly time to reflect; the great cause was in crisis.

Two days after his decision Blake had written to Mills, and the letter was to be shown to Laurier. Relieved of the old tensions, recovering the old friendship, it was warm, nostalgic, and familiar as a balance sheet of his mind. His first duty was to Canada, he wrote without reproach, "but my differences with my friends being found, after every effort to adjust them, irreconcilable, the opportunity of service here is not open."[9]

As to the other service and the speculations of newspapers, he was as irritable with windy friends as he was with hostile critics. He knew better than any of them the limitations he went with. The night thoughts of the debit side were all carefully set down. "My financial resources would be greatly diminished while my expenses would be greatly increased, and I owe $25,000. . . .

"I am quite too old and too little informed on Home and Imperial questions . . . the absurd suggestions of my taking the leading part in the Irish party, and the still more ridiculous idea of my taking such a part in the British Liberal party are only calculated to make me a laughing stock, and to impair any chance I may have of making my way to a modest position of usefulness in the ranks.

"The divisions in the Irish party have greatly weakened them, and render the prospect of acting along with them much less agreeable than it might have been. . . .

"I could not bear the thought of turning my back permanently on my own country, and this attitude is not calculated to advance me elsewhere."

Yet after these came the counter-balancing credits, and they had proved to be more than enough. "I could not help feeling that the call, coming as it did without the slightest effort or communication or sign of present interest in the struggle, and in face of the fact that I had ceased corresponding with my friends on the other side, and had been prevented from visiting them for several years, and of the fact that I had failed to retain a seat here, seemed very remarkable and not such as should be slighted. . . .

"Nor could I conceal from myself that I had a certain reputation, however undeserved, owing to which my accession might in the present very critical position of the party in the three Kingdoms, add, however little, yet some little energy to the impulse needed in the election. . . .

"Again I have long felt deep interest in the great question, both in its local aspect as affecting the country of my origin, and in its Imperial phases, including that of Canada, and in the gallant struggle of Mr. Gladstone, not only against the Tory hosts but also against old friends, adverse fortunes and time itself. I think that the approaching may be one of the most important parliaments of modern days, to be a member of which would be no small thing. . . .

"So that on the whole, within an hour after I heard I had decided to accept."[10]

"My dear Blake," the reply had come from Laurier, "the one consideration with me which towers up above all others is that in the Imperial Parliament you will find an arena worthy of yourself. A very young country like Canada might and should afford vast horizons, but it has been dwarfed by political debauchery. I verily fear that the great questions to which we might have looked will not come up in our day." For all their warmth, to one who thought of return, there was a bleak hint of finality lurking behind those words, yet it was swept away by others. "My dear Blake, this is the opportunity of your life . . . be true to yourself and the brightest portion of your career is just opening."[11]

It was to be brief in its first phase. Gladstone, at eighty-two, was fighting his last election on the issue of Home Rule. Six years out of office and faced by entrenched Conservatism, his sixty Irish Nationalists were his one hope of a majority. By July 9, as the candidate for South Longford, Blake was one of that hope. On July 10, quite secure in a carefully chosen riding, he was driven out in a long, triumphal procession to confront his new electors. "Longford had never seen such a gathering . . . the bands played their loudest, cheer followed cheer, and many went forth to meet the hero of the day. No royal conqueror could have had a better or more hearty reception."[12]

By the 13th, proclaimed as "the Gladstone of Canada", he was in possession of his safe seat. He was a member of the Imperial parliament and the original Gladstone could claim to have won the election, but nothing was yet quite clear. The Irish party, still fragmented into anti- and pro-Parnellites, could abate none of its confusion and unite none of its factions. The Conservative party in parliament hung on for several weeks, refusing to concede defeat. On August 14th, with the Tories at last turned out, Gladstone came to office only to adjourn the session. There were by-elections required now to confirm his new ministers, and Home Rule must wait. The member for South Longford, though he had been well received in London and spoken to impressive gatherings of leading Liberals, had not addressed a syllable to Mr. Speaker. By the 18th he was on his way to Canada.

He arrived at Murray Bay, and there were congratulations from Laurier. "You must not suppose," Blake replied to them, "I have made any great success. I do not think so. But I have not failed, and have the prospect of a moderately useful work before me. That is all I care for; and so I am satisfied."[13]

It was well for him, if true, since he had little else to look for on his own side of the Atlantic. To Justin McCarthy in London, who had listened to Blake in Canada, he was "one of the finest parliamentary debaters I ever heard . . . I feel perfectly bashful at having to be the leader of such a man."[14] In Toronto, however, it was different. The Young Liberals, who had been inclined to welcome his arrival, found their plans for a large reception countered by other friends. It was Irish Home Rulers, most of them Roman Catholics, who intended to receive him now. For two weeks, as a great political brawl was fought out in the newspapers, Tories moved to the attack on the new Blake. Protestants were duly warned of him, whatever their political faith, and the lost first name of his youth was revived for emphasis. He was now Dominic Blake, the Irish Home Ruler, friend of Catholics and the Pope. Party support dwindled, Liberals retreated in confusion, and speeding the flight of fugitives were the efforts of alleged friends.

The Tory Toronto *Mail*, always ingeniously vindictive in earlier attacks on Blake, produced an intriguing tidbit for its issue of September 12. Ostensibly a letter from one, Ignatius Loyala Murphy, at present involuntarily domiciled in Kingston penitentiary, it was a warm salute to "Mr. Dominic Blake (God bless him!) MP for South Longford (my native county) on his return to this country after his noble efforts to secure Home Rule for old Ireland." It was the writer's hope that the oppressed and deprived of Canada might adapt Irish methods, preferably with Blake at their head. "Why should it be considered a crime here to shoot an unjust and exacting landlord?" Mr. Murphy himself, removed by his Ontario landlord for non-payment of rent, had taken his own measures. "I hough his cattle and burn his barn in order to warn him and others like him that the rights of tenants must be respected." Given fourteen years for that by "wretched Saxon hirelings", he was urgent that all true Irishmen should attend the meeting for Blake, as he certainly would himself "had circumstances permitted."[15]

On September 19, in the familiar, sweaty spaciousness of the Horticultural Pavilion, the demonstration took place. It was hugely attended, with hundreds turned away. But it was sponsored by Irish Nationalists rather than by Young Liberals, and both the guests prominent on the platform and the notable absentees provided emphasis of the fact. Laurier was not present, and the portrait dominating the stage was of William Ewart Gladstone. It was of Ireland rather than of Liberalism that "the Gladstone of Canada" spoke, and the choice was highly acceptable to his old friends of the party. He spoke easily and well, a man adapted to change, perhaps still seeing beyond it the prospect of change again. Four out of five Canadians, he told his audience, supported the Irish cause. He was abroad in their service; he hoped for ultimate return, perhaps for ultimate reward. He believed, he said, that "we will see a good Home Rule bill introduced in the Imperial parliament. . . . I am giving to that cause these two or three years of my life."[16]

Even as he spoke he was preparing for departure again. There were limp plans by Liberals to arrange a banquet in his honour, but he was soon informed that they had been allowed to "lie over". He wrote expressing relief; he did not comment on the cause. Goldwin Smith did. To the old friend of the Aurora days, now the acidulous acquaintance, "the Canadian Champion of Home Rule" was a source of Protestant hostility and of fresh and deeper division in the Liberal party. "Mr. Blake," he wrote Laurier, "probably does not fail to see this, but he has already shown that he thinks of nobody but himself."[17]

In any case, to the Irish member of parliament the going now was a relief rather than a wrench. He had a Home Rule meeting in Boston for October 28, and on November 2 he was sailing again for England, this time with Margaret. He was to speak at a banquet in Bristol on November 14, and on the whole it was better than Toronto. He was nearing sixty now; it was late for sinking the roots of a political life. But if there were to be roots they must go down in the soil of the old country, for they had been torn up in the new.

CHAPTER ELEVEN

"THE GOVERNOR"

THERE WERE, in fact, never to be roots again in the soil of politics. He was a member of the imperial parliament but he was also an Irish Nationalist, the heart of his cause a dispute with British rule. It barred his way to the cabinet, for it was a first principle of the Nationalists that they could not accept office. He might be noticed by Gladstone, he might and did confer on Irish affairs with men like John Morley and James Bryce, but he could never hope to be associated with them in the government of the United Kingdom. Nor could he hope, even if he had wished for it, to become head of his own party. Perpetually faction-ridden and perennially bankrupt, it was prepared to grant him every other eminence. He was immediately a principal spokesman and soon a distracted peacemaker in "squalid and disgusting"[1] quarrels. He could advise the British on federalism as it might be applied to Ireland, and he could often direct the Irish in their own tactics and strategy. He could strain his personal resources and he could comb North America in the unending quest for funds. But he was not native to the turf nor bred of the older battles; he was the benevolent Trans-Atlantean who could help but never lead.

All this and much more was confirmed by his first full session in the British parliament. On February 13, 1893, Gladstone outlined the terms of the bill for Irish Home Rule which he intended to introduce in the House. On September 2, after seven stormy months the measure passed, only to be overwhelmed in the House of Lords. The strong walls of Toryism stood up with hardly a breach, Gladstone's health was failing, and there would not be another like him to revive hope in defeat. The Irish cause was again at a seething standstill, and so was the career of Blake. He had spoken twice in the debate, and had been admired in the friendlier sections of the British and Irish press. The *Globe* was predicting in Canada that he would be leader of the Irish party. He found that only an irritant, for he was already sensing his fate. In two hours, in his elaborate maiden speech, he had made the mark that would cling to him for the next thirteen years. The able outsider, too well aware of his abilities, he could impress and delight the listener who shared his view. "He has, after Gladstone himself, no superior in the House of Commons,"[2] exclaimed Justin McCarthy. But he could not sway the mind of the imperial parliament. His very eminence in Canada, his appreciation of the eminence, and the habits of a quarter-century told against him. His speech, said a British journalist, saying all, had been "a compendious effort with something subtly colonial in its character".[3]

By September 10, as the bill went down in the Lords, he was at sea bound for Canada. There was a rest at Murray Bay, a brief visit to Toronto, and a month or more of speech-making in Canada and the United States. He was still prominent, always immersed in business, and much in demand for many elaborate occasions. As a barrister resident in London he had more briefs than ever now for appeals to the Privy Council. Yet the old friends seemed different, the new friends less congenial, and the whole of his public effort was restricted to one cause. He was advancing Home Rule, he was raising money for the Irish, and always a little too much of it was required from his own pocket. By mid-February of 1894, with another session of the imperial parliament in prospect, he was sailing again for London. For him and Margaret, the indispensable companion, the pattern of years ahead was taking shape. "I suppose on Monday," she wrote from on board *Umbria* to her young friend Wylie Grier, "I will begin to hunt for lodgings. Oh dear! if a certain artist I know were only there to meet us, how different I would feel!"[4]

The future Sir Edmund Wylie Grier, already a painter whose work was attracting notice, was then just thirty-two. He had studied in Europe and begun his career in Europe, but he maintained his links with Canada. A trans-Atlantic commuter like the Blakes themselves, he had been for three years a friend and often a welcome house guest. His first stay with the family had been at Murray Bay, in the depths of the gloomy summer of 1891. Witty, pungent, engaging, and still a promising unknown, he had been received with warmth and had formed some lasting impressions. He was to remember long afterward his first coming to the wharf, his sight of "the big man" and of "his gentle and kindly wife".[5] There was a confusion of friends and relatives that he could never quite sort out, and there were prominent visiting Canadians and equally important Americans with "bifurcated beards". There was *Maison Rouge* itself, high above the St. Lawrence with its sweep of pine and water, and usually out on a balcony there was the absorbed and silent host.

He was more a study to the artist even than the view itself. Grier would be impressed forever by Blake "the mental giant", but he would be equally intrigued and exasperated by some of the giant's moods. He came to appreciate sooner than most of his elders, the breadth and clarity of the mind, the reserves of hidden warmth, the rare, sardonic flashes both of gaiety and understanding. But they were all too well-concealed, particularly in that dark summer, by the man shut in on himself. Shy with "a shyness which he did not confess and which amounted almost to a nervous disease . . . an acerbity of manner of which he was unconscious . . . a habit of sarcasm which was a defence", Blake was a prisoner of qualities from which he had no means of escape. Hospitable without reserve, he was never the host at ease; he could speak but not converse, he could impart but never share. He was a passionately devoted parent whose sons spoke when they were spoken to, and whose wife seemed "rendered dumb" by his very presence. There were unforgettable evenings at the long family board when talk suddenly languished and frivolity fled away, when a single word from the master "reduced the table to the condition of a wheat-field after a cloudburst". Fantastic as it seemed to Grier, "I am inclined to think that, with all his appreciation of wit, his whole being and the sum of all his aptitudes and accomplishments were attenuated by his lack of humour. Without it there is none more solemn than an Irishman."

Yet there were other sides to life at *Maison Rouge*. Grier was attracted instantly to Sammy, the youngest son, who was twenty-three years old, and who wrote verse in secret. That "blend of poet and athlete", that "face of rare spiritual beauty" seemed to cry out to be sketched, and in spite of a lack of drawing-paper sketched at last it was. Grier had charcoal with him and he had the cooperation of Sammy, who was familiar with the general store. Rummaging there, the two discovered a biscuit tin, abstracted a sheet of cardboard, and the sketch was done on that. It was a warm and appealing work, and the turning point of a career. It delighted the shy father who idolized the shy son, and he transmuted much of his feeling into a new regard for the artist. "Benevolently planning for my advancement, taking great pains about my welfare, and paternally advising me for my good . . . Edward Blake assured me that if I should decide to spend a winter in Toronto I could count on success . . . Mrs. Edward Blake was my first sitter . . . commissions followed, and I was launched on a stream of Canadian portraiture which has kept me busy to this day."

Out of it all grew a warm and unique relationship between the Blakes and the artist. In this urbane young sophisticate, there was much that each of them lacked and he supplied a want in their life. Both sat for him often and were tireless friends and sponsors. They were more than that in their almost parental concern, their frank delight in his company, and he returned affection for affection. Yet he dissected subjects as a painter of them, and he had a quick and merciless eye. "One could almost weep," he wrote of Blake in the last days of his ascendancy, "to see him laying waste the ranks of those who would fain love and follow him."

Grier was himself a witness to the decline of one friendship and to a somewhat graphic result. He was painting without much pleasure, and frequently under the criticism of Mrs. Goldwin Smith, a portrait of her famous husband. During the same period he was also painting Blake. Both portraits were to be displayed by the Royal Academy in London, and the subjects' sittings were arranged in immediate sequence, with Blake following Smith. "I derived a good deal of amusement," Grier recorded, "as I noted the dread on the part of each of my sitters that he might meet the other. My studio . . . was in the, then, head office of the Imperial Bank of Canada. On one occasion Goldwin Smith, lingering in my apartments rather beyond his allotted time, heard a knock on my door, and in his hurried attempt to secrete himself or gain an exit, he opened a door which gave access to a light well and almost pitched himself down a shaft designed to illuminate the desks of toiling bank clerks beneath." The unavoided meeting is a blank in Grier's recital, but the two completed portraits were shipped to London together "appropriately back to back".

Observant not only at sittings but on many other occasions, Grier had numerous assessments of his favourite subject. The Blake aura came through to him "as originally a thin, colorless, misty outline which time gradually congealed into ice". He listened, benumbed, to speeches with their interminably involved parentheses and waited for the suspended verb, like "a sportsman who sees his retriever emerge from the tangled underbrush with a woodcock in its mouth". As the Blakes' ship reached England in the winter of 1894 he was not there to meet them. But he came later, and he remained the shrewd observer.

"Blake," he wrote, "was a rare figure in London." The cosmopolitan atmosphere seemed to have relaxed some minor scruples. Though he did not touch wine in Canada Blake took port here, occasionally and in small quantities "because of the English climate". He dressed with more care, and was better groomed than at home, though he was never able to bring himself to adopt the top hat. He mixed with the legal fraternity and was heard on formal occasions at some of the London clubs, though he was already known as the colonial who talked too much too long. "His tall, well-built figure, his leonine head and colonial hat . . . made him a marked personality in the street." He was obviously conscious of it all and determined to support the image; he was the distinguished Canadian called to the Irish cause. What else could he be now — why else was he here — far from Humewood, far from *Maison Rouge*, living in rented lodgings? "To him London was opportunity, stimulus, a major step in his career." For once Grier's shrewdness failed him; it was a half-truth at best, and there was more of his old perception in his view of Margaret, "with her pretty grey hair . . . her beautiful, rather sad grey eyes — one of the sweetest and most loveable of women." To her London was exile — "nobly endured and bravely continued with some show of cheerfulness — but exile none the less."[6]

"I go to Ireland tomorrow for about 3 weeks — then argue 3 cases — then expect Parlt, to meet about end of August — probably stay on it a little — then home home home."[7] Blake wrote the letter in 1895, and it was a capsuled glimpse of the life he led in England. He was indispensable to the Irish, he was a known and respected figure to the Lords of the Privy Council, and he was bored, depressed, and ineffective in parliament. Gladstone was now gone, the limp government of Rosebery had just tottered to its fall, and Home Rule and Liberalism were alike in the slough of despond. There was no prospect ahead of Blake but years in opposition, years of party squabbles and of dismal scratching for funds. He would keep alive the cause, he would do his share and more, but he was homesick and heartsick and he would remain so to the end.

"I can't tell you," he wrote to Wylie Grier in that same summer of 1895, "how I weary for home and friends or how sad and lonely a life we lead in this Babylon among 'new men, strange faces, other minds.' God grant it may soon end for us."[8] Yet within six weeks he was writing another letter this time to the family. "I have a chance of going to New Zealand and making £2,000 this fall . . . I hate the idea but there is a prospect of money in it."[9]

He had career enough, and more here, for any ordinary man. Though Irish leaders could agree on little else, they were agreed on the ability of Blake, and on the disastrous effects of his loss. Ineffective as he was, he was as powerful as any of them in parliament and he was the link between their factions. He was their first man on the committee established in 1894 to study the financial relations between the United Kingdom and Ireland, and he would be the pre-eminent figure in the work. There was the same pre-eminent excellence in his work before the Privy Council. From Manitoba, where the minority had appealed to the courts against the abolishment of separate schools, the brief came to Blake. It was his argument that produced the decision of the Lords. And it was the report of that decision that determined Laurier's stand.

"Blake," wrote J. S. Ewart, the Toronto lawyer associated with him in the pleading, "was probably the only man in the world who could do the work as well as he did it . . . it was the most satisfactory preparation that I ever saw given to a case during my whole experience."[10] The judges, Blake was told by the registrar of the Privy Council, "agreed that you had argued your case in the most marvellously able way."[11]

The invitation to New Zealand, and the eventual result of the trip, were another proof of his standing. The colonial barrister was invited to go to Wellington and act as arbitrator in a dispute between the government and the New Zealand Midland Railway Company which involved some $8,000,000. In less than four weeks he completed proceedings that had been expected to drag for months, and produced a decision on which even the losers congratulated him. As usual, in matters of law and the grasp and relation of facts, he was one of the few masters.

Yet he went to New Zealand, came home around the world and returned to London with his thoughts fixed on Canada, yearning with family affections and seething with family problems. Margaret had not gone with him and was sadly missed. His long letters chronicled every day, every sight seen, every symptom of his various traveller's ailments, and breathed on every page of his incessant loneliness for her. He woke in the nights dreaming of her and reported the dreams in full, always centred in the familiar scenes of home. The warmth he could not show, the words he could not say — or was never heard to say by any outsider — were all here released in the sprawled writing. There were jokes and kisses for the grandchildren, there was sharp, observant wit, and there was wry acceptance of himself for what he was. If he was sometimes taken for an actor or a bishop incognito he did not blame his fellow-passengers in the ship. He could not mix, he could not bend, and he posed in self-defence. "I . . . fear I have on the whole only added to my well known indifferent character as a reserved and standoff sort of gent."[12]

The best times for Blake were the times when he was unobserved. "There was a very fine sunset . . . and just on the port or left-hand bow was a beautiful young moon, hung low in the sky . . . after dinner I went right into the eyes of the boat, close over her stem and lay there for an hour . . . I could hear the water cut by the stem and the two different kinds of *swish* it sent out as it broke on the weather and lee bows; the sounds were delicious and then the little bit of moon gave a great deal of light, and there was a soft, balmy air; and I enjoyed that dark, silent, lonely hour more than any moment I have had since I left."[13]

One of the family problems he had taken with him, and he

returned with it still unsolved. The young Sammy, now a member of the law firm and heartily detesting his work, had been a cause of much concern. Edward Francis, the second son, as the resident worrier in Toronto, had conveyed misgivings to "The Governor" which brought immediate response. Blake had work in London, he wrote with careful tact, on which Sammy's help would be useful, and the change might do him good. The boy's reply had been very much in character. "I don't exactly know what Ned has written . . . but . . . there is nothing much the matter with me except 'local depression' . . . it is perfectly true that I have no heart in my work and in fact such distaste that it is all and perhaps more than I am equal to keep from shirking, but if I was to go away now for a holiday trip on account of my health or down-in-the-mouthness . . . I would be worse fitted for work than ever . . . dearest father, I have written all this believing that your first and main object in sending for me was my own interests . . . I seem to have had holiday all my life . . . if I thought that apart from my own good you wanted me to do anything I would be on the way now. . . ."[14]

Eventually he had been persuaded to come, and had gone along to New Zealand. Yet he had remained throughout, as he would always, the beloved, charming, unhappy, self-depreciating enigma. "Sammy seems well and has no headaches . . . Sammy and I have played merry games with dominoes . . . Sammy seems torpid toward night and goes to his berth and lies down . . . I have invited him to study my case, but he does not seem very keen about it . . . Sammy had one of his attacks, tiredness and indigestion . . . Sammy turned in, feeling a little cold — cold on the night we crossed the line!"[15]

The father's reports for the mother, recorded on the long voyage, were a fever chart of concern, relentless and ineffective. It weighed the son down, walled him into his silences, and was only to be resumed in London. Set up in practice there as a solicitor to the Privy Council, Sam was reasonably successful on the strength of his father's name. He was diligent by fits and starts, oppressed with generosity, and still the lost young dreamer who was locked away from fulfillment. There was much Blake understood, and he was not the possessive father, but he could find no key for the lock. There were only the "changes" and holidays, the renewed travels for health, and a poignant cry from "The Governor" which seemed the sum of the result. "Sammy not well; much neuralgia, dreadful blues and speechlessness, and I fear a *giving way* which leaves him with work undone and a general state of misery which breaks my heart. But I am helpless."[16]

At home in Canada Humewood was standing closed, vacant for most of each year. There were occasional openings at Christmas or to celebrate family reunions, but maintenance was becoming expensive. The house was old, constantly in need of repair, and Blake had disposed of much of the surrounding land. That phase of his life was nearly over. There were several homes for the family now, closely grouped in the city. On Jarvis Street, in the days of its first elegance, Edward and brother Sam had each built houses. There had been another for Edward Francis when he married Ethel Benson, the daughter of Judge Thomas Benson of Port Hope. A little later still another had been built for Sophia and George Wrong. All of them stood in satisfying proximity, with Sam at 256, Edward Francis and his family at 449, Sophia and the Wrongs at 469, and Edward and Margaret's house, which was usually rented in their absence, cheek by jowl with the Wrongs at 467. Only Hume, the eldest son, who had married Georgie Manning, was a little apart from the group. His residence, at 94 St. George Street, was the finest home of all, yet there was something characteristic in the separation. It was a house built on drygoods and breweries and street railways by an Irish immigrant father who had become Toronto's mayor. Alexander Manning was a sizeable and respected man, but his wealth derived from commerce. The mild and gentle Hume, marrying into commerce, had left the firm to administer some Manning interests.

He was neither particularly successful nor particularly happy in his work, and he was the only Blake who was not allied with the professions.

Over it all The Governor presided from a distance, worrying about every child, fretting over every property, endlessly concerned with fees, mortgages, and investments. He lived on a system of remittances designed to flow from Canada, while his fees flowed back to restore the family coffers. Established on the one principle that there must never be idle money, it was elaborate, intricate, demanding, and subject to constant revision. Delays in the remittance of fees, demands for help from the Irish and the expenses of travel and rest cures would upset his calculations. He would rearrange them all, discourse on the need for the changes, and forward peremptory instructions to adjust the balance in his books. Certain shares must be sold, certain shares must be bought, always within ranges stipulated and subject to new conditions. The letters teemed with figures, with his own reflections on business, and concluded with much affection and the latest word on his health. "I don't like to risk money in the loan companies and I had rather not touch the banks while I am away. Therefore I have decided to ask you to look out for *first class* mortgages of moderate amount on *productive* property. . . . I am a believer in small rather than large mortgages . . . I am very weak and have lost about 12 pounds but have got back my appetite and got rid of my cough and will be all right soon . . . tell Will I have just dosed myself with his cocaine . . . goodbye my darling boy."[17]

The luckless recipient of the letters was Edward Francis Blake, now entering his thirties. He was depressed in his own condition as the last of the three sons who remained with "Blakes". His father's connection for years had been merely nominal. Edward Blake's was the first name at the masthead, but he was now apart from the business. He was sought too much for himself; there were too many briefs with accompanying large retainers he could not be expected to share. Sam,

Zebulon Lash, and Walter Cassels were the remaining senior partners, and each of the three had sons. "Ned" Blake seemed somehow lost in the shuffle, consigned to the junior work and a junior's share in the profits. Yet he could not complain of idleness for he was his father's agent in Canada, devoted, sometimes protesting, but always the prop and stay.

It was the level-headed Ned who received the stream of instructions, and bought and sold and administered and remitted as required. He was often impatient with the process, for it was niggling beyond all reason, creating a bogey of money where there was always money enough. He was weighed down with the endless concern for the family, for the state of the family properties, and the satisfaction of newly imagined needs. He dealt with bankers and brokers, and carpenters, builders, and painters, and was never sure that he had given the final word. He was financial, rental, and repair agent and never quite the free agent, for there was no disposal of assets, no dispute with a tenant and no change in a house-fitting that was not subjected to trans-Atlantic discussion. Whether it was a new furnace for Humewood, a roof for *Maison Rouge* or a bay window on Jarvis Street the father's instructions came, to be ignored at proper peril. Yet they were always quite as generous as they were unrelentingly detailed, and the guiding purpose was reflected in other letters. "The Governor," wrote Ned in one of them, reporting to his brother Sammy, "has given me absolutely my house with 40 feet frontage on Jarvis Street . . . he has transferred to the Trust Company for Sophia upon certain trusts her own house . . . he has also transferred to each of us and to yourself 556 shares of 20% stock in the Huron and Erie. . . ."[18]

There was Hume Blake, established and happily married, to a wealthy heiress. But he had little joy in his employment, and he had no resources of his own. He loved horses and sport, he did not love breweries and railways, and he did not believe that he was advancing the Manning interests. The Governor knew that too, and worried about it too. On the way home from

New Zealand with the large fee warm in his pocket he sent his instructions to Ned. "You remember that I determined to make dear Hume an allowance of $500. a year. Well, I think in lieu of this I will give him ten thousand dollars out and out . . . enter in my books the receipt of £2,500. as fees in the award and . . . pass the $10,000. for Hume through your mother's book."[19]

It was to provide "a little *income*, however small, from us,"[20] and the acknowledgment must have been satisfying. "My dearest father," wrote Hume, "I really do not know how to thank you for your generous kindness. I need hardly say that your present will make the greatest difference to me. It relieves me from a feeling of dependance which I must confess has worried me considerably . . . the one extravagance which I have committed on the strength of your present is the purchase of a saddle horse. The mare I used to ride went wrong last summer and I have not done any riding since and have felt the want of it a good deal, so I bought a horse the other day which I think will turn out very well."[21] The beloved first son, closer to the imposing father than the father could ever betray, was joined by another link.

Meanwhile, year by year, interspersed with the trips to Canada, the London life went on, the life in lodgings. They were always good lodgings, they were usually chosen by Margaret, and there was never a real home. Blake complained of it often, and he knew the cost to his wife. Yet he did not want permanency, he could not endure the thought of it; home was decaying Humewood, or the houses along Jarvis Street, or the balcony at Murray Bay. Home was that House in Ottawa, that chamber on Parliament Hill; it was not this parliament of Westminster where he spoke and was not heard. "It may surprise you to know," he wrote to J. G. Bourinot, the clerk of the Canadian Commons, "that so casual do I feel my situation I have never read the rules of this House."[22] He was in parliament but he was not of it, he was high in legal circles but he remained the esteemed stranger. He was the invaluable friend of Irishmen who longed to escape his friends.

In addition to all that, both he and Margaret were usually in wretched health. There were lengthy visits to some of the English watering-places or to continental spas. Considering the frequent absences, permanency would involve waste. It was cheaper to vacate when leaving and search about on return. Transience as well as loneliness were a part of the pattern of life, and figured in the calculations. "Remember," he could write Ned, "that there is money in the stocking and don't spare any expenses and call on me."[23] In his own case, however, which necessarily involved Margaret, he harped on a different theme. For all the large fees, for all the eminence at the bar of the Privy Council, "I live in an uncomfortable London lodging and look twice at a shilling before spending it on myself."[24]

There was a spectral familiarity with the life of his father before him, and the son in Canada protested as Blake had done himself. "I do hope that you will make yourself and mother comfortable, I wish you could see your way to taking a nice flat and keeping it all the time . . . it is so very trying for both yourself and mother to have to hunt for some abode each time you go back to London."[25] In another and later outburst there were even more forceful words: "As the poorest of your children. I want to urge you as strongly as possible not to continue forcing yourself to work when you do not feel up to it. . . . I find that I have over $17,000. in cash . . . you gave me between $14,000. and $15,000. . . . Sam has done better than I have. You know Hume's and Sophia's positions and prospects as well as I do. I do not think any of us or of our children would starve if you gave us nothing more."[26]

It was of no use. Instructions came, as they had always come, from 40 Ebury Street, from 12 Carlyle Mansions, from 112 Ashley Gardens, from 15 Chelsea Court, from 44 Emperor's Gate, from 20 Kensington Gate . . . "if you see any signs of

Sophia wanting money make her a remittance." . . . "you must make a great effort at the proper time in the fall to get an abatement in the taxes of Humewood . . . I intend to make you a present of whatever is saved, so you can remember you are fighting for yourself" . . . "sickness expenses must have been heavier than I supposed, and I want you to take another $100. from my funds" . . . "I hope you are having a merry Christmas; for us, who have seen so many years, *merriment* is past. . . ."[27]

At the general election of June, 1896, the Liberal party in Canada was returned to power. After eighteen years of Torydom, Laurier succeeded to the place Mackenzie had left, and that Blake had once refused. When the member for South Longford returned on his autumn visit it was to salute his friend in the office of Prime Minister.

He was warmly welcomed, he was asked for advice and gave it, and he was once more back in England when a letter from Mowat followed. His old friend from Ontario was now Minister of Justice in the federal cabinet, and he had matured his hopes with Laurier. There was a prospect of approaching vacancies both on the Ontario Court of Appeal and on the Supreme Court of Canada. "Laurier authorizes me to say to you that either of the two Chief Justiceships will be open to you for acceptance when the time comes . . . I need not say that you could have no rival for consideration as regards either."[28]

There was more than that. "Our Premier," Mowat added, "has always had some hope that when you once more make Canada your home you would again enter political life here, and he is such a politician that I quite see he would personally rejoice more at your return to Canadian politics than even at your taking the Chief Justiceship of the Supreme Court of Canada . . . I should like to have you in Canada again in any position, but most of all in a judicial position worthy of you."[29]

They could hardly have been warmer words, and even the fact that the offer lay in the future seemed only to reinforce them. "I do not want a present answer from you. I should rather not have a present answer, lest it should be 'no'."[30]

It was the expected call to Blake, and he received it without surprise, returning warmth for the warmth. "I obey your wish as to answering now, *for the reason which you assign.*"[31] With the other thought, however, he was not so ready to part. "Laurier's wish that I should return to Canadian political life is like what I have always found him. I cannot conceive myself once again immersed in all the details of party strife, though if it were well understood that I was irrevocably detached from them I might perhaps be able to do some service to my country in the House of Commons." It was the old spectre of Blake the independent, and it must have been chilling to Laurier. In the farewell words to Mowat, however, it was lost in benevolent mist. "Whether I stay here to fight the battle as I am generally minded to do as long as there is a party to fight it with; or whether I return soon; and whether in my return I rest or labour; and whether, if I labour I do so in the one or the other Canadian field; I shall always gratefully remember and carefully treasure your letter."[32]

He wrote with the breadth of a man of many options, as indeed he was that year. He was more than ever in demand by his Irish friends. In the Anti-Parnellite faction the Dillonites warred with the Healyites, but both sides turned to Blake. So did John Redmond, leader of the Parnellite Party and the rising hope of the movement. In March of 1897, when the financial relations between the United Kingdom and Ireland became the subject of acrid debate, it was Blake who presented the Irish case in the House, "before an audience overwhelmingly hostile and with the other sections of Irishmen not supporting but carping at my heels and putting the blame of defeat on me."[33] After two years of work on the committee studying the problem he had recoiled from making the speech. "The thing will come up on 4th March, I believe, a dry, dull discussion of technical details and figures, impossible to make interesting, and in which the best that can be hoped is to be allowed to make the statement."[34] But "Dillon implored me to undertake it . . . Healyites, for certain reasons, supported my choice after I had told them they could do me no greater favour than to choose someone else,"[35] and in the end he had a minor triumph. "I had warm congratulations from Healyites, Parnellites, Irish Unionists as well as Tories and Liberals . . . I fully expected to empty the House, but it is not true that it emptied, and it was interested and receptive to the very end, tho' of course quotations and figures, however inevitable, were a weariness to the flesh."[36]

He had stirring days before the bar of the Privy Council, and more from there to include in his reports to Ned. "I have had very good luck with my P.C. cases, both in their fortune and in the strife with the judges, which waxed mighty hot for the last three days."[37] Beyond that, opening out wider vistas, there was a brief and creditable moment on the stage of imperial affairs. The Jameson Raid in the Transvaal, the prelude to the Boer War, had involved the Conservative government in a parliamentary inquiry. It had involved Cecil Rhodes and it had threatened to involve Chamberlain, and Blake as an attacking Liberal had been a powerful figure in the assault. He had exposed the gaps in the evidence, he had hinted at suppressed evidence, and he had cross-examined Rhodes. It had been a well-noted performance and a promise of greater things. For the first time, not as a mere colonial but as one of Her Majesty's lawmakers, he had duelled with a great imperialist and had more than held his own.

Yet more than ever in his own mind he was the Canadian on leave abroad, hoping for the end of his mission. It had only been bearable at all for him when he viewed it in that light. He saw himself now as enhanced by service abroad, and there were changed conditions at home. Forced from politics in Canada by the errors of his own party, he had seen those errors corrected. Formally and in full convention, during the first year of his absence, Liberals had reduced their trade policy to the limited hopes of Blake. They were the government now and they were tinkering with imperial tariffs, but these were political gestures which changed nothing at the core. The great obstacle was removed, the twin heresies of Commercial Union and Unrestricted Reciprocity had been equally rooted out. The new opportunities of Liberalism were reopening wide horizons and Blake could accept recall.

It remained, however, for the new position to be realized. Friends of the old days wrote to Blake, and they all spoke of his return. But they were a close band and a narrowing one, and they were not in the highest quarters. Mowat wrote for Laurier, but Laurier did not write, or only on rare occasions. Mills wrote, but with regretful casualness rather than invitation, and it was the same with too many others. What was required was something else; something perhaps neglected. It was reminder and appreciation of the servant labouring abroad, a stirring of the forgetful silence of the great Canadian constituency.

From the first weeks of 1897 reminders began to be despatched. John Willison of the *Globe* and John Cameron, the friend in London, Ontario, who was now owner of the *Advertiser*, had been often tried and had proved worthy of the trust. They had been cooperative within reason in the publication of news of Blake from England, and their reward now was a shower of English cuttings. "I am rather disposed to believe," the letter went to Willison with accompanying reports of speeches, "that from a Canadian liberal point of view it is worthwhile to show the Irish Canadians that the *Globe* retains an interest in their fortunes, and in the Canadian whom they look on as their representative in these quarters." One could admit to personal feelings and accept the restrictions of space, but Blake must also think of those who had sent him. "Almost all my work for some years has been from painful necessities private and behind the scenes, and the few friends who continue to correspond with me so often hint the wish that I should do something, and convey the impression that I am doing nothing, that I can't but fear this impression is widespread. And this fear makes me anxious that on those rare occasions on which I do publicly intervene those whom I love and whose judgment I value should know."[38]

Spring came on, and he grew a little more pressing. The faithful Ned became the recipient of bulky parcels. "I have sent a few *Daily News* and many Freeman's *Journals* . . . you can pass them round and then to London where I daresay John Cameron would publish if Willison can't find space" . . . "I am sending *Daily News* and *Daily Chronicle* with Rhodes exam. I also send copies to Willison and John Cameron. I hope they will publish the commendatory allusions to my examination. It will be useful to me. Do anything you can with W. and ask Uncle V. to do anything he can with C."[39] The W. referred to Willison, whom Ned found quite obliging, and the C. to John Cameron, with whom Uncle Verschoyle Cronyn had also reasonable success.

June came on, and with it Victoria's Jubilee and the mighty celebration of the world-wide empire. Laurier came to London as Prime Minister of Canada. He rode as the be-plumed Sir Wilfrid in the great procession and he spoke as the guest of honour at many of the dazzling banquets. At one of them Blake spoke too. "I enclose copy of dictation of my speech on Dominion Day," he wrote Willison, "which I am for several reasons very anxious should be reproduced in the *Globe* while it is yet fresh. It took only about 12 minutes, so won't take much space." He was in haste and almost wheedling, and there was a hint at least of some of the several reasons. "I spoke so late that the reporters had given up, and anyway a mere Irish member does not get much reported in London now . . . Laurier is having a great reception . . ."[40]

August came, and Blake was in Murray Bay. He arrived in Toronto in September. Willison and Cameron had cooperated, there had been considerable space in the newspapers, and he seemed to be looked for now. Amid the welcoming correspondence and the welter of prospective occasions he moved with selective care. There were Irish Funds to be raised and he made the required speeches until he had "taken all the nuggets and nearly exhausted the mine."[41] Yet there was a new readiness, and even a new anxiety, to be heard on Canadian affairs. Mowat wrote, cordial and warm as always, reviving the matter of the judgeships. "I think that we can get the offer made," he ventured, "if it would be of any use."[42] It would not be, or at least it would not be accepted, but he was sharply brought to book.

"I understood," Blake replied, "you had already (with Laurier's approval) made me the offer; and indeed, little as I am disposed to stickle upon such questions, I will say frankly that I might have felt somewhat mortified had the Ministry not renewed to me the offer Mackenzie made twenty-one years ago. It was of course of some consequence to me that my professional position should be thus recognized; and I am disposed to think that it will do no harm to the Administration with the public that this recognition should have taken place."[43] The offer should be made known; everything should be heard and read of that would restore and enhance prestige. Nor could Mowat be left in doubt on the matter he had not revived. "I would most gladly, did I feel free to consult my personal inclinations, resign my seat in the House of Commons and return to Canada at once."[44] It was not possible "just now", but the time had come for the indispensable prelude, the awakening of the call for Blake.

One by one the occasions came, to end in the same result. He remained the distinguished Canadian whose views deserved to be heard, and whose time was now of the past. On one platform, after a brisk dispute for the place with William Mulock, he stood with Laurier again. But he was there as Chancellor of the University of Toronto, presenting the Prime Minister with an honorary Doctorate of Laws. He had been challenged even in this precedence by the ambitious Vice-Chancellor, and he left the hall alone.

"Convocation is over," recorded the young Clara Benson, who was sister-in-law to Blake's second son, in her diary for October 7th. "Sir Wilfrid is now a LLD of Toronto University . . . everything was most successful but . . . it makes me just a little sad. Mr. Edward Blake was the chairman and the Chancellor of the University and next to the graduates the hero of the day and yet he has walked home with only me."[45]

On November 24, at a Liberal reunion in Strathroy, he had the place of honour to himself. There was the flag-bedecked hall, the mass of upturned faces, and the old gusts of enthusiasm that were almost reverential. He was the man justified; and he justified himself again, telling the oft-told story in its undiminishing length. He had been the prophet driven forth, he was the exile still detained, but he spoke with hope of return now and with trust in those who heard him. It was his dearest aspiration, if events should make it possible, to serve them once again in their own parliament. "Still I look and long, earnestly desiring that the path of duty may some day approximate closer to the path of comfort and pleasure, and may lead me back to the land of my birth . . . nor have I ever doubted for an instant that the great mass of my Canadian fellow countrymen, whom I have loved and served so long, would love or trust me less because it has happened to me to take a course in respect of which I have never had occasion to retract a single step, and on which I am now able to appeal to time and events as my adequate and ample vindication."[46]

Yet it all withered in newspaper reports that were neither adequate nor ample. He complained to Cameron of the *Advertiser* of Willison's treatment of the speech. "The mutilation it underwent in the *Globe* report has diminished its effective circulation . . . I am very strongly inclined to print a pamphlet containing some former speeches and addresses, and closing with the Strathroy speech in vindication of my position."[47] Time pressed, however, there were other occasions pending, and he still had hopes of the *Globe*. On December 8 he turned to Willison again.

"I am to speak tonight at the National Club dinner in response to the toast of 'Canada and the Empire' . . . I take leave to enclose you a copy whereby your reporter's notes may be corrected . . . I am obliged, unexpectedly, to leave for Ireland by the *Teutonic* on 29th December, so this is the last occasion on which I shall be able to speak to my own people."[48]

It was not quite the last; there was another the following night, and on each occasion Willison did his best. He was defeated by Blake, however, and by fate and his own composing room, and the sum of both was almost complete disaster. At the National Club dinner, in the presence of Lord Aberdeen, the Governor General, and surrounded by the elite of loyal and imperialist Toronto, Blake delivered his views on the federation of the Empire. They rounded out, in severe and measured eloquence, to a flat rejection of the plan. He had once had hopes for it himself, it was much in fashion now, but its proponents "have not solved the insoluble . . . have not revealed the unknown, nor have they thrown one gleam of light on the problem of Imperial federation."[49]

On the hubbub following the speech, as the loyal leaped to their feet in fierce rebuttal, it appeared that one reporter had closed his notebook; little appeared in the *Globe*. Whatever lacked, there, however, was much more than made up for by other organs of opinion. The august *Mail and Empire*, though it was coolly reserved in its editorial comment, gave full space in its columns to the wrath of eloquent dissenters. Few of the other newspapers were content to leave it at that. By the evening of December 9, as Blake stood up again to address a banquet given by the medical faculty of the University of Toronto, the air crackled about him with the echoes of lively phrases. His hearers had come from their homes and favourite journals fortified before the dinner by a diet of printed spleen.

"Alas poor Yorick!" lamented the *Toronto World*, "Mr. Blake has put his foot in it again." In his "doleful, dispiriting tale, conceived on the ultra-humanitarian, peace-at-any-price tone of the Little Englander, of a disbeliever in that great wave of imperial unity now sweeping over the Empire, Mr. Blake trod the Via Dolorosa with crape on his hat for the movement that he himself inaugurated years ago in his Aurora speech."[50] He had come home, said the *Evening Star*, "aching with the dissensions of Irish politics . . . to preach blue ruin."[51] It was no wonder, in the eyes of the *Evening News*, "that the Liberal Government in Ottawa does not want Edward Blake to enter Canadian politics again."[52] The crocodile *Evening Telegram* came in on another tack. "When Edward Blake speaks some people fancy they can hear his disappointed ambition sobbing in every utterance." It was hardly fair or just to an eminent Canadian, it was necessary to respect his sincerity, to "treat him at least as a mistaken fellow countryman and not wrong him by the supposition that he is a sour and disgruntled partisan going about in search of a hole through which he can crawl to the leadership of some Canadian party."[53] There had been much more and it remained for the Hamilton *Spectator*, writing a few days later, to present the summing-up. "Ireland's cause is under one of its periodical eclipses, and now this political carpetbagger turns up again in Canada and tries to earn a foothold by telling the people what a patriot he was to desert it in 1891 . . . When his warning should have been heard, he closed his mouth and carpet-bag and slunk off to Ireland. He thought then that he could serve Ireland better by his presence. Canada thinks so now."[54]

With all this in print or bound for the presses, Blake standing at the banquet table was framing his last nuance. His complex intimations to the great Canadian constituency must be brought to their final point. It must inform but not press, it must induce its own deductions, and they were to mean to a waiting people that it could have Blake back on terms. He would never be minister in a cabinet, he would never again be leader of a political party; these were the things which "I have always detested, have kept away from when possible, and have got away from as soon as possible."[55] But it would be far different under other and better conditions. Delayed though it might be, difficult though it might be, the return as a free servant, serving in the House of Commons, was still as it had been at Strathroy, "the dearest aspiration of my life".[56]

He woke next morning to open the still-damp *Globe.* Its report was mildly but not fatally garbled; for discerning readers the sense of the speech was there. But the headline crushed it out, brutal and heavy-handed, destroying the hopes of months. "Mr. Blake's Intentions. Will Not Return to Canadian Public Life. A Definite Statement."[57]

His anguished protest to Willison was met with flustered apology, and the correction appeared next day: "The newspaper reports of Mr. Blake's speech at the dinner of the medical faculty of the University, and particularly the headlines, do not correctly represent what Mr. Blake said. He did not say he would not return to public life in Canada. He did say that he would not resume the leadership of a political party in Canada; but he has repeatedly spoken in distinct terms of his readiness to serve as an independent Liberal member of the Canadian parliament."[58]

"Pray," Blake had begged, "let it be as brief as possible, but also as decisive."[59] It was all that but it was late, and could not undo the harm. *Teutonic* waited in New York, and there was no delaying outcry. There were no remonstrances from Laurier and there could be now no help from Mowat. He had resigned as Minister of Justice and the man in his place was Mills, always friendly in letters yet somehow a little remote, unable to arrange a meeting. One no longer thought of Cartwright though Cartwright thought of Blake, and delivered his sour epitaph in a letter to John Willison. "All that I can say of it," he wrote, commenting on the Strathroy speech, "is that it is charitable to believe that his memory has failed him in a very great number of particulars. On the whole the best course, I think, is to ignore him."[60]

There were the well-worn bags to be packed, the familiar

tears and farewells, and the member for South Longford was at sea bound for London. Among the many letters he had despatched in the past month there had been another to West Durham. This time it was to the editor of the Bowmanville *Statesman*, still disposed to be friendly but plagued with a careless typesetter. Or so one wished to believe, for his columns had carried the Strathroy speech with certain portions omitted. "I am going to ask you to do me the great favour of printing the whole of my personal statement, or at any rate of supplying the gap . . . I suppose it is extremely unlikely that I shall ever meet my old friends face to face again, but I think the longer I live the warmer my feeling grows for them, and the more anxious I am that they should retain a kindly recollection of the past . . . my old subscription to the *Statesman* must have expired long ago, and I enclose you a cheque. . . ."[61]

CHAPTER TWELVE

"A WRECK UPON THE SHORE"

THERE WAS NOT to be much more, though he had fifteen years to live. The Irish member continued to serve his party. The London barrister retained his eminence in the profession. The Governor pursued his fees, mortgages, and investments, concerned and consumed with fears and hopes for the family. There were the periods of relentless work, the breakdowns and departures, the trooping-off for holidays and for rest cures on the continent. There were visits home and there were more from home to visit him as the young grew up and travelled. There was Margaret, essence of all, the one unchanging solace. But beyond that were the lees; the wine of life was drawn.

Sammy practiced in London as an intermittent solicitor, all too often on forced leaves for his health. Often his father forced them for the boy was moody and vague, indifferent to his own needs. One could not fathom him, one could not cure him, one could only love him more. He gave love in return, yet it was a troubled, impatient love, resentful of its impositions on paternal bounty and care. He seemed to long for escape, yet the question remained to what; one could only hope that marriage, when it came, might change him.

Sophia was happy in Toronto, and Hume was still involved with the Manning interests. If he was unfulfilled in his career he would have no material worries, and one had to leave it at that. There was no dictating to life, above all to the lives of sons. One sometimes thought of Ned, wishing it were different. He had four young children now and he slogged along in the law firm, with no improvement in his prospects. Brother Sam's son and the sons of the other partners were politely moving ahead. The father could change nothing, yet his own dependence grew. Ned was the essential man, the major link with home. The unending stream of the instructions still went to him; he bought, sold, and supervised, administered and ran the errands; he was the eyes and hands of the man who could not let go. He was easy, generous, selfless; the wailing wall, the comforter, and the composer of family differences, and he had the least means of any. It was not quite fair; it was one of the father's night thoughts; yet still the instructions went, the adjustment remained in prospect. Ned would be cared for some day, but for now what must be, must.

In London there were still lodgings, but in Murray Bay there was change. There was another house, by the beginning of the 1900s, "for a tired old man like me".[1] He did not see it often, and it was Ned who had seen to the building, but the absent father loved it as his own work. Much of it was his own, for he had planned for it, prescribed for it, and altered it in multitudinous detail. It was wide, gawky, and roomy, built for children and grandchildren. It was three stories high, each with a protruding gallery, and it climbed up in defiance of the principles of architecture to a fourth gallery extended above the roofline. It was generally in deplorable taste and it was exactly as Blake wished it, even to the sign at the gate. "The new house," Ned had informed the builder, "is to be called La Caprice, and Mr. Blake has requested me to see that it is generally known by this name."[2] Yet almost two years later, from an inn in the Swiss Alps, the owner wrote with a final alteration. "Thanks for confirmation about the cost of *Le* Caprice. For *Le* Caprice it is, not *La* Caprice . . . I find in Molière and elsewhere that Caprice is *not* feminine. Let the sign I ordered — if it was ever put up — be taken down and put by inside; and let Hume and Georgie know . . . and tell Ethel, and generally correct the error, which is shameful."[3]

As usual, Ned obeyed. It was *Le* Caprice that the grandchildren would remember, along with the summer turmoil when the master and his wife returned. There were the great arrivals from England, the opening of trunks and boxes, the stir of assembling visitors. There were always plentiful gifts to be repaid with dutiful kisses, and on evenings when there were no visitors there was sometimes more than that. There would be the massive form of grandfather, still in his black frock coat, seated in the middle of the floor. There would be growls, screams, laughter, and the glint of light on his spectacles as the children raced around him and his great arms reached out for them, playing "Bear".

Yet it was less and less often that he was to be seen in moods like that. They became the fading memories, dimmer with each return. There were more of the lonely walks, more of the sombre silences and brusque dismissals. Through many hours he was a remote figure on the balcony, that highest balcony reserved for him when he came. One was free of tumult here, one was almost free of thoughts. His own century was gone; there was nothing he could now change. He looked out across the tops of the pine trees to the sweep of the mighty river, letting the new come on.

He had attacked the inspirers of the Jameson Raid, and he detested the Boer War. In February of 1900, when his Irish party moved that the war be brought to an end and the Boer states recognized, he cast his vote for the motion. From his aroused homeland, throbbing with renewed imperialism and cheering on its contingents, a surge of hostile shock waves crossed the Atlantic. For almost the last time, before it was time for the obituaries. Blake was again in headlines. "I suppose," he wrote Ned, as the letters and cuttings came to him, "I am the most unpopular man in Canada."[4]

In the same month he resigned as Chancellor of the University of Toronto. By the end of another year, with his last scholarships paid up, his last gifts fulfilled, he had completed his obligations. "Accordingly my financial relations, as well as all other relations with the University of a special nature are now closed."[5]

He had closed relations and completed his gifts to Wycliffe College and Havergal. He had been President for twenty years of the Toronto General Trusts, and he was now free of that. There was still a "Blakes" dominating the Toronto legal world, but it was severed from its founding partner. The notice of dissolution, in May of 1901, had appeared in all the newspapers. "Of course I am now, or rather my name is now, useless to the firm."[6]

In 1902, with the Boer War concluding, Sammy went off to South Africa in pursuit of rest and change. He returned to London married to an army nurse, an Ontario girl who had served with the Canadian forces. For both partners it was obviously a disaster from the first, only to be eased by frequent separations. The son's moods and phases became darker and less predictable, and there was little else in the London scene to improve the mood of his father. There was always Irish politics and there were often the large cases, but there were long gaps between fees. There had always been, and he had always complained to Ned . . . "I am very short of business" . . . "I have been earning hardly a shilling."[7] Penury was quite imaginary but now it fretted him more, remembering the plans for the family, aching with the thought of Sam. Worry had become a habit like gout and headaches, companion of the old man.

It was February of 1903, after years of rare and all too casual greetings, when cables and letters began to arrive from Laurier. Canada and the United States were disputing the massive question of the Alaska boundary. It was old, involved, and intricate, bespiked with history and geography, and the discovery of gold in the Yukon had added a new dimension. The determination of borders and the control of access to the gold fields had become a dangerous dispute. There was to be a court of arbitration and there was a Canadian brief required. It could only be prepared by Blake, it could only be presented by Blake; there was pressing urgency in Ottawa that Blake accept the commission.

He was instantly alight with the prospect, and he responded in the old way. For three weeks his demands and stipulations and his threats to withdraw a first tentative acceptance went back across the Atlantic. He must have more time than was offered, he must have libraries of information, he distrusted the sketchy promises of staff and assisting counsel. Yet one by one, amid a cloud of soothing rejoinders, each condition was met. He would have all the staff he asked for, his books and documents were on the way from Canada, and Clifford Sifton, the able Minister of the Interior, would serve as his right hand. The fee required had been agreed to, and it was $30,000.

On that point his instructions to Laurier were precise. "I must ask you to give directions that as early as possible in the financial year, and at the latest before the end of July next, I be put in funds here in London to the amount of $5,000. and that $25,000., the balance of my fee, be remitted within the same time to my agent and attorney, Edward F. Blake of Blake, Lash and Cassels, Toronto."[8] There were instructions to Ned, equally precise, regarding the investment of the money; and in the glow of the coming windfall the work on the brief began.

He had promised Laurier the devotion of his "entire energies", and he was more than good as his word. It was to be the greatest case of his life, a large supplement to his means, it might mean a change for Ned. For five months, surrounded by the heaped-up books, the ancient charts and maps, the reports of bygone diplomats, and yellowing, beribboned treaties, he drove his clerks and law officers with the old, demonic force. He was merciless with himself and Sifton and he even conscripted Sammy, in the hope that work might prove a cure for the moods. Alaska devoured everything, there was no relief or distraction; there was time only for an occasional report to Ned. For Willison, the *Globe* and friendship there was now no time at all. The cable came from the editor that Oliver Mowat was dead, the old, devoted companion, the writer of the treasured letter. The *Globe*'s columns, so often besought before, were open to Blake for a word of appreciation.

He would not send it; he had only time for his own incredible reasons. "I am so absolutely severed from the life of the province and have lost so many friends that I feel as good as dead myself, and an old-fashioned reluctance to obtrude myself in public has thus become intensified. . . . I could not do what you asked."[9]

He was well on with the brief by late July. The scrawled notes were becoming the typed drafts, re-turned re-scrawled with masses of new revisions. His hand shook and the papers blurred before him; he had worked at the pace of the old days and he was nearing seventy now. But there was the urge of the great case, the thought of the fat fee. Ned, writing in Toronto, was gently reminding Laurier that the money had not yet come. Laurier was promising to send it. It was required now, for Ned had invested on the strength of it, borrowing funds to do so. On July 31 the cable arrived from England: "Stop investing. Cable round total sum. Don't ask Ottawa funds."[10]

There would be half the fee and the rest must be de-invested, used to repay the loan. "Dear Sir Wilfrid," Blake was writing Laurier that same day, "It is with a very heavy heart that I write to tell you that I have been obliged to give up further association with the Alaska case. I have devoted to it all my time and energies since my retainer, but with ever increasing difficulties . . . at last and within a few days the malady became so acute that my energies and powers of concentration, recollection and continuous application . . . so far failed that I was driven to consult the best physician available."[11] It was severe "*neurasthenia*"; there would have to be six months rest, and it was the least part of the disaster. Whether from the work or marriage, Sammy had collapsed too, and his state was worse than his father's. The six months they were to spend together in Switzerland would not be enough for him. There would be another year in an American sanitarium.

The Alaska boundary question was settled on October 20. Theodore Roosevelt, President of the United States, had said that it would be settled his way, and settled his way it was. Sifton had replaced Blake as the leading Canadian counsel and had presented his case before a board of arbitration on which Elihu Root, the American Secretary of War, and two American senators sat with A. B. Aylesworth and Sir Louis Jetté for Canada and with Lord Alverstone, the Lord Chief Justice, as the representative of Great Britain. It was Alverstone's vote, cast with those of the Americans, that brought the final decision, four to two. For Canada there was to be no access by sea to the Yukon gold fields, and for Roosevelt it was "the greatest diplomatic victory of our time".[12] To Laurier and most Canadians the American big stick, and the old imperial expediencies had cost them their precious strip of Alaska coastline. "The difficulty as I conceive it to be," Laurier told the Commons in words that might have been Blake's, "is that so long as Canada remains a dependency of the British Crown the present powers that we have are not sufficient for the maintenance of our rights."[13] Later and less politely he was to inform a Governor-General that the word "Alverstonize" had acquired as unsavoury a place in the Canadian vocabulary as the word "boycott" in the English."[14] In any event, as it seemed, it had been a foredoomed case. The ailing barrister in Switzerland, though deprived of his great moment and his $15,000, was perhaps as well out of it.

By 1904 he had resumed his usual round, "working at half speed". In October of that year it was extended to new territory. Plagued as usual with his autumn cough and bronchitis, he sailed for St. John's, Newfoundland, on another arbitration. It was "a case in which it is proposed to establish the probable profits, or the net earning of a telegraph line in one country for about half a century to come",[15] and it commanded a substantial fee. Yet still there were needs unmet, hopes unfulfilled, pneumonia, neuralgia, gout, and lessening powers. He was in London again in June of 1905 when the letter came from Ned. The son who had never complained was unhappy and giving up. He was thinking of leaving the law firm, if only he could find a partner. Yet the obvious partner, aching for the opportunity, could not be of service now; the time for that was past. "Ah me, my heart is full to bursting as I write. If I were as I was even 10 years ago I would offer my name and some poor professional help. But my dear boy *I am done*, and can only lie as a wreck upon the shore so far as law is concerned."[16]

There was one last ambition shaping in his mind. If there had been success anywhere — complete and satisfying success — it had been in the sessions of the Judicial Committee of the Privy Council. There was scope for his powers here, the powers were recognized by his equals, and it was a field worthy of the work. Since the days of Aurora thirty years before, he had been groping for some conception of a developing empire. He no longer found it in Imperial Federation, in that dream of the great arbiter, the parliament of many colonies that would legislate round the world. It was not in Chamberlain's hopes for enclosed imperial trade, common imperial defence. The world was too wide, the colonies were too diverse; they had neither common quarrels nor common interests. Yet there was the link of British law, that one majestic gift, somehow binding the whole. The word "Commonwealth" had often figured in his rhetoric, and without conveying much; one could not yet see so far. Yet if Commonwealth there were to be, it would be a Commonwealth based on law, with the freed daughters freely turning to the motherland as the ultimate guide of all.

He had not come easily to the view, as he moved away from his first Toronto Britishness. He had resented Governors-General and rejected British colonialism as much as any. He had been for a while for an ultimate Canadian judicial authority, a Supreme Court that was wholly supreme in Canada. Yet there had always been the old bond, always the old reverence for the best that England might be, and it had grown on him of late years. During the blaring rites of the Jubilee in 1897 he had been mostly silent and morosely thrust aside. He had disliked, distrusted, and feared those legions of the subject peoples, that pride of the armed empire that had gone thundering down the Mall. His own conception of its grandeur he had given three years later.

He had spoken as a colonial member of the British legal profession at a banquet given to visiting American barristers. "Well, my Lord Chancellor," he had said, "the place to which I would like to take our friends of the United States Bench and Bar is a quiet little room in Downing Street, rather dingy, with no pretence about it, where they would see sometimes six or seven, sometimes four or five gentlemen, without wigs, without gowns, dressed in morning apparel, not sitting under the names of judges but hearing the prosy arguments . . . and dealing with questions arising under the laws of very nearly seventy distinct political communities, each flying the British flag . . . in Europe, in Africa, in Asia, in America, in Australia, and including in their systems various laws, law from the ancient customs of France, the old customs of the Monarchy, the Civil Law, the Roman, Dutch law, the Brahminical laws, the laws of the Mahomedans — all disposed of in this dingy room. I know no greater, no more practical, no more significant proof of the vitality of the British Empire."[17]

It was in that dingy room, amid that quiet of exalted equals, that a man called could serve his country and the empire. He wanted the call now, and felt it was his for the asking. It was a matter for arrangement by Laurier as Prime Minister of Canada, but there would be few difficulties there. Nor was there prospect of anything here but a respectful welcome. The London *Morning Post*, writing of the Privy Council as a bond of imperial unity, had discussed the appointment of resident colonial judges and suggested the name of Blake. The noble jurists themselves were warm and pressing. Lord Herschell had said to a friend "very emphatically, that I had no equal in argument at the English bar."[18] "Will you not join us?" another of the Lords had asked him.[19]

He came home late in July of 1905, nursing the idea along with his fatigues and ailments. From Toronto Ned came down, obviously tired too, to join him at Murray Bay. They worried together about Sammy who was better now and out of his sanitarium, but resting in the southern states. They talked of Ned's own difficulties, but only with the usual result. They talked long of the hope of the new appointment and the prospective letter to Laurier. Then with the needs of the business shortening his summer holiday, Ned went back to Toronto.

He had seemed frail and even a little unwell, but it was a family inured to that. One worried and went on working, and there was now the letter to write. By August 30 it was done. It was again to "My dear Laurier". The stiff "My dear Sir Wilfrid" that had marked some earlier exchanges had gone with the Alaska case. It had been a disappointment shared; nothing could have been more tactful, more filled with regretful sympathy, than Laurier's handling of that. One was writing again to a friend, the old man to the aging.

The suggestion of the *Morning Post* had just been reprinted in the *Globe*, and it was the immediate cause of the letter. But the idea was older than that. It would involve a request, transmitted by the Canadian government, for a Canadian jurist to be called to the Privy Council. Blake's name had been mentioned and had been favourably received by many. He mentioned his invitations from some of the present Lords and the opinion expressed by one "that there was nothing to interfere with the power of the Crown to appoint to the Privy Council and to summon any Privy Councillor to the Judicial Committee." The salary for present Law Lords was £5,000 per year, but it would not be so with Blake. He was as firm now on that matter as he had been in pursuit of fees; he would accept no salary at all. "No money is involved."[20]

There was the entanglement of parliament and politics, and he was still besought to remain with the Irish party. For five years now its factions had been reunited under John Redmond, and Redmond had need of Blake. With the Irish cause strengthening and a Conservative government falling, there was the immediate prospect of another general election. Blake would be expected to stand for South Longford, he had no doubt of his election, and he felt himself bound in duty to serve as long as he could. But he had had to give up his law practice, and he feared the strain of the sessions. "I must own to you that I gravely doubt whether I can stand the night work . . . my impression is that I shall find myself obliged very soon — far sooner than I wished or expected — to give up parliament."[21]

If he did, what then? He could have his home in Toronto, and his pied-à-terre in London. He could commute as he had done for years on the large, important cases and the fees would pay him well. He would always be the man in demand, always the potential earner, but he was almost done with that.

"I own I would greatly prefer, when obliged to leave parliament, to give the last of my life to our own country, for which I laboured while I could in days gone by . . . I have not the least wish or claim to interfere with the legitimate aspirations of others who have borne the burden and heat of the day in Canada. But it does not seem to me that a mere summons to the Privy Council with a view to judicial work, without indemnity of any kind, could interfere with any other plan or person. And as I could in my simple way of living manage the financial part for a few years, this is what I should be very ready to do."[22]

There was a different summons while he was still reviewing the proposal. It would be November 9 before his letter was mailed. For over two months it lay forgotten on his desk, while he and Margaret agonized in Toronto. The tired son had been more than overworked, more than merely depressed, more than suffering from the usual Blake ailments. "Leukemia" — one had hardly even heard of it, but it was the name of Ned's disease. It ran its course and he was dead.

There was nothing wanting in Laurier when the letter finally reached him. For the bereaved friend there was all he asked and more. The Supreme Court was open to him. "The feeling is universal that nothing would so strengthen the Court as your acceptance of its presidency as Chief Justice." On the other hand, if Blake preferred the appointment to the Privy Council, "let me assure you that the Government here will be only too happy to secure your services in such a high and important capacity, and we will at once make application to the Imperial authorities."[23]

It was a reply to a benumbed man who had cleared his desk from habit, and who replied again from habit. The new letters to Laurier were in the way of the old Blake, turning in the old grooves. "Blow after blow has fallen upon us."[24] There was no Ned, the mother of the four children was in a state of total collapse, Margaret had given way. For over two months more, amid the chaos of distracted homes, Blake pondered, delayed, obstructed, and reconsidered. There would perhaps, after all, be constitutional difficulties in the way of the new appointment. He had been re-elected in his absence as the member for South Longford; there were the urgent pleas of the Irish and the claims of conflicting duties. There were a widow and four children now, increasing his responsibilities. As to the Supreme Court of Canada he had only one wish, prevailing and automatic, "that at a convenient time it should be made known that this honour, which I was regretfully obliged to decline, had been proposed to me."[25] For the rest it hardly mattered, and he had no strength left to decide; the worn paths were the easier. By February of 1906 he had returned to the chills of London.

By the autumn he was back in Canada, fiddling with dusty papers. "I have been engaged," he wrote Laurier from the study on Jarvis Street, "in the task — rather melancholy in the majority of cases — of re-reading all, and destroying the great bulk of my Canadian political correspondence"[26] . . . "I send you by concurrent post . . . some speeches on constitutional questions, colonial questions and points of parliamentary practice which I have got together. I know of nothing deader than dead speeches. . . . "[27] It was true, Laurier replied, but the rule was not absolute. "I read again your speech on the Pacific scandal and I can truly say that my enthusiasm was almost as great as when I read it first many years ago, before I knew you and before I had entered Parliament."[28]

"Almost", that inevitable word. Inevitably enthusiasm dwindled as the band of the friends decreased. There were no longer letters from Mills; Mills was dead. Edgar had died as Speaker of the House of Commons. Mackenzie was long dead and he had hardly died as a friend, yet one thought of him as that now. "Most of my old friends and contemporaries have joined the majority."[29] For the few, the living and loyal, the rememberers of the old scars, there were still unwearying discussions and the mounds of yellowing reprints. "These things were explained by me in my West Durham letter, of which I send you a copy."[30]

"I leave for England in time for the session of 1907."[31] How many times before had he written the same words, with only the year changed? There was the January voyage eastward, the search for London lodgings, the rush and renewal of politics with Liberals again in power. There was an Irish party revivified under Redmond, and there were the hopes of Campbell–Bannerman for Home Rule "step by step". And for Blake it was abruptly over. On May 24 came the "effusion of blood on the brain".[32] On May 26 his letter went to Redmond. With "paralysis of the left arm and leg, with some other minor consequences . . . I *must* go."[33]

It was late July before he could be allowed to travel, and August when he reached Toronto. At the railway station, as he was lifted from the coach in his wheel chair and installed in the waiting carriage, Sammy walked beside him. The companion on the voyage from London, Sammy had escaped at last to responsibility; he was the man who had taken charge.

The last home on Jarvis Street was to be Number 449. It had been Ned's house but Blake had bought it from the widow, who wished to return to her family home in Port Hope. It would provide funds, along with more he provided, for the raising of the four children. It stood then across from Havergal College, but it would be sold and times would change. It is now known as the Celebrity Club, across from the CBC. Actors, writers, and comedians, political commentators, and pop-singers are there renowned and recognized, but it knows not Edward Blake.

"I . . . appoint . . . Samuel Verschoyle Blake and Professor George M. Wrong my literary executors in order that some selections from my political despatches and writings, and from my political, university, legal and other speeches may be published in a popular form."[34] It was all he proposed to leave of himself, and the project was not completed. Whatever the work had meant, whatever he had been or done, must be found ingrained in the nation.

His first memory in life, he once said, was of the Lower Canada rebellion. He would then have been four years old. He had matured as man and lawyer with the maturing of Confederation, and his work began with the opening of the first parliament. He had prepared himself for the making, and his hopes were centred then, on the new Dominion of Canada. He welcomed it with clear eyes — with clearer eyes than most — and endeavoured for half a lifetime to expound and impose his view. It was the one goal, and the sum of his final failure. Through more than a quarter-century he was the man marked out as a leader, the man that leaders looked to. There was no phase of development, there was not a facet of nationhood with which he was not commandingly concerned. Yet at too many vital crossroads he was the man of the other way.

He had no illusions, as Macdonald had, that the shape of

federalism was temporary, that time and growth and manoeuvring would dilute the essence of the pact. He had no hope, and he had no wish, for the reduction of provincial powers, the super-imposed unity, the "strength" of central rule. What strength there was in the nation had come from a common wish, a pooling of common interests. They were far too vaguely established, they had been perhaps proclaimed too soon; and standing quite apart from them was the reservation of others. The provinces were still diverse; there were still the diverse peoples. Blake was a man of Ontario, and he would never forget that. He was the successor of George Brown, he was to be the superseder of Mackenzie, but wide as his ways diverged from them he began as an Ontario Grit. He was jealous for the rights, jealous for the growth, jealous for the needs and character of the people of his own province. Yet he began where Brown left off and he went beyond Mackenzie in his recognition of other interests in Canada. There would be a west one day to be accommodated with all its wild unknowns, there were eastern provinces to be reconciled in union; there would always be, and he accepted them, the unrelenting French. A union made to protect, and itself preserved by, diversity; it was to become a tired cliché. It would be a never-ending problem, it was the perpetual enemy of centralizing, and it was the base of the entire frame. Blake saw that fact and fought for its recognition, and it can be counted one of his victories that the problem is still a hope.

He fought Macdonald to a finish, and was well bloodied in the process, over the granting of better terms to Nova Scotia. At the other end of the country he became the skinflint ogre in the way of British Columbia. What then, of this friend of the diverse provinces? His answer was that he was a friend of union too. Provinces were being bribed by the central government, against the general interest of the Dominion and ultimately against their own. They would be found complaining one day, as the central provinces were complaining in the 1870s, of being milked for gifts and subsidies they were not invited to share. In the matter of Nova Scotia, as it seemed to Blake's contemporaries, he had the thinnest case of all. Yet he did not grudge Joseph Howe that "pension" of two millions that went to the men by the sea. He was a lawyer expounding the real values of a contract, the assurance and permanence of agreements that were openly made and held to. The British North America Act had established the terms of union. It confirmed an agreement made by the four provinces. If there were change it should be by amendment, by the common consent of all. To the founding fathers who had made the Act, and been three years in the process, the thought of re-opening the embroglio was an occasion of raucous laughter. Yet if there had been more discussion then there would have been a saving of breath since, and there would be better accord between the provinces and the central government.

The great myths of the railway duel will always haunt Blake's name. He was the grim, grey parson in the way of high adventure; the block to be overridden for the sake of the national dream. The explored realities point to something else. In 1873, when he brought down a government, there was a corrupt bargain with a sleazy entrepreneur; there was neither plan nor means. It was the work of the next five years, for the men who had made the bargain, to squirm away from its terms. Meanwhile building went on, approved and supported by Blake, in a government dominated by Blake. The eastern provinces were knitted together by rail, the road was opened to settlement in Manitoba, the west beyond was mapped.

Macdonald returned with his National Policy, his new plans for the railway and his drums against the Americans. All of it Blake opposed. It was all linked to the idea of the closed-off continent, the eternally competing nationhoods, the war of friends and cousins. He was for roads but he was not for walls, and he would have used American roads, as Americans used Canadian. There would have been inter-locking traffic, there would have been open competition, and there would have been an equal chance for Canadians to draw from the American west.

There were not two million people yet in the western states along the Canadian border. They had been drawn from a dozen nations and they were hardly yet of any; they had come for land and grain. It would be the same with the new Canadians, those English, Russian, German, and Scandinavian-speakers, when they filled the neighbouring north. Here was the immediate problem and the immediate opportunity; British Columbia could wait. The men of the central prairies should not be the pawns of nationhood, they should be served by common steel, reaching west as required. They would farm as neighbours and they could ship their grain as neighbours, without regard for the flag. But the flag came to prevail; Blake was brushed aside. And he saw the results he had said he would in the early 1890s. Over-strained, over-taxed, pulled apart by its regionalisms rather than drawn together, the junior partner of the Americans went out on the search for trade.

Trade policy, for Blake, had been shaped by the framing of the National Policy and the building of the Pacific Railway. He had wanted a compact east, a decade of intensive growth, a move from strength toward freer trade with the Americans. Instead there had been the wall, and the industries grown behind it, to be sustained only by protection. Along the line of the railway there was the over-extended country, demanding and devouring an investment it would not repay for years. For both needs tariffs were the only answer. It had been imposed by the other man, but was equally a fact for Blake. He was almost as cool as Macdonald toward the hope of reciprocity. If he was less cool toward Commercial Union with the Americans, he at least believed with Macdonald that it was not a possibility. He was caught with the old man in the same dilemma and stalemate, and it would hold to the end for both. The one was to die in harness and the other depart from politics with none of the problems solved. They remained to confront Laurier, to perplex his years in power; and the attempt at a great solution would be a major cause of his fall. There could be no great solution, no swift severing of the knot; only a slow unravelling that would be work for generations. Blake with his stiff pomposities and his grey deliberation had foreshadowed the actual course.

He taught Laurier and he learned from him, and the rich exchange was a major gift to the country. The speech on Political Liberalism, made in Quebec in 1877, was Laurier's answer to the interfering priest. On at least two occasions, as he prepared to deal with interfering Orangemen, Blake wrote for copies of the speech. The two men echoed each other in their respect for religious opinion, their respect for temporal concerns, and their firm demand for the separation of each. Blake was English as Ontario, Laurier French as Quebec, yet they accommodated on Riel and they bridged the rift in the country. They shared trust, they bred trust, and their own enduring relationship was a bond between distrustful peoples. It was a guide for colony and empire at the great councils in London, though they were observed by then from a distance by a half-forgotten lawyer. The Prime Minister of Canada, tracing the course of a new imperial relationship, was using the chart of Blake.

The man goes down in the history books as a tragic, brooding failure, frozen away from his kind. It is a half-truth but it is true of the central fact, measured by his own rule. Laurier of the sunny ways, Laurier the all-adaptable, knew as much as Blake of the bitter fruits of politics and the dregs of lost endeavour. What he did not know was the image formed in the womb, the generations before it, the frame of growth and training. The child born on the backwoods plot in Ontario had the wars and the changed religions and the griefs of Ireland in his genes. He had the guilts and prides of the gentry, the sense of place and privilege, and the God of the Evangelicals to see that he kept his place. He had the Victorian Toronto establishment as his ever-surrounding ambience, and he had William Hume Blake and Catherine Blake as mentors. Driven, prayed, and provided for, seething with worth and duty, he rose in his own closed circle to his own conception of himself. All doors opened easily, he required means and success, and

Providence soon complied. Pre-eminence became his portion, his goal, his fate, and his goad. There could be no escape from destiny and there could be no rest in the pursuit. It broke, rebuffed, and bewildered him for there were common men to be dealt with, coarse and demanding, sinful and stupid, bawdy and corrupt men. They would accept him on their terms, but they would never comply with his. He could give them love as a redeemer, but he could not like them as a man. They were the rubbery mass of politics, the ooze that would not mould. Or not to his hand, not in his time. Yet the coming home in the wheel chair, the useless left leg, and the lonely study on Jarvis Street were not the sum of it all. He had seen much and he had said much that would shape the future shapers; there would be his mark on the clay.

"We have not communicated since more than 3 years ago." The letter went to Laurier on December 15, 1909, a wavering scrawl in pencil. "Politics which used to engage me" was now a distant echo; he was writing on behalf of his secretary who would require a new position. Laurier's reply was back with the next mail. There would be instant consideration but there was the question of the girl's name; Blake had forgotten to mention it. He apologized and sent the name, sending the last note. "My wife joins me in new year's greetings. I cannot hope ever to see you again."[35]

He walked a little now, but for the most part sat in his study with a nurse always in attendance. That summer, and the summer of the year before, there had been visits to Murray Bay. There had been the breath of the river again, the balcony at Le Caprice, the special railway car provided by the Prime Minister. There had been the family and the growing children. "Grandfather walked through the drawing room and up to his room" . . . he has been sitting on all his verandahs . . . "he seems wonderfully well" . . . "he seems delighted to be here. . . ."[36]

The next spring came, however, and "my disease which follows the slowly appointed course"[37] had imposed its limitations. There were the four walls of the study, the window looking on Jarvis Street and the ranks of books and dockets. The memories recalled by the grandchildren were now of a grey recluse, often formidable and grim, sometimes strangely kind, reading papers and destroying them, putting the files away. The general election came in 1911 — again on reciprocity — echoing the old cries, changed with the inevitable changing, and bringing Laurier's downfall. He grieved for Laurier but could now no longer write; one of the family wrote for him, sending love.

The end came on March 1, 1912, at the close of another long day in the study. He roused himself for the trip to the adjoining bedroom, and the nurse moved to help him. At the door he paused, wavered, and abruptly sank in a chair. "I am feeling very sick."[38] In another hour, with Margaret and the family round him, he had passed to join the majority.

For the last time, and in satisfying profusion, the newspapers ran their headlines and the columns filled with his photographs. He had loved photographs, of himself, the family, the children, of every familiar scene. Above all, of Murray Bay, and of the gatherings and places there. "Imagine," said one granddaughter, "a man who wanted every room of his house photographed!"[39] He had vanities enough but there was not vanity in this; it was a grasping at the loved moment, a holding to cherished things. There had always been too much work, always too much to think of, always too little time really to enjoy them. They were all relinquished now, left behind to the minority. Humewood stood with its echoes and its solitude and decay. The study waited on Jarvis Street for the oncoming celebrities. The high, ugly balcony jutting from Le Caprice looked out across snowy pine woods and the river bound for the sea.

A NOTE ON SOURCES

The Blake Papers in the Ontario Provincial Archives have been a principal source of material for this work. So have other collections in the Public Archives of Canada, such as the Laurier Papers, Alexander Mackenzie Papers, and others. A large selection of Blake letters and other documents made by the late Professor Frank H. Underhill and deposited with the Public Archives of Canada was made available to me through the kindness of Mrs. Underhill and Professor H. Blair Neatby. Members of the Blake family have supplied me with a history in manuscript, largely concerned with the life of William Hume Blake, and with a number of private letters and other papers. Archivists in charge of various other collections have been consulted, and have been kind and cooperative.

For the work of research in the larger collections I have had extensive help, made possible by a grant from The Canada Council. Mr. Peter Yurkiw of the Public Archives of Canada and Mrs. Marion Beyea of the Public Archives of Ontario have been unwearying and invaluable assistants. M. Marcel Caya gave much help in investigating Blake's correspondence where it was concerned with Quebec politics, Mr. Daniel Livermore supplied me with material on Alexander Mackenzie, and Mr. Alan Bowker provided a special study of Blake's relations with the University of Toronto. Through the kindness of Mr. Arthur Pattillo and Mr. W. O. Chris Miller of Blake, Cassels and

Graydon, I was given access to considerable material on Blake held by the firm.

I should like here to acknowledge the assistance of Mr. Edward Phelps, Regional History Librarian of the University of Western Ontario; M. Jacques Prémont, Directeur de la Bibliothèque de la Législature, Québec; Mr. D. W. Rudkin, University Archivist, Department of Rare Books, University of Toronto Library; Dr. C. Bruce Ferguson, Provincial Archivist, Public Archives, Nova Scotia; Mr. K. R. MacPherson, Supervisor of Private Manuscripts, Public Archives of Ontario; Miss Edith Firth of the Baldwin Room of the Toronto Public Library; and Professor Henry C. Klassen of the University of Calgary. My thanks go to the numerous members of the Blake family who have patiently endured questioning, and to the equally patient business officers of the Department of History, University of Toronto — Miss Eileen Utterson, Mrs. Geraldine Rerup and Mrs. Erene Stanley.

Manuscript sources consulted are given below:

BP Blake Papers, in Ontario Public Archives and University of Toronto. (All references in the notes are to the Public Archives of Ontario.)

BFP Blake Family Papers, presently retained in the possession of the family.

BFH Refers to the manuscript history of the Blake family, a copy of which is among the Blake papers in the Ontario Archives.

PAC Public Archives of Canada
George Brown Papers
William Buckingham Papers
Carnarvon Papers
Charles Clarke
Dufferin Papers
Hayes Family Papers
Laurier Papers
John A. Macdonald Papers

John Sandfield Macdonald
Alexander Mackenzie Papers
R. W. Scott Papers
Goldwin Smith Papers
Sir John Thompson Papers
F. H. Underhill Papers
J. S. Willison Papers
Record Group 13 (Department of Justice), 1867-1906

OA Public Archives of Ontario
Sir Alexander Campbell Papers, 1855-1908
Cartwright Family Papers, 1779-1913
J. D. Edgar Papers
Sir E. W. Grier Papers
T. C. Patteson Papers
Goldwin Smith Papers

David Mills Papers — University of Western Ontario
A. G. Jones Papers — Public Archives of Nova Scotia
W. S. Fielding Papers — Public Archives of Nova Scotia
Lande Collection, McLennan Library, McGill University (various pamphlet reprints of Blake speeches)
Newspaper sources consulted are generally indicated by the notes.

Of the published materials, those continually at hand for much of the work were such books as *Alexander Mackenzie: Clear Grit* by Dale C. Thomson; *Brown of The Globe* by J. M. S. Careless: *John A. Macdonald* by Donald Creighton; *Canada, 1874-1896: Arduous Destiny* by Peter B. Waite; and, particularly in relation to tariff questions, *Canada's National Policy, 1883-90* by Robert Craig Brown. *Edward Blake: Irish Nationalist* by Margaret A. Banks, was indispensable in dealing with Blake's years as a member of the British parliament and must still be consulted as a study of his actual involvement with the Home Rule movement. Also much consulted were the many writings on Blake by the late Frank H. Underhill.

A list of the principal secondary sources follows:

ADAMS, C. MERCER. *Canada's Patriot Statesman: Sir John A. Macdonald.* Toronto: Parrish, 1891.

ARMSTRONG, CHRISTOPHER. "The Mowat Heritage in Federal-Provincial Relations." In *Oliver Mowat's Ontario,* edited by Donald Swainson, Toronto: Macmillan, 1972.

BANKS, MARGARET A. *Edward Blake, Irish Nationalist: A Canadian Statesman in Irish Politics, 1892-1907.* Toronto: University of Toronto Press, 1957.

———. "The Change in Liberal Party Leadership: 1887." *Canadian Historical Review,* June 1957.

———. "Edward Blake's Relations with Canada During His Irish Career, 1892-1907." *Canadian Historical Review,* March 1954.

BARTHE, ULRIC. *Wilfrid Laurier on the Platform.* Quebec: Turcotte & Ménard, 1890.

BERTON, PIERRE. *The National Dream.* 2 vols. Toronto: McClelland & Stewart, 1970, 1971.

BIGGAR, C. R. W. *Sir Oliver Mowat,* 2 vols. Toronto, 1905.

BORDEN, ROBERT LAIRD. *Memoirs.* 2 vols. Toronto: Macmillan, 1938.

BOWKER, ALAN FRANKLIN. "Edward Blake and the University of Toronto, 1863-1900." Thesis in preparation.

BOYD, JOHN. *Sir George Etienne Cartier, Bart.* Toronto: Macmillan, 1917.

BROWN, ROBERT CRAIG. *Canada's National Policy, 1883-1900: A Study in Canadian-American Relations.* Princeton, N.J.: Princeton University Press, 1964.

BUCKINGHAM, WILLIAM, and ROSS, HON. GEORGE W. *The Honourable Alexander Mackenzie: His Life and Times.* Toronto, 1892.

BURKE, SISTER TERESA AVILA. "Mackenzie and His Cabinet, 1873-8." *Canadian Historical Review,* June 1960.

CARELESS, J. M. S. *Brown of The Globe.* 2 vols. Toronto: Macmillan, 1959, 1963.

———. "Frontierism, Metropolitanism and Canadian History." *Canadian Historical Review,* March 1954.

———. *The Union of the Canadas, 1841-1857.* Toronto: McClelland & Stewart, 1967.

———, ed. *Colonists and Canadians, 1760-1867.* Toronto: Macmillan, 1971.

———, and BROWN, ROBERT CRAIG, eds. *The Canadians, 1867-1967.* Toronto: Macmillan, 1967.

CARRINGTON, PHILIP. *The Anglican Church in Canada.* Toronto: Collins, 1963.

CARTWRIGHT, SIR RICHARD. *Reminiscences.* Toronto: Briggs, 1912.

COLLINS, J. E. *Canada Under the Administration of Lord Lorne.* Toronto: Rose, 1884.

CREIGHTON, DONALD. *Canada's First Century.* Toronto: Macmillan, 1970.

———. *John A. Macdonald.* 2 vols. Toronto: Macmillan, 1952, 1955.

———. "The Victorians and the Empire." *Canadian Historical Review,* June 1938. Reprinted in Donald Creighton, *Towards the Discovery of Canada.* Toronto: Macmillan, 1972.

CROWFOOT, A. H. *Benjamin Cronyn, First Bishop of Huron.* Incorporated Synod of the Diocese of Huron, 1957.

CURNOE, LORNE J. "John Charlton and Canadian-American Relations." M.A. thesis, University of Toronto, 1938.

DAFOE, JOHN W. *Laurier: A Study in Canadian Politics.* Toronto: Thomas Allen, 1922.

DALES, J. H. *The Protective Tariff in Canada's Development.* Toronto: University of Toronto Press, 1966.

DAVIN, N. F. *The Irishman in Canada.* Toronto: MacLean, 1877.

DAWSON, R. M. "The Gerrymander of 1882." *Canadian Journal of Economics and Political Science,* May 1935.

DENISON, G. T. *Soldiering in Canada.* Toronto, 1900.

———. *The Struggle for Imperial Unity.* London, 1909.

DENT, JOHN CHARLES. *Canadian Portrait Gallery.* Toronto: Magurn, 1880.

DURAND, CHARLES. *Reminiscences of Charles Durand of Toronto, Barrister.* Toronto: Hunter-Rose, 1897.

FIRESTONE, O. J. *Canada's Economic Development, 1867-1953.* London: Bowes, 1953.

FOSTER, W. A. *Canada First, or Our New Nationality.* Pamphlet. Toronto: Adam, Stevenson, 1871.

FRASER, BARBARA. "The Political Career of Sir Hector-Louis Langevin." *Canadian Historical Review,* June 1961.

GLAZEBROOK, G. P. de T. *Life in Ontario: A Social History.* Toronto: University of Toronto Press, 1968.

GRAHAM, W. R. "Liberal Nationalism in the 1870's." Canadian Historical Association *Report*, 1946, pp. 101-19.

———. "Sir Richard Cartwright." PH D. thesis, University of Toronto, 1950.

———. "Sir Richard Cartwright, Wilfrid Laurier and Liberal Party Trade Policy, 1887." *Canadian Historical Review*, March 1952.

GRAYDON, ALAN. *Some Reminiscences of Blake's.* Privately printed, 1970.

HAM, GEORGE H. *Reminiscences of a Raconteur.* Toronto: Musson, 1921.

HEISLER, J. P. "Sir John Thompson. PH D thesis, University of Toronto, 1955.

HODGINS, BRUCE W. *John Sandfield Macdonald.* Toronto: University of Toronto Press, 1971.

HOPKINS, J. CASTELL. *The Life and Work of Sir John Thompson.* Toronto: United Publishing Houses, 1895.

HOUGHAM, G. M. "Canada First: A Minor Party in Microcosm." *Canadian Journal of Economics and Political Science,* May 1953.

de KIEWIET, C., and UNDERHILL, F. H. *The Dufferin-Carnarvon Correspondence.* Toronto: Champlain Society, 1955.

KLASSEN, HENRY CORNELIUS. "L. H. Holton, Montreal Businessman and Politician, 1817-67." PH D thesis, University of Toronto, 1970.

LANDON, FRED. "The Canadian Scene, 1880-90." Canadian Historical Association *Report*, 1942, pp. 5-18.

LANGTON, W. A., ed. *Early Days in Upper Canada: Letters of John Langton from the Backwoods of Upper Canada.* Toronto: Macmillan, 1926.

LEDERLE, J. W. "The Liberal Convention of 1893." *Canadian Journal of Economics and Political Science*, February 1950.

LONGLEY, J. W. "Reminiscences." *Canadian Magazine*, October 1920-February 1921.

LOUDON, J. W. "Edward Blake." *University of Toronto Monthly*, May 1912.

———. Manuscript of unpublished autobiography in the University of Toronto Archives.

LOWER, ARTHUR. *Canadians in the Making.* Toronto: Longmans Green, 1958.

———. *Colony to Nation.* Toronto: Longmans Green, 1946.

MAC DONALD, NORMAN. *Canada: Immigration and Colonization, 1841-1903.* Toronto: Macmillan, 1966.

MAC INTOSH, A. W. "The Career of Sir Charles Tupper in Canada, 1864-1900." PH D thesis, University of Toronto, 1960.

MAC KIRDY, K. A. "The Loyalty Issue in the 1891 Federal Election Campaign and an Ironic Footnote." *Ontario History*, September 1963.

MAC NUTT, W. S. *Days of Lorne.* Fredericton: Brunswick, 1955.

———. "The 1880's." In *The Canadians, 1867-1967*, edited by J. M. S. Careless and R. Craig Brown. Toronto: Macmillan, 1967.

MAXWELL, J. A. "Lord Dufferin and the Difficulties with British Columbia." *Canadian Historical Review*, December 1931.

MORRISON, J. C. "Oliver Mowat and the Development of Provincial Rights in Ontario." M.A. thesis, University of Toronto, 1947.

MORTON, W. L. *The Critical Years: The Union of British North America, 1857-1873.* Toronto: McClelland & Stewart, 1964.

———. *Manitoba: A History.* Toronto: University of Toronto Press, 1967.

NEATBY, H. BLAIR. "Laurier and a Liberal Quebec." M.A. thesis, University of Toronto, 1956.

———, and SAYWELL, JOHN T. "Chapleau and the Conservative Party in Quebec." *Canadian Historical Review*, March 1956.

Ontario Historical Society. *Profile of a Province: Stability and Progress in Ontario*, 1967.

ORMSBY, MARGARET. "Prime Minister Mackenzie, the Liberal Party and the Bargain with British Columbia." *Canadian Historical Review*, June 1945.

OSTRY, BERNARD. "Conservatives, Liberals and Labour in the 1870's." *Canadian Historical Review*, June 1960.

POPE, JOSEPH. *The Correspondence of Sir John A. Macdonald.* Toronto: Oxford, 1921.

———. *Memoirs of the Right Honourable Sir John Alexander Macdonald.* 2 vols. Ottawa: J. Durre & Sons, 1894.

POPE, MAURICE, ed. *Public Servant: The Memoirs of Sir Joseph Pope.* Toronto: Oxford, 1960.

PRESTON, W. T. R. *My Generation of Politics and Politicians.* London: Eveleigh Nash, 1915.

READ, D. B. *Lives of the Judges.* Toronto: Rowsell & Hutchison, 1888.

ROSS, G. W. *Getting into Parliament and After.* Toronto: Briggs, 1913.

ROSS, P. D. *Retrospects of a Newspaper Person.* Toronto: Oxford, 1931.

SAGE, W. N. "Federal Parties and Provincial Groups in British Columbia, 1871-1903." *British Columbia Historical Quarterly,* April 1948.

SAYWELL, JOHN T. "The Crown and the Politicians: The Canadian Succession Question, 1891-6." *Canadian Historical Review,* December 1956.

———. "The 1890's." In *The Canadians, 1867-1967,* edited by J. M. S. Careless and R. Craig Brown. Toronto: Macmillan, 1967.

———, ed. *The Canadian Journal of Lady Aberdeen.* Toronto: Champlain Society, 1960.

SHRIVE, NORMAN. *Charles Mair, Literary Nationalist.* Toronto: University of Toronto Press, 1965.

SKELTON, O. D. *The Day of Sir Wilfrid Laurier.* Chronicles of Canada Series. Toronto: Glasgow Brook, 1916.

———. *Life and Letters of Sir Wilfrid Laurier.* 2 vols. Toronto: Oxford, 1921.

SMITH, GOLDWIN. *Reminiscences.* Edited by Arnold Haultain. Toronto: Macmillan, 1910.

STAMP, ROBERT. "The Public Career of Sir James David Edgar." M.A. thesis, University of Toronto, 1962.

STANLEY, GEORGE F. G. *Louis Riel.* Toronto: Ryerson, 1964.

SWAINSON, DONALD, ed. *Oliver Mowat's Ontario.* Toronto: Macmillan, 1972.

THOMSON, DALE C. *Alexander Mackenzie: Clear Grit.* Toronto: Macmillan, 1960.

TUPPER, SIR CHARLES. *Reminiscences of Sixty Years.* London: Cassells, 1914.

TYLER, J. E. *The Struggle for Imperial Unity, 1868-1895.* London, 1938.

UNDERHILL, FRANK H. "Edward Blake." In *Our Living Tradition,* edited by Claude T. Bissell. Toronto: Carleton University and University of Toronto Press, 1957.

———. "Edward Blake and Canadian Liberal Nationalism." In *Essays in Canadian History,* edited by R. Flenley. Toronto: Macmillan, 1939, pp. 3-38.

———. "Edward Blake, the Liberal Party, and Unrestricted Reciprocity." Canadian Historical Association *Report,* 1939, pp. 133-41.

———. "Edward Blake, the Supreme Court Act and the Appeal to the Privy Council." *Canadian Historical Review,* September 1938.

———. *The Image of Confederation*. Reprint by Canadian Broadcasting Corporation of the Massey Lectures, 1963.

———. "Laurier and Blake, 1882-1891." *Canadian Historical Review*, December 1939.

———. "Laurier and Blake, 1891-2." *Canadian Historical Review*, June 1943.

———. "Political Ideas of the Upper Canadian Reformers, 1867-78." Canadian Historical Association *Report*, 1942, pp. 104-15.

———. *In Search of Canadian Liberalism*. Toronto: Macmillan, 1960.

WADE, MASON. *The French Canadians*. Toronto: Macmillan, 1955.

WAITE, PETER B. *Canada, 1784-1896: Arduous Destiny*. Toronto: McClelland & Stewart, 1971.

———. "The 1860's." In *Colonists and Canadians, 1760-1867*, edited by J. M. S. Careless, Toronto: Macmillan, 1971.

———. "Reflections on an Un-Victorian Society." In *Oliver Mowat's Ontario*, edited by Donald Swainson. Toronto: Macmillan, 1972.

WALLACE, ELISABETH. *Goldwin Smith, Victorian Liberal*. Toronto: University of Toronto Press, 1957.

WALLACE, W. STEWART. *The Memoirs of the Rt. Hon. Sir George Foster*. Toronto: Macmillan, 1933.

———. "The Mystery of Edward Blake." *Canadian Magazine*, September 1912.

WARD, NORMAN. "The Formative Years of the House of Commons." *Canadian Journal of Economics and Political Science*, November 1952.

WATT, JAMES T. "Anti-Catholic Nativism in Canada: The Protestant Protective Association." *Canadian Historical Review*, March 1967.

WESTERN, MAURICE. "Edward Blake as Leader of the Opposition, 1880-87." M.A. thesis, University of Toronto, 1939.

WILLISON, SIR JOHN. *Reminiscences Personal and Political*. Toronto: McClelland & Stewart, 1919.

———. *Sir Wilfrid Laurier and the Liberal Party*. Makers of Canada Series, 2 vols. Toronto: Oxford, 1927.

WILSON, BECKLES. *The Life of Lord Strathcona*. London: Cassells, 1915.

YOUNG, JAMES. *Public Life and Public Men in Canada*. 2 vols. Toronto: Wm. Briggs, 1912.

NOTES

CHAPTER ONE

1 *House of Commons Debates*, March 18, 1881, p. 1443.
2 *Ibid.*, pp. 1453-55.
3 Blake Papers (hereafter cited as BP), Laurier to Blake, November 26, 1880.
4 *Ibid.*, Huntington to Blake, January 6, 1881.
5 BP, Pamphlet, *Address to Young Men's Reform Club*, Montreal, March 29, 1881.
6 *Ibid.*
7 *Ibid.*
8 *Ibid.*
9 BP, John Maclaren to Blake, April 8, 1881.
10 PAC, W. E. Buckingham Papers, Mackenzie to Blake, May 31, 1881.
11 BP, Laurier to Blake, May 21, 1881.
12 *Ibid.*, Laurier to Blake, June 3, 1881.
13 Blake Family Papers (hereafter cited as BFP), 283, Blake to Carmichael, June 10, 1881.
14 *Mail* (Toronto), Nov. 22, 1881.
15 *Ibid.*
16 BP, Laurier to Blake, December 7, 1881.
17 *Ibid.*,Mercier to Blake, January 17, 1882.
18 *Ibid.*
19 *House of Commons Debates*, February 9, 1882, pp. 1-2.
20 *Ibid.*, February 10, 1882, p. 14.
21 BP, Mills to Blake, January 2 and January 10, 1882.
22 *Ibid.*, Cartwright to Blake, 2 letters, January 2, 1882.
23 *House of Commons Debates*, April 14, 1882, p. 914.
24 *Ibid.*, p. 919.
25 *Ibid.*, April 20, 1882, pp. 1035-8.
26 *Ibid.*, p. 1046.

27 PAC, Kimberley Papers, PC/B/6, Kimberley to Lorne, May 25, 1882.
28 *House of Commons Debates*, April 21, 1882, pp. 1068, 1073, 1074.
29 BP, Blake to Edgar, April 22, 1882.
30 *House of Commons Debates*, April 28, 1882, p. 1203.
31 *Ibid.*, p. 1207.
32 *Ibid.*, May 8, 1882, p. 1394.
33 *Ibid.*, pp. 1387, 1396.
34 *Ibid.*, p. 1390.
35 *Ibid.*
36 *Globe* (Toronto), May 29, 1882.
37 BFP, 288, Blake to Carmichael, June 25, 1882.
38 BP, Blake to Laurier, July 24, 1882.
39 *Globe*, May 20, 1882.
40 PAC, Macdonald Papers, PP. 185085-7, Robert Armour to Macdonald, December 31, 1882.
41 BP, Laurier to Blake, December 20, 1882.

CHAPTER TWO

1 BP, Blake "my dear friend" (draft), January 2, 1883.
2 W. T. R. Preston, *The Life and Times of Lord Strathcona* (London: Eveleigh Nash, 1915), pp. 151-5.
3 G. Mercer Adam, *Canada's Patriot Statesman: Sir John A. Macdonald* (Toronto: C. R. Parrish & Co., 1891), p. 409.
4 *House of Commons Debates*, February 12, 1883, p. 16.
5 *Ibid.*, March 16, 1883, p. 234.
6 *Ibid.*, p. 237.
7 PAC, Laurier Papers, 160-1, Blake to Laurier, December 1, 1883.
8 *House of Commons Debates*, January 18, 1884, p. 12.
9 *Ibid.*, p. 15.
10 *Ibid.*, February 5, 1884, p. 12.
11 *Ibid.*, p. 127.
12 John W. Dafoe, *Laurier: A Study in Canadian Politics* (Toronto: Thomas Allen, 1922), p. 16.
13 BP, Blake to Carmichael, January 26, 1884.
14 *Ibid.*, Edgar to Blake, March 2, 1884.
15 *Ibid.*, Blake to Edgar, March 3, 1884.
16 *House of Commons Debates*, March 17, 1884, pp. 904-19.
17 Maurice Western, "Edward Blake as Leader of the Opposition." Unpublished MA thesis, University of Toronto, 1939, p. 280.
18 BP, Fiset to Blake, March 29, 1884.
19 *Ibid.*, Blake to Edgar, March?, 1884.
20 *Ibid.*, Edgar to Blake, March 27, 1884.
21 PAC, Laurier Papers, P185-7, Blake to Laurier, May 24, 1884.
22 *Statesman*, (Bowmanville), June 27, 1884.

23 PAC, Macdonald Papers, PP. 195738-40, Prower to Macdonald, June 25, 1884.
24 *Ibid.*
25 *Ibid.*, PP. 122204-7, Stephen to Macdonald, February 29, 1884.
26 PAC, Laurier Papers, 207-15, Blake to Laurier, November 10, 1884.
27 *Ibid.*

CHAPTER THREE

1 BP, Laurier to Blake, December 10, 1883.
2 *House of Commons Debates*, December 10, 1880.
3 OA, Edgar Papers, Edgar to wife, May 3, 1885.
4 Sir Richard J. Cartwright, *Reminiscences* (Toronto: Wm. Briggs, 1912), p. 252.
5 OA, Edgar Papers, Edgar to wife, March 3, 1885.
6 *House of Commons Debates*, June 10, 1885, p. 2560.
7 *Ibid.*, June 17, 1885, p. 2607.
8 *Ibid.*, July 6, 1885, p. 3077.
9 *Ibid.*, p. 3108.
10 *Ibid.*, p. 3110.
11 *Ibid.*, July 7, 1885.
12 BP, Edgar to Blake, July 31, 1885.
13 *Ibid.*, Blake to Edgar, August 1, 1885.
14 *Ibid.*
15 *Ibid.*
16 PAC, Laurier Papers, 207967-70, Blake to Laurier, August 15, 1885.
17 *Ibid.*
18 *Ibid.*
19 *Ibid.*
20 *Ibid.*
21 BP, Blake to Edgar, September 7, 1885.
22 *Ibid.*
23 PAC, A. G. Jones Papers, Mackenzie to Jones, September 18, 1885.
24 PAC, Laurier Papers, Edgar to Laurier, October 5, 1885, pp. 252-4.
25 OA, Edgar Papers, Laurier to Edgar, October 22, 1885.
26 PAC, Laurier Papers, Cartwright to Laurier, October 23, 1885. pp. 275-7.
27 *Ibid.*, Cartwright to Laurier, October 23, 1885, pp. 281-5.
28 *La Presse* (Montreal), November 16, 1885.
29 PAC, Laurier Papers, Edgar to Laurier, November 18, 1885, pp. 286-8.
30 *La Presse*, Nov. 23, 1885.
31 *Ibid.*
32 PAC, Laurier Papers, 207974-6, Blake to Laurier, November 21, 1885.
33 Mason Wade, *The French Canadians* (Toronto: Macmillan, 1968), p. 419.
34 PAC, Laurier Papers, 207958-62, Blake to Laurier, December 27, 1885.

35 *Ibid.*, 207952-7, Blake to Laurier, December 23, 1885.
36 *Ibid.*, 207958-62, Blake to Laurier, December 27, 1885.
37 BFP, Pamphlet, Blake speech, London, Ontario, January 14, 1886.
38 *Ibid.*
39 *Liberal* (Essex, Ont.), Jan. 21, 1886.
40 *Globe*, Jan. 16, 1886.
41 *News* (St. Catharines), Jan. 19, 1886.
42 *Herald* (Guelph), Jan. 15, 1886.
43 *Journal* (Ottawa), Jan. 15, 1886.
44 *Herald* (Bruce), Jan. 20, 1886.
45 *Gazette* (Montreal), Jan. 18, 1886.
46 BP, Scrapbook, no name, no date.
47 *La Patrie* (Montreal), no date.
48 BP, Laurier to Blake, February 10, 1886.
49 *Leader* (Regina), n.d.

CHAPTER FOUR

1 BFP, Mrs. V. Cronyn to Blake, February 11, 1886.
2 *House of Commons Debates*, March 22, 1886, p. 267.
3 *Ibid.*
4 *Ibid.*, March 16, 1886.
5 *Ibid.*, March 19, 1886, p. 237.
6 *Ibid.*, pp. 237-65.
7 Cartwright, *Reminiscences*, p. 265.
8 PAC, Thompson Papers, MG26D-3ca, Vol. 289, pp. 505-6.
9 PAC, Laurier Papers, 208005-7, Blake to Laurier, October 14, 1886.
10 *Ibid.*
11 BP, Laurier to Blake, November 13, 1886.
12 *Toronto World*, December 11, 1886.
13 Ulric Barthe, *Wilfrid Laurier on the Platform* (Quebec: Turcotte & (Ménard, 1890), p. 338.
14 *Ibid.*, p. 310.
15 PAC, Laurier Papers, 208075-6, Blake to Laurier, December 30, 1886.
16 BP, Blake to Mowat, January 8, 1887.

CHAPTER FIVE

1 BP, Blake to Mowat, January 11, 1887.
2 *Ibid.*, Blake to Mowat, January 12, 1887.
3 *Ibid.*, Blake to Mowat, January 9, 1887.
4 BP, Pamphlet 15, *Malvern Speech*, January 22, 1887.
5 *Ibid.*
6 *Ibid.*
7 BP, Pamphlet, *1887 Campaign Speeches*, "Speech at London, Ontario", p. 222.
8 *Ibid.*, Blake to Laurier, January 17, 1887.

9 *Ibid.*, Blake to John Hallam, February 19, 1887.
10 *Ibid.*, Blake to F. A. Lawrence, February 12, 1887.
11 *Ibid.*, Blake to James Somerville, February 24, 1887.
12 *Ibid.*, Laurier to Blake, February 24, 1887.
13 PAC, Laurier Papers, 403-4, Blake to Laurier, February 28, 1887.
14 Margaret A. Banks, "The Change in Liberal Party Leadership, 1887," *Canadian Historical Review*, June 1957, quoting circular in Cartwright Papers, Queen's University, Kingston.
15 Queen's University, Cartwright Papers, 411-8, S. A. Fisher to Laurier, March 6, 1887.
16 *Ibid.*, 427-9, Cartwright to Laurier, March 10, 1887.
17 BP, Laurier to Blake, March 16, 1887.
18 *Ibid.*
19 *Ibid.*, S. H. Blake to Edward Blake, March 14, 1887.
20 *Ibid.*, P. A. Chaquette to Blake, March 12, 1887.
21 *Ibid.*, G. Amyot to Blake, March 15, 1887.
22 *Ibid.*, Amyot to Blake, March 18, 1887.
23 *Ibid.*, M. Beausoleil to Blake, March 15, 1887.
24 *Ibid.*, Draft, March 28, 1887.
25 *Ibid.*
26 PAC, Laurier Papers, 432, Blake to Laurier, March 28, 1887.
27 *Ibid.*, 433, Blake to Laurier, March 28, 1887.
28 *Ibid.*
29 OA, Edgar Papers, Laurier to Edgar, March 29, 1887.
30 BP, Laurier to Blake, April 2, 1887.
31 *House of Commons Debates*, April 13, 1887, p. 2. (Blake went a little far in this. The Speaker of the Canadian House was not accorded to rank of First Commoner.)
32 *Ibid.*, May 26, 1887, p. 569.
33 *Ibid.*, p. 576.
34 O. D. Skelton, *Life and Letters of Sir Wilfrid Laurier* (Toronto: Oxford, 1921), I: 341.
35 *Ibid.*, I: 342.
36 BP, Laurier to Blake, June 10, 1887.
37 *Ibid.*, Laurier to Blake, June 18, 1887.
38 BFP, Blake to Carmichael, September 21, 1887.
39 BP, Laurier to Blake, July 14, 1887.
40 BFP, Blake to Carmichael, September 21, 1887.
41 *Ibid.*, Blake to (Margaret?), partial letter, undated.
42 *Ibid.*, Blake to Margaret, November 13, 1887.
43 *Ibid.*, Blake to Sophia or Margaret, December 4, 1887.
44 *Ibid.*
45 *Ibid.*
46 *Ibid.*, Blake to Sophia, November 24, 1887.
47 *Ibid.*, Blake to Margaret or Sophia, November 13, November ?, November 24, December 22, 1887.

48 *Ibid.*, Blake to Margaret, October 25, 1887.
49 PAC, Laurier Papers, 611-6, Blake to Laurier, December 22, 1887.
50 *Ibid.*

CHAPTER SIX

1 BP, Laurier to Blake, January 16, 1888.
2 Skelton, *Life and Letters of Sir Wilfrid Laurier*, 1: 358.
3 *Handbook of Commercial Union*, published by Commercial Union Club of Toronto, 1888. Extract here is quoted from Robert Craig Brown, *Canada's National Policy, 1883-1900* (Princeton, N. J.: Princeton University Press, 1964), *q.v.* for a complete study of the Commercial Union movement.
4 *Globe*, Oct 14, 1887.
5 *Ibid.*, Nov. 15, 22, 29, 1888. Open letters by Edgar addressed to Erastus Wiman.
6 BP, Laurier to Blake, January 16, 1888.
7 BFP, Letters, Edward Blake to family, January 23, 25, and February 6, 1888.
8 *Ibid.*
9 PAC, Laurier Papers, 663-8, Blake to Laurier, March 6, 1888.
10 *Ibid.*
11 BP, Laurier to Blake, March 29, 1888.
12 *Ibid.*
13 PAC, Laurier Papers, Blake to Laurier, May 6, 1888.
14 All material on "The Ontario Lands Case, 1888" is taken from reports in BP. (I am indebted to Senator H. Carl Goldenberg, Q.C., for pointing out references to this case in the recent case of Calder *v.* Attorney-General of British Columbia, involving rights of the Niska Indians.)
15 BFP, Blake to Margaret, July 21, 1888.
16 *Ibid.*, July 25, 1888.

CHAPTER SEVEN

1 *Mail*, Oct. 17, 1887.
2 PAC, Laurier Papers, 208297-301, Cartwright to Laurier, October 25, 1888.
3 BP, Blake to B. E. Swazzie, November 16, 1888.
4 PAC, Laurier Papers, 208330-2, Edgar to Laurier, November 25, 1888.
5 *Ibid.*, 790-2, Cartwright to Laurier, December 10, 1888.
6 *Ibid.*
7 BP, Laurier to Blake, December 15, 1888.
8 *Ibid.*, Laurier to Blake, December 24, 1888.
9 PAC, Laurier Papers, 823-5, Blake to Laurier, January 1, 1889.
10 BP, Blake to Jaffray, Mar 19, 1889.
11 *House of Commons Debates*, April 30, 1890, p. 4217. Blake, quoting letter.

12 *Ibid.*
13 PAC, Laurier Papers, 922-5, Cartwright to Laurier, May 31, 1889.
14 *Ibid.*, 188-93, Blake to Laurier, July, 1889.
15 From a speech delivered by D'Alton McCarthy at Stayner, Ontario, July 12, 1899. Quoted by John Willison, *Sir Wilfrid Laurier* (Toronto: Oxford, 1927), II: 53.
16 PAC, Laurier Papers, 1067-9, Blake to Laurier, September 13, 1889.
17 Ulric Barthe, *Wilfrid Laurier on the Platform* (Quebec: Turcotte & Ménard, 1890), pp. 535ff.
18 PAC, Laurier Papers, 1005-7, Cartwright to Laurier, August 18, 1889.
19 *Ibid.*, 1063-4, Cartwright to Laurier, September 3, 1889.
20 *Ibid.*, 1164-8, Cartwright to Laurier, December 30, 1889.

CHAPTER EIGHT

1 *House of Commons Debates*, February 14, 1890, p. 674.
2 *Ibid.*, p. 670
3 *Ibid.*, 670-88.
4 *Ibid.*, February 18, 1890, pp. 878ff.
5 *Ibid.*, April 29, 1890, p. 4084.
6 *Ibid.*, April 30, 1890, pp. 4210-28.
7 PAC, Laurier Papers, 1244-51, Blake to Laurier, February 24, 1890.
8 *Ibid.*, 1298-1303, Blake to Laurier, June 2, 1890.
9 *Ibid.*, 1304-9, Blake to Laurier, June 15, 1890.
10 *Globe*, July 3, 1890.
11 BP, Laurier to Blake, September 9, 1890.
12 PAC, Laurier Papers, 1446-8, Blake to Laurier, September 13, 1890.
13 BP, Laurier to Blake, December 5, 1890.
14 PAC, Laurier Papers, 208419-20, Cartwright to Laurier, December 13, 1890.
15 BP, Draft Letter, Mowat to Laurier, January 14, 1891.
16 *Ibid.*, Blake to Mowat, January 16, 1891.
17 Willison, *Sir Wilfrid Laurier*, II: 158.
18 D. G. Creighton, *John A. Macdonald* (Toronto: Macmillan, 1955), II: 553.
19 BP, Blake to D. Burke Simpson, January 28, 1891.
20 *Ibid.*
21 *Ibid.*, James Young to Blake, January 28, 1891.
22 Sir John Willison, *Reminiscences Personal and Political* (Toronto: McClelland & Stewart, 1919), p. 230.
23 *Ibid.*, p. 233.
24 BP, Laurier to Blake, February 2, 1891.
25 PAC, Laurier Papers, 1598-1600, Blake to Laurier, February 9, 1891.
26 BP, D. Burke Simpson to Blake, February 10, 1891.
27 *Ibid*, Blake to Simpson, February 11, 1891.
28 *Ibid.*

29 Willison, *Reminiscences*, p. 214.
30 BP, Blake to Wells, February 11, 1891.
31 *Ibid.*, Blake to D. A. Fiset, February 26, 1891.
32 *Ibid.*, Blake to D. Mitchell, February 25, 1891.
33 *Ibid.*, Blake to Willison, February 12, 1891.
34 *Ibid.*, Blake to Wells, February 11, 1891.
35 *Ibid.*, Blake to Willison, February 12, 1891.
36 *Ibid.*, Blake to D. McIntyre, February 26, 1891.
37 *Ibid.*, Blake to Carmichael, February 6, 1891.
38 *Ibid.*, Blake to D. McIntyre, February 26, 1891.
39 *Ibid.*, Blake to Willison, February 12, 1891.
40 *Ibid.*, Blake to Willison, February 27, 1891.
41 *Ibid.*, Laurier to Blake, March 3, 1891.
42 *Ibid.*, Kirkpatrick to Blake, March 3, 1891. See also Lande Collection, McLennan Library, McGill University, Montreal, "Correspondence between Mr. Blake and Mr. Kirkpatrick as to the Inverary Meeting," March 2-5, 1891.
43 *Ibid.*, Blake to Laurier, March 4, 1891.
44 *Ibid.*, Pamphlet, *Letter of Edward Blake to the West Durham Reform Convention*, March 5, 1891, in *Globe*, Mar. 6, 1891.

CHAPTER NINE

1 PAC, Laurier Papers, 1667-70, Willison to Laurier, March 11, 1891.
2 *Ibid.*, George E. Casey to Laurier, March 12, 1891.
3 Willison, *Reminiscences*, p. 243. *Globe*, Mar. 12, 1891.
4 OA, Edgar Papers, Laurier to Edgar, March 11, 1891.
5 PAC, Laurier Papers, 1725-7, Edgar to Laurier, March 22, 1891.
6 BP, Wells to Blake, February 12, 1891.
7 *Ibid.*, Blake to Mills, July 14, 1891.
8 *Ibid.*, Blake to Laurier, July 24, 1891.
9 *Ibid.*
10 *Ibid.*, Laurier to Blake, August 1, 1891.
11 *Ibid.*, Blake to Laurier, August 4, 1891.
12 *Ibid.*, Laurier to Blake, August 1, 1891.
13 *Ibid.*
14 *Ibid.*, Blake to Laurier, August 4, 1891.
15 *Ibid.*, Laurier to Blake, December 29, 1891.
16 PAC, Laurier Papers, 2055-60, Blake to Laurier, January 2, 1892.
17 BP, Blake to A. F. McIntyre, March 11, 1892.
18 PAC, Laurier Papers, 2117-21, Blake to Laurier, March 8, 1892.
19 *Ibid.*, 2120-1, Laurier to Blake, March 9, 1892.
20 BP, Draft of Circular from Blake, March 23, 1892.
21 *Ibid.*
22 *Ibid.*
23 *Ibid.*, Mills to Blake, March 24, 1892.

24 *Ibid.*, Mills to Blake, March 26, 1892.
25 *Ibid.*, Blake to Mills, March 28, 1892.
26 *Ibid.*
27 *Ibid.*, Mills to Blake, March 29, 1892.
28 *Ibid.*, Blake to Mills, March 31, 1892.
29 *Ibid.*, Laurier to Blake, April 9, 1892.
30 *Ibid.*
31 *Ibid.*, Blake to Laurier, April 12, 1892.
32 *Ibid.*, Blake draft, dated April 12, 1892.
33 *Ibid.*, Laurier to Blake, April 13, 1892.
34 PAC, Laurier Papers, Blake to Laurier, April 16, 1892.
35 BP, Blake to Laurier, April 23, 1892.
36 *Ibid.*
37 *Ibid.*
38 *Ibid.*, Laurier to Blake, April 29, 1892.
39 *Ibid.*, Blake to Laurier, May 2, 1892.
40 *Ibid.*, Blake to J. S. Smith, May 5, 1892.

CHAPTER TEN

1 BP, Section II, no. 14, Scrapbooks.
2 *Ibid.*
3 *House of Commons Debates*, February 14, 1890, p. 681.
4 University of Toronto Archives, James Loudon, *Memoirs*, unpublished, quoting Blake, p. 327.
5 James Loudon, "Edward Blake." *University of Toronto Monthly*, May, 1912.
6 BP, Blake to Ross, June 13, 1892.
7 Margaret A. Banks, *Edward Blake, Irish Nationalist* (Toronto: University of Toronto Press, 1957), p. 11. This is a complete and valuable account of Blake's career in Ireland and in British politics, which is not covered in the present work.
8 *Ibid.*, p. 11.
9 BP, Blake to Mills, June 16, 1892.
10 *Ibid.*
11 *Ibid.*, Laurier to Blake, June 17, 1892.
12 Banks, *Edward Blake, Irish Nationalist*, p. 27.
13 PAC, Laurier Papers, 2222-7, Blake to Laurier, August 31, 1892.
14 Justin McCarthy, *Our Book of Memories: Letters of Justin McCarthy to Mrs. Campbell-Praed* (London: Chatto & Windus, 1912), p. 324. (Hough — to cut the sinews or tendons of the hock.)
15 *Mail*, Sept. 12, 1892.
16 *Globe*, Sept. 20, 1892.
17 PAC, Laurier Papers, Goldwin Smith to Laurier, October 7, 1892.

NOTES

CHAPTER ELEVEN

1 PAC, Hayes Family Papers, Blake to F. B. Hayes, May 11, 1894.
2 McCarthy, *Our Book of Memories*, p. 343.
3 Sir Henry Lucy, *A Diary of the Home Rule Parliament, 1892-95* (London: 1896), p. 58.
4 BP, Margaret Blake to Wylie Grier, February 18, 1894.
5 OA, Grier Papers. Quotations and descriptions from Wylie Grier are in *Sir Wylie Grier: Reminiscences*, MS. See also MS. of unpublished novel dealing with "Mr. Bland", obviously Blake.
6 *Ibid.*
7 PAC, Underhill Papers, Blake to Edward Francis Blake, July 2, 1895.
8 BP, Blake to Grier, June 5, 1895.
9 PAC, Underhill Papers, Blake to E. F. Blake, July 17, 22, 1895.
10 PAC, A. Caron Papers, J. S. Ewart to Alex Ferguson, February 5, 1895.
11 PAC, Underhill Papers, Blake to E. F. Blake, December, 1894.
12 *Ibid.*, Blake to Margaret Blake, October 24, 1895.
13 *Ibid.*, Blake to Margaret Blake, October 18, 1895.
14 BP, S. V. Blake to Blake, May 3, 1894.
15 PAC, Underhill Papers, Blake letters to Margaret Blake, October-November, 1895.
16 *Ibid.*, Blake to E. F. Blake, February 8, 1900.
17 PAC, Underhill Papers, Blake to E. F. Blake, March 9, 11, 1895.
18 BP, E. F. Blake to S. V. Blake, October 24, 1896.
19 PAC, Underhill Papers, Blake to E. F. Blake, January 9, 17, 1896.
20 *Ibid.*, Blake to E. F. Blake, January 17, 1896.
21 BP, Hume Blake to Blake, March 12, 1896.
22 PAC, Sir John G. Bourinot Papers, Blake to Bourinot, May 25, 1894.
23 PAC, Underhill Papers, Blake to E. F. Blake, March 10, 1893.
24 BP, Blake to Benjamin Cronyn, March 11, 1895.
25 BP, E. F. Blake to Blake, April 11, 1896.
26 BP, E. F. Blake to Blake, May 5, 1901.
27 PAC, Underhill Papers, Blake to E. F. Blake, May 11, June 9, December 29, 1894.
28 BP, Mowat to Blake, November 24, 1896.
29 *Ibid.*
30 *Ibid.*
31 BP, Blake to Mowat, December 8, 1896.
32 *Ibid.*
33 PAC, Underhill Papers, Blake to E. F. Blake, February 13, 1897.
34 *Ibid.*
35 *Ibid.*
36 *Ibid.*, Blake to E. F. Blake, March 20, 1897.
37 *Ibid.*, Blake to E. F. Blake, February 13, 1897.
38 PAC, Willison Papers, Blake to Willison, January 17, 1897.

39 PAC, Underhill Papers, Blake to E. F. Blake, February 24, March 31, 1897.
40 PAC, Willison Papers, Blake to Willison, June 30, 1897.
41 BP, Section II, NO. 9, Blake to W. O'Brien, October 29, 1897.
42 BP, Blake to Mowat, October 4, 1897.
43 *Ibid.*
44 *Ibid.*
45 BFP, Note for diary by Clara Cynthia Benson, October 7, 1897. Clara Benson was one of the first women to take a PH D degree at the University of Toronto. The Benson women's athletic building is named after her.
46 Margaret A. Banks, "Edward Blake's Relations with Canada During His Irish Career, 1892-1907." *Canadian Historical Review* 35, March 1954, p. 36. Quoted from *Advertiser* (London), Nov. 26, 1897.
47 BP, Blake to John Cameron, November 30, 1897.
48 PAC, Willison Papers, Blake to Willison, December 8, 1897.
49 *Globe*, Dec. 9, 1897.
50 *Toronto World*, Dec. 9, 1897.
51 *Evening Star* (Toronto), Dec. 9, 1897.
52 *Evening News* (Toronto), Dec. 9, 1897.
53 *Evening Telegram* (Toronto), Dec. 9, 1897.
54 *Spectator* (Hamilton), Dec. 13, 1897.
55 PAC, Willison Papers, Blake to Willison, December 10, 1897.
56 *Ibid.*
57 *Ibid.*
58 *Globe*, Dec. 11, 1897.
59 PAC, Willison Papers, Blake to Willison, December 10, 1897.
60 *Ibid.*, Cartwright to Willison, December 15, 1897.
61 BP, Blake to M. A. James, December 9, 1897.

CHAPTER TWELVE

1 PAC, Underhill Papers, Blake to E. F. Blake, September 13, 1898.
2 BP, E. F. Blake to John Warren, April 19, 1898.
3 PAC, Underhill Papers, Blake to E. F. Blake, January 2, 1900.
4 *Ibid.*, Blake to E. F. Blake, February 23, 1900.
5 *Ibid.*, Blake to E. F. Blake, December 31, 1901.
6 *Ibid.*, Blake to E. F. Blake, December 6, 1900.
7 *Ibid.*, Blake to E. F. Blake, January 3, 10, 1891.
8 PAC, Laurier Papers, Blake to Laurier, May 23, 1903.
9 PAC, Willison Papers, Blake to Willison, April 20, 1903.
10 BP, E. F. Blake to Blake, July 31, 1903.
11 BP, Blake to Laurier, July 31, 1903.
12 Skelton, *Life and Letters of Sir Wilfrid Laurier*, II: 153.
13 *Ibid.*, II: 156.
14 PAC, Grey Papers, 2114-5.

15 BP, Blake to Martin J. Griffin, December 15, 1904.
16 BP, Blake to E. F. Blake, June 5, 1905.
17 Lande Collection, McLennan Library, McGill University, Pamphlet, *Blake Speech to Visiting American Bar, London, July 27, 1900.* Pamphlet also in possession of Blake, Cassels and Graydon, Toronto.
18 PAC, Underhill Papers, Blake to E. F. Blake, November 21, 1898.
19 BP, Blake to Laurier, August 30, 1905.
20 *Ibid.*
21 *Ibid.*
22 *Ibid.*
23 PAC, Laurier Papers, Laurier to Blake, November 11, 1905.
24 BP, Blake to Laurier, October 23, 1906.
25 *Ibid.*, second letter, November 20, 1905.
26 PAC, Laurier Papers, Blake to Laurier, October 23, 1906.
27 *Ibid.*, Blake to Laurier, November 17, 1906.
28 *Ibid.*, Laurier to Blake, November 21, 1906.
29 BP, Blake to Senator McMullen, October 24, 1906.
30 *Ibid.*
31 *Ibid.*
32 BP, Section II, NO. 9, Blake to Redmond, May 26, 1907.
33 *Ibid.*
34 BP, undated copy.
35 PAC, Laurier Papers, Blake to Laurier, December 15, 20, 1909.
36 Family letters held by Mrs. C. H. A. Armstrong, *née* Agnes Wrong.
37 PAC, Laurier Papers, Blake to Laurier, December 15, 1909.
38 *Globe*, Mar. 2, 1912.
39 Family letters held by Mrs. C. H. A. Armstrong.

INDEX